THE LITERATURE OF GUILT

The Literature of Guilt

From *Gulliver* to Golding

PATRICK REILLY

University of Iowa Press Ψ Iowa City

To the memory of my father and mother

Contents

Acknowledgements

I am grateful to my colleague Professor Philip Hobsbaum for advice and encouragement throughout the writing of this book. I should like to thank the Editors of *Was: Hefte für Kultur and Politik* for permission to use material that first appeared in that journal. I am especially indebted to Miss Ingrid Swanson for her skill and patience in preparing the typescript for publication.

1

Introduction: the Dark Epiphany

Only Matthew of the four evangelists describes the two epiphanies, positive and negative, redemptive and destructive, connected with the life and death of Jesus. The positive epiphany, that celebrated by the Church, is, of course, the coming of the Magi to the stable, where, penetrating with the eyes of faith the disguise of the homeless infant, they recognised the lord of the universe and the hope of mankind. The moment is one of salvation in which the self attains new, breathtaking dignity by virtue of its newly revealed kinship with the incarnate God. The negative epiphany is the sudden blasting awareness of his own vileness that broke upon Judas after his act of betrayal – so sickened was he at the taste of his true self that he went and hanged it. 'I am gall, I am heartburn . . . my taste was me.'[1] Hopkins, at the nadir of despondency and self-disparagement, makes the same discovery as Judas, though escaping the ultimate despair. This Judas moment when the self gags at its own corruption has become a salient, almost a defining, characteristic of modern literature. It is especially interesting because here, as in so much else, our own century has shockingly challenged the assumptions and pieties of its predecessor.

'Thou didst think too highly of men';[2] the Grand Inquisitor's rebuke to Christ is not one that could legitimately be levelled against the writers of our time, but the great nineteenth-century writers might have had some difficulty in refuting the accusation. Graham Greene declares that 'in all writers there occurs a moment of crystallisation when the dominant theme is plainly expressed', and goes on to discover such a moment in Hardy's phrase about the President of the Immortals torturing Tess.[3] If we were to risk extending Greene's dictum from the *oeuvre* of an individual artist to the literature of an age, we would find the moment of crystallisation in nineteenth-century literature to be very different from that de-

1

tected in Hardy. If the dominant theme in Hardy is the human animal harried to destruction, that of nineteenth-century literature is the rescued sinner, the near-ruined individual plucked from the brink of moral catastrophe. Not crime and punishment, but crime and redemption is the leit motiv of the age from the Ancient Mariner onwards:

> The self-same moment I could pray;
> And from my neck so free
> The Albatross fell off, and sank
> Like lead into the sea.

To which of us is prayer forbidden, what sinner so abandoned as to be beyond the claim of grace? The redemptive mythology, whether religious or secularised, favoured by the nineteenth century excluded the idea of the doomed culprit, the man like Macbeth or Claudius or Marlowe's Faustus, the man sundered from grace, who, wanting to pray, cannot. In the hour of truth the criminal will be possessed with creative remorse – the crime will be undone, the error rectified. Some such optimistic conviction sustains works such as *The Ancient Mariner*, Goethe's *Faust* and Hugo's *Les Miserables*.

The idea of reclamation is central to the literature of the age. The theme of the nineteenth-century novel from *Jane Eyre* onwards ('Reader, I married him') is rescue, and its major practitioners are all strenuously involved in the salvage industry. *Janet's Repentance*: all it needs is the change of possessive to make the title applicable to so many key works of the time. In their pages we contemplate a gallery of escapees, a series of lives recovered from crime, despair and waste. Jean Valjean is simply the most dramatic of the reprieved, and Hugo's preface makes it plain that crime is as much a commodity as coal, produced by society in much the same kind of way. If we wish to discontinue the supply of violent men and prostituted women, his book will tell us how to do it. The all-sufficient deterrent is, of course, love. 'Those to whom evil is done / Do evil in return.'[4] Auden's lines are almost platitudinously irrefutable, and the savage Valjean reflects the savage society that has so consummately succeeded in making him what he is. 'Do your duty towards me, and I will do mine towards you and the rest of mankind.'[5] So declares the Creature to Frankenstein and the book shows the terrible results of not responding to this appeal. But the converse is also blessedly true, as the strategy of Hugo's saintly bishop so amply demonstrates. Love is stronger than hatred; *amor vincit omnia*. This is as true of Pip and Sydney Carton and the penitent Dombey as it is of Silas Marner and Dorothea Brooke. Each of these characters is a brand saved from the burning, a potential castaway rescued by love.

'I believe that people are almost always better than their neighbours think they are.'[6] Dorothea Brooke, instinctively defending Lydgate from the insinuation of bribery, simultaneously makes a larger point on her creator's behalf. George Eliot holds to the fundamental decency of the human being, to his capacity for generosity and his ability to stand upright again after a fall. The compassionate conclusion of Chapter 74 of *Middlemarch* makes this clear when a rather commonplace woman, not remarkable hitherto for virtue or intelligence, nobly sustains in the hour of crisis her fallen husband: 'Look up, Nicholas.' So great is the power of love that it can dispense with words: 'the confession was silent, and her promise of faithfulness was silent . . . a movement of new compassion and old tenderness went through her like a great wave'.[7] Dostoevsky shows a similar belief in the power of speechless love at the end of the 'Legend of the Grand Inquisitor': the startling kiss instead of the verbal defence that both we and the old man expect, the gesture of love which shakes if it does not convert the accuser – what more dramatic exemplification could there be of the maxim that actions speak louder than words, what more cogent demonstration that love can disarm where reprisal merely inflames? The silent reconciliation of the Bulstrodes recapitulates the even finer, because more dramatically rendered, conclusion of Chapter 42 when Dorothea overcomes a natural sense of resentment and wounded pride to sacrifice herself for her insensitive, offending husband. Her generosity evokes in turn a reciprocal magnanimity from the usually egotistic Casaubon. Treat people well and they will behave well – it is Hugo's lesson all over again. Dorothea realises fearfully how close she has come to 'hurting a lamed creature', and the final scene is of selfishness routed by love: 'she put her hand into her husband's, and they went along the broad corridor together'.[8] It is the central article of George Eliot's creed: we must love each other because there is no God to whom the duty can be delegated; we *must*, therefore we will. Man is his own and his only redeemer.

The indignant Dorothea, smarting from her husband's slights, might so easily have toppled irrecoverably into the pit (Gwendolen

Harleth, provoked into far greater peril by far greater injuries, is plucked from the same precipice) – it is *philanthropia*, sacrificial love, that stays the fall. Sydney Carton, similarly inspired, goes gladly and even gratefully under the guillotine's blade. *A Tale of Two Cities* moves in a direction completely opposite to that of a modern text such as *The Fall*. Camus's tale begins in success and heads for demoralisation; Jean-Baptiste Clamence exposes himself as a fraud who has duped himself and others into regarding him as a virtuous man. There is no virtue, no altruism, no love, merely a world full of impostors – such is the book's cynical conclusion. Dickens's novel, by contrast, takes a ruined man, given to alcoholism, squandering his talents, trapped in self-contempt, and brings him, improbable as it initially seems, to redemption. Admittedly, the price is death, but Dickens makes it plain that that's an acceptable price for integrity of life and significance of existence. Carton is already destroying himself for want of a reason to live when Lucy Manette enters the wasteland of this life and makes it fruitful. The book ends in a secularised resurrection: 'They said of him, about the city that night, that it was the peacefullest man's face ever beheld there. Many added that he looked sublime and prophetic'.[9] There is a dual expiation, at once individual and collective, Sydney's and the age's; the revolutionary evil will work itself out and a new age of love and harmony will dawn. Sydney on the scaffold sees the blessed future made possible by his sacrifice – the boy, born because Sydney dies, who will appropriately bear his saviour's name. It is as close to being the father of Lucy's child as will ever be granted Sydney, and he unhesitatingly embraces both the opportunity and its attendant penalty. The boy will grow up to become a highly respected, honourable man to father in turn a third Sydney – what future immortality will a sensible man expect or demand?

This redemptive mythology implied a radical critique of the notion of guilt, and borrowed heavily from Rousseau in making it. Bad education or bad society was the real culprit, with the erring individual unjustly punished for the defects of his environment or upbringing. What seemed evil was really a failure of intelligence, imagination or sympathy; when we recoil in revulsion from the strange or unusual we risk creating the monsters we fear – from *Frankenstein* to *Silas Marner* and *Les Miserables* the lesson is driven home. Silas is restored to the community by the same infallible method that rescued Jean Valjean: love instead of ostracism. The alien must be embraced as a friend, not shunned as a leper.

Throughout Dickens we find the essential elements of this re-demptive mythology, the same recurring pattern of sin, expiation and redemption, with love as the agent of salvation. *Hard Times*, like *A Tale of Two Cities*, ends with a vision of the beautiful, blessed things to be, of the healing that follows the hurt. Part of Louisa's expiation is never to have children of her own – but her fate is milder than Sydney's, for she will have Sissy's children to love and to love her in turn. The book ends with the authorial encourage-ment to the readers to achieve in their own lives similar happy results: 'Let them be!', and the exhortation is delivered with confi-dence.[10] The conclusion of *Great Expectations* promises no shadow of a future parting – exactly, in Bulwer-Lytton's estimation, what the Victorian public wanted to hear. The avoidance of tragedy is the age's requirement; the change of heart denied Macbeth and Faustus is always an option available to the Victorian sinner and death itself need not be an annihilation. *David Copperfield* manages to trans-form the anticipated death-bed into a blessed consummation with the hero's prayer to his beloved Agnes to 'still find thee near me, pointing upward!'[11] It is simply Dickens's secularised equivalent of the religious prayer for a happy death, where Joseph, dying in the consoling presence of Jesus and Mary, is taken as the paramount example of this enormous privilege.

However harsh the narrative, the end is always a reconciliation. Eugene Wrayburn is as 'saved' by marriage to Lizzie as Rochester by marriage to Jane, and Twemlow bravely puts the sneering Pod-snap in his decidedly inferior place for attacking what he can only see as a shocking *mésalliance*. The book ends with Mortimer Light-wood's joy: 'Mortimer sees Twemlow home, shakes hands with him cordially at parting, and fares to the Temple, gaily.'[12] The reader is no more permitted to doubt the future of the marriage than he is to speculate about the innocent Miranda's fate when she leaves her father's island for corrupt Milan. Little Dorrit and her husband, breaking the prison, Adam and Eve in Victorian dress, 'went quietly down into the roaring streets . . . went down into a modest life of usefulness and happiness'[13] – not with great expectations, but with the measured, decently disciplined desires of good people peopling the good earth. In *Dombey and Son* the erstwhile arrogant man has turned penitent, the harsh father now treasures his grand-daughter, proving by this devotion that the prayer he prayed has been munificently answered: 'Oh, my God, forgive me, for I need it very much!'[14] Ask and it shall be given; the assurance is implicit in every Dickens novel and in this he is simply the outstanding spokesman of the redemptive mythology of his age.

> And my ending is despair,
> Unless I be relieved by prayer.

Prospero's appeal for rescue is generously answered in Victorian literature – where before Hardy is a genuine plea for forgiveness or mercy rejected? Even the tragedies are muted – they consent to a tranquilly subordinate status within the reassuring structures of these fictions. What happens to Little Em'ly and Hetty Sorrel is both sad and irreversible – the fallen woman does not, apparently, have the same recuperative resiliency as the fallen man – but not to the extent that it irredeemably darkens the books. Whether it be the theme of fruitful remorse that runs from Coleridge to Wagner or the theme of love triumphing over world and self that informs the major fiction of the time, somewhere in this literature, exultant or restrained, sounds the seraphic assurance of Dame Julian of Norwich: 'Sin is behovely, but all shall be well and all shall be well and all manner of things shall be well.'[15]

All shall be well. We are right to be shaken when we quit the protective pinfold of this fiction for the shocking and pitiless disclosures of modern literature. It is not entirely fanciful to imagine that a major objective of this literature has been to expose and explode what it interpreted as the unearned optimism of the preceding century. In one of the major texts of our time this deliberate programme of demolition is, in fact, explicitly proclaimed, the intention to cancel the nineteenth century remorselessly announced by its hero. In 1905 Thomas Mann outlined his sketch for a novel which only came to be published more than forty years on: 'Figure of the syphilitic artist: as Dr Faust, pledged to the devil. The poison works as intoxicant, stimulant, inspiration; he is filled with ecstatic enthusiasm and creates works of genius; the devil guides his hand. But finally the devil fetches him: luetic paralysis.'[16]

The reappearance of the diabolic is, as Angus Wilson has demonstrated, a distinguishing feature of modern literature, reestablishing a tradition that persisted through the Middle Ages and Renaissance until its dying English expression in the work of Samuel Richardson.[17] The devil has successfully reaffirmed his visiting rights in modern literature; it is the flights of angels escorting the dead Hamlet to felicity who remain unwelcome, the chorus of spirits carrying the ransomed Faust, 'no more the thrall / Of evil cares',[18] to celestial bliss who are still very much *personae non gratae*. Mann's idea of the artist as a lost soul doomed to everlasting torment reinforces our contemporary view of tragedy as a catastrophe stripped of consolation. Works such as *Samson Agonistes*, *Die Jüngfrau von Orleans*, *St Joan*, *Murder in the Cathedral*, seem too optimistic for admission to the tragic canon – in each there is gain to balance the loss, and we prefer our tragedy neat, its tang undiluted by any dash of reassurance. It is not, as is sometimes mistakenly said, that the idea of a life after death is lethal to the tragic experience. The truth is, as the Mann quotation proves, that our modern view of tragedy can easily accommodate a future existence provided it is restricted to hell – it is the hint of heaven we cannot abide. If Macbeth laments having given his eternal jewel to the common enemy of mankind, if Othello in anguish foresees himself hurled into hell at the Last Judgement, that intensifies rather than attenuates the tragedy; to imply that either has passed to a place of torment does not provoke the uneasiness that the notion of Cordelia or Lear translated to beatitude so damagingly does. The promise of redemption undercuts the finality of tragedy, whereas the threat of damnation sharpens the sense, already experienced, of irremediable loss. The literature of our time is attuned to hell; it is the heavenly chord that jars.

In Mann's rendition of the diabolic pact, love is the forfeit for infernal inspiration. Adrian Leverkühn destroys wherever he loves, a monstrosity before which even Hugo's saintly bishop might have stood appalled and helpless. Adrian's final, most heart-rending victim is his nephew, an angelically adorable little boy whose hideous death from cerebro-spinal meningitis is presented as almost a form of possession. This, at least, is how Adrian interprets it – as the satanic exchange-rate for his artistic genius. In nineteenth-century literature love is the infallible cure for our condition; in Mann's story love itself becomes the agent of destruction. Just as the nineteenth century had its secularised equivalents for the religious concepts of resurrection and beatitude – the life-to-be that Sydney Carton anticipates in Lucy's unborn son, the blessed death-bed with Agnes as attendant angel, the victory over petty egoism which is George Eliot's way of showing the rising from the dead – so Mann's novel similarly has its secularised equivalents for the religious concepts of damnation and possession: the hero's fearful descent into, not hell, but luetic paralysis, the dying child's seizure, not by devils, but by the spasms of disease. This paralysis and this disease are, of course, as terrifying as any of the nightmare visions of hell that vexed the mind of medieval man.

The proof of this is that the now bleakly enlightened hero feels impelled to compose his hell-fired masterpiece annihilating the consoling lie of the nineteenth century, the delusion that love and virtue are stronger than any other elements in existence. During the little boy's death-agony, Leverkühn speaks to his decent, pedestrian, uncomprehending friend to communicate his discovery: 'I find . . . that it is not to be.' He explains his riddling remark. 'The good and noble . . . what we call the human, although it is good, and noble. What human beings have fought for and stormed citadels, what the ecstatics exultantly announced – that is not to be. It will be taken back. I will take it back.' Still his unimaginative friend is baffled: ' "I don't quite understand, dear man. What will you take back?" "The Ninth Symphony," he replied.'[19]

The reference to the ecstatics might easily apply to Dame Julian of Norwich, but the specific citation of the Ninth Symphony puts the entire statement into a precise historical context. The Ninth Symphony and Goethe's *Faust* date from the same period and share a fundamental attitude towards human life and its aspirations and possibilities. Both are trustfully optimistic, filled with belief in human nobility. Goethe's Faust is saved because of his unremitting exertions to perfect the nobility inherent in man. Beethoven's chorus proclaims with Schiller's words its faith in the coming kingdom of joy and brotherly love. The 'Ode to Joy' is buoyantly, exhilaratingly confident:

> Allen Sündern soll vergeben
> Und die Hölle nicht mehr sein.

Leverkühn knows how fatuously idealistic this is: sinners are not always forgiven and hell has no end. The fruit of this bleak insight is Leverkühn's masterpiece, 'The Lamentation of Dr Faustus' – *not* a hymn of exultation, a *Fidelio* or a Ninth Symphony, but the revocation, the taking back, the negation of the Ninth. 'The Lamentation' fulfils Leverkühn's destructive promise; it is the reverse of the 'Ode to Joy', the counterpart to Beethoven, 'the negative, equally a work of genius, of that transition of the symphony into vocal jubilation. It is the revocation.'[20]

In its rejection of the redemptive mythology of the previous century, Mann's novel clearly shows the imprint of the harsher, more pessimistic age in which it was conceived. The damnation of Leverkühn is explicitly linked to the fate of Germany under Hitler as well as to the doomed sinner depicted by Dürer – the two nightmares, medieval and modern, merge together. Not Goethe and the 'Ode to Joy', nor Weber's *Der Freischütz* with its theme of sin and forgiveness, but Dante and Dürer and Marlowe seem the more appropriate, more reliable guides to Mann as he grapples with the foul mysteries of twentieth-century German history. His was not an eccentric or perverse reaction, but was rather, if we can trust Jaspers, representative: 'We came face to face with experiences in which we had no inclination to read Goethe, but took up Shakespeare, or the Bible, or Aeschylus, if it was possible to read at all.'[21] It was precisely Goethe's embarrassment in the face of tragedy, his helplessness before the manifestations of sin and evil, that so devastatingly disqualified him as the Virgil who could guide us through the hell of modern history.[22] It is the optimistic eschatology of Goethe that Leverkühn resolves to revoke, shattering for ever 'the lie of its godliness.'[23] The shocked narrator makes plain the relevance of this hellish art to the wider cultural catastrophe: 'We children of the dungeon dreamed of a hymn of exultation, a *Fidelio*, a Ninth Symphony, to celebrate the dawn of a freed Germany'. Instead they get 'the Lamentation of the son of hell, the lament of men and God'.[24]

For obvious historical reasons the twentieth century has not been so hospitable as its predecessor to the themes of salvation and reclamation; those who believe that man is inherently noble, with the gift of redemptive love forever at his disposal, have been increasingly forced onto the defensive in the face of modern iniquity. It is, paradoxically, often disillusioned liberals who are most Augustinian in presenting evil as ontological reality, even if they sometimes give the impression that this evil is peculiar to our own times, a twentieth-century invention unknown to previous ages. Sartre lays claim to our attention by his portentous use of the capital letter:

'We have been taught to take Evil seriously. It is neither our fault nor our merit if we lived in a time when torture was a daily fact. Chateaubriand, Oradour, the Rue des Saussaies, Dachau and Auschwitz have all demonstrated to us that Evil is not an appearance, that knowing its cause does not dispel it, that it is not opposed to Good as a confused idea is to a clear one. . . . In spite of ourselves, we come to this conclusion, which will seem shocking to lofty souls: Evil cannot be redeemed'.[25]

The final categorical assertion, with its tone of defiant, unassailable discovery, is advanced as though Shakespeare had never created Iago nor Milton conceived the Satan of Mount Niphates; but, apart from its untenable claim to have unearthed a hitherto unapprehended truth, the assertion is clearly designed to rout Rousseau, Goethe, Hugo, the whole *amor-vincit-omnia* school of moral philosophers, and to restore us to the harsher, more realistic outlook of Dürer, Marlowe and Shakespeare.

It has been a bad period for Pelagians – the boot in the face forever is an image that fits more easily into Augustinian categories. The appearance of Eliot's *The Waste Land,* Barth's *Epistle to the Romans* and Freud's *Beyond the Pleasure Principle*, all within a few years of each other, mark a significant shift in the *Weltanschauung* of twentieth-century man. As always, the tendency, here as in so much else, is to swing to the other extreme: from *laisser faire* to Big Brother, from Victorian prudery to full-frontal provocation, from utopian humanism to an obsession with total depravity, from presumption to despair. At a perverse extreme there is even the temptation, irresistible to some on the Augustinian wing, to indulge a shameful *Schadenfreude*, gloating with twitching nostrils over each fresh atrocity, each new evidence of man's finitude and nastiness. The waning of utopia and its associated humanistic hubris is apparently so pleasing to some that hell itself is welcomed as a preferable alternative, Gehenna celebrated as a refuge from Dostoevsky's crystal palace.

Such a mentality is depicted with abhorrent perfection in the sneering monologist of *The Fall* – Camus's *juge-pénitent* is diabolic (*diabolos* is, etymologically, a mud-slinger) both in his malign resolve that belief in goodness shall not survive and in his strategy of procuring a sadistic joy in infecting others with his own disease. He is glad that corruption prevails, is wickedly elated to recount the crucifixion of the simpleton who trusts his fellow men – isn't this the appropriate recompense for such folly? Jean-Baptiste Clamence, as much as Adrian Leverkühn, is bent upon a programme of revocation, with each, appropriately enough, attacking deluded optimism in the person of a fellow-countryman: the German attacks

Beethoven, the Frenchman, Hugo. The target of Clamence's nihilistic derision is quite clearly Hugo's saintly bishop and his strategy
of reclaiming sinners through love; Clamence knows where love
finally gets you; nailed through the hands and feet, dying on a
cross:

> I knew one pure heart who rejected distrust. He was a pacifist
> and a libertarian and loved all humanity and the animals with an
> equal love. An exceptional soul, that's certain. Well, during the
> last wars of religion in Europe he had retired to the country. He
> had written on his threshold: 'Wherever you come from, come in
> and be welcome.' Who do you think answered that noble invi-
> tation? The militia, who entered and made themselves at home,
> and disembowelled him.[26]

This, we infer, is how Jean Valjean will really respond when you
fatuously think to tame his savagery with kindness – as well be
compassionate to a shark.

But the indictment of such *naïveté* is not merely that it injures the
simpleton who entertains it; far graver is the charge that it also
destroys other people – people who, had they ever been consulted,
would not have confided so disarmingly in human nature. When
Greene's Quiet American declares that 'a man becomes trustworthy
when you trust him', the worldly-wise narrator, aghast at such
murderous innocence, finally decides that the speaker must not be
allowed to live and begins to conspire his friend's assassination.[27]
Pyle *is* a foolishly dangerous man, not to himself but to the many
innocent people who will die as a direct result of his lethal gulli-
bility. Trusting too easily is a recipe for massacre, that of other
people in *The Quiet American*, one's own in *The Fall*.

The Fall is, of course, an Augustinian nightmare, showing how a
superficial trust in human goodness, clashing with the real world,
turns into a shockingly indefensible exposé of human depravity –
indefensible, above all, because it exhibits an unholy joy in the
revelation it brings. Jean-Baptiste Clamence is the diabolic extreme
of the Augustinian onslaught, accomplice to the atrocities he
parades. In similar, only less slightly shocking fashion, Evelyn
Waugh condemns *his* simpleton, the luckless Tony Last of *A Handful of Dust*, to life-long imprisonment in the Brazilian jungle where
he is forced to read and re-read Dickens to an illiterate madman; the
implication is that those who share Dickens's optimistic delusions

deserve to be immured in his books forever. That Tony is the nicest character in the book, far from saving him, ensures his retribution for being so gullible, so foolishly unwary towards that treacherous animal, man.

The fear of being a fool, the dread of being undone through trusting too easily, has become almost an element of the realist atmosphere which we presently breathe. It emerges, for instance, in Orwell's curiously eccentric reading of *King Lear* wherein he finds the moral that if you give away your power you have no right to complain when it is inevitably used against you. Don't trust anyone or you'll get your teeth kicked in.[28] To begin with, this sounds too uncomfortably like the defence that the wicked daughters advanced against the old man's reproaches. True, the Fool says much the same thing to his enraged master, but to reduce the 'moral' of the play to an argument in favour of wary self-preservation is surely a depressing circumscription of Shakespeare's greatest triumph. What Orwell sees is certainly there but not, surely, as the central preoccupation he takes it to be. It is a sign of our times that Orwell should identify a failure of circumspection, the foolish credulity of a silly old man, as the heart of this great play. Our alacrity in condemning credulousness as the truly inexcusable sin is a measure of our own adamantine resolve that we ourselves shall never be taken in.

Even when the cynical complicity of Clamence is absent, the works of our time continue to rebuke the previous age for its naïve optimism and avoidance of tragedy. Leverkühn, affirming his intention of taking back the Ninth, simultaneously announces the programme of twentieth-century literature in its adversarial stance towards the work of its predecessor. Everything is taken back. Where was once salvation is now damnation; where love once ruled, there is the boot in the face forever. In place of the reclaimed sinner, Carton or Dombey, we confront the doomed criminal, Conrad's Kurtz or Mann's Aschenbach. The fruitful remorse of Jean Valjean cedes to the cynical despair of Jean-Baptiste Clamence. Instead of the serene optimism of Dame Julian's assurance, we hear the disconcerting challenge at the end of *Lord of the Flies:* who will save the officer and his ship, who will save *us?*[29] Prospero faces despair unless prayer comes to the rescue. But Prospero believes in the efficacy of prayer and the God to whom it is directed. We today are in Prospero's case without equal hope of amendment. Our experience is closer to that of Judas than to that of the Magi. We live in the time of the dark epiphany.

The following pages will pursue this negative epiphany through certain major works of twentieth-century literature: *Heart of Darkness*, *Death in Venice*, *Nineteen Eighty-Four*, *The Fall* and *Lord of the Flies*. As prolegomenon to this discussion, Swift's 'Voyage to the Houyhnhnms' will be examined for its paradigmatic significance, its relevance as a frame within which these later texts will assume a sharper definition. Swift, too, over two and a half centuries ago, challenged the Pelagianism of his time, and presented in his great satires a far bleaker view of human nature, a view with certain affinities to our own contemporary variants of Augustinianism. He was rebuked for this, not by an enemy but by a friend. Bolingbroke, his personal and political ally, faulted *Gulliver's Travels* on the ground that it was a bad design to depreciate human nature.[30] Man was basically good and was capable of becoming better – he was *animal rationale*, uniquely privileged among creatures as participant in the divine gift of reason. It was, so Bolingbroke judged, scandalously offensive to besmirch the *imago dei* with the filth of the Yahoo. Swift's masterpiece, even in our atrocity-benumbed century, still has the power to unnerve, but Bolingbroke's sense of outrage at the insult to human nature understandably finds fewer sharers today. Rather, the experience of Swift's alienated protagonist strikes us, in certain aspects, as peculiarly pertinent to that of the central characters in the texts being appraised: to Marlow detecting the fraud of western civilisation in distant places; to Aschenbach on a voyage that disconcertingly merges self-discovery with self-destruction; to Orwell's brainwashed victim who ends up loving Big Brother as Gulliver does the Houyhnhnms; to Camus's erstwhile lover of humanity turned mordant misanthrope; to Golding's boys cruelly discovering on the island that there is no recourse from corrupt civilisation in Yahoo nature.

Yet Swift, it must be remembered, is a man from another age, a voice vaulting a chasm – between the great Augustan and ourselves lies a yawning historical divide, in particular that profound transformation of norms and values which we call the Romantic Revolution. It schooled men to think, perhaps even more decisive, to feel, differently; those who come after, ourselves included, are changed, if not utterly, at least significantly. Near the end of his life, Swift is alleged to have broken a long silence with the heartrending words, 'I am what I am.' It is otherwise with us. A discontinuity or mutation has occurred in the evolution of post-romantic humanity:

we are not as we were. But here, too, the preliminary investigation of *Gulliver's Travels* can help to illuminate the problems of our time – where we differ from Swift can also be as informative as where we agree. What follows will be an attempt to demonstrate the truth of this proposition.

2

Gulliver's Travels: Looking into the Pool

T. S. Eliot rightly describes the 'Voyage to the Houyhnhnms' as one of the greatest triumphs that the human soul has ever achieved, and the time is happily past for having to urge on resistant ears the continuing relevance of Swift's masterpiece.[1] Its inclusion in the present argument is, however, less for its perennial pertinence than for its value as a template against which a special experience in certain twentieth-century texts can be aligned – this is the justi-fication for the discussion of the *Travels* about to be initiated. Yet, however relevant as paradigm or useful as propaedeutic, *Gulliver's Travels* differs from our modern texts in one significant respect: it comes before, where they come after, an age of optimism, marking the end of an era where they signal the emergence of a new sensi-bility. Swift's book is a last, brilliant Augustinian sortie against the armies of Enlightenment massing for the final assault upon the ruined fortress of seventeenth-century ideology. It was a sortie at once devastatingly successful and inexorably doomed; doomed, because not even the genius of Swift could check the juggernaut of history, successful in that it evoked from those attacked a chorus of disapprobation so fierce and so widespread as to indicate just how painfully it had struck home. It was almost as if the expiring seven-teenth century had gathered together all its force and concentrated it in the person of Swift to launch one parting onslaught upon the deluded optimism of its successor.

That even in his own day Swift was already a man of the past is so well established as to be the essential departure-point from which all serious criticism must begin. He was a seventeeth-century man, all of whose major attitudes on religion and politics had been hardened in the mould of that turbulent time. Nowhere is this conservative temper more manifestly demonstrated than in his old-fashioned, 'reactionary' view of human nature and of the ex-pectations we may reasonably entertain concerning it. The modesty

15

of his own expectations explains his impatience with those whom he derisively described as 'empiricks', by which he meant people who advanced inanely inappropriate solutions to problems, like advising a cripple to go jogging every morning for the good of his health. Nothing angered him more than the spectacle of the utopian dreamer posing as wise man; he fumed when people ignorant of Ireland put forward their ostensibly rational proposals for the amendment of that perversely unhappy country, projects faultless in every respect save one – they would not work. They were worthless because they ignored the realities of the Irish situation, of what one might sensibly ask the Irish people to do with any reasonable hope of being heard and heeded. The controlled fury of the 'Modest Proposal' is fired by a bleak realism: 'Therefore, I repeat, let no man talk to me of these and the like expedients, till he hath at least a glimpse of hope, that there will ever be some hearty and sincere attempt to put them in practice.'[2] He had little time for fools and was the more bitter because he felt that he had become one in offering for so many years those 'vain, idle, visionary thoughts' which the sottish, insensate Irish either would not or could not comprehend. Politics, the art of persuading people, is no different from any other art in demanding that its practitioner must know his material, what it can and what it cannot be made to do, the opportunities it affords and the limits beyond which it cannot be coerced. 'A Modest Proposal' reflects a dual and contradictory anger – the anger of the politician-artist at his recalcitrant material and an anger with himself for so completely misjudging it. Milton had delivered a similar caution against sequestering 'out of the world into Atlantic and Utopian polities, which never can be drawn into use' and hence 'will not mend our condition'.[3] Swift, however, touched depths of pessimism unfound in Milton.

Swift's anguish was intensified when he realised that Ireland was not so exceptional after all, that the limitations of Irish man are those of man everywhere – the blunder of misjudging Ireland was compounded when it deepened into the catastrophe of misjudging man. Swift clearly believed, as the *vous autres* letter to Pope and Bolingbroke shows, that the new, optimistic view of man, built on the ruins of original sin, was dangerously misguided.[4] In *Gulliver's Travels* he issued his deliberately provocative challenge to developing, buoyant Pelagianism.

The enemies he attacked were many and varied: deists, rationalists, freethinkers, benevolists, sentimentalists – but all were united in an avowed or tacit denial of the doctrine of original sin and a determination to absolve human nature of corruption. Peter Gay calls them 'the party of humanity' (a title which is at least revelatory of his own bias, since it implies a party of inhumanity made up, presumably, of those who did not share the *philosophes'* optimism) and warns us against an over-simplified and therefore incorrect judgement about them.[5] For example, it is not true that the *philosophes* as a body held an exalted view of the status and efficacy of reason – many of them agreed with Pascal that human reason was a severely circumscribed faculty, and used their own reason to prove how limited reason was; the so-called Age of Reason is also the age of repeated attacks on the rationalistic, metaphysical constructions of previous centuries. Attitudes are, admittedly, far more various than they appear at a distance and some accepted commonplaces need to be reversed. It is, nevertheless, possible to identify one shared characteristic decisively separating them from the men of the previous age: they were practically all men of sentiment, pre-ferring the heart to the head, relying upon the emotions rather than upon reason.

If Vico is right in asserting that each culture expresses its own collective experience, we may conclude that the eighteenth-century Enlightenment was distinguished by its hostility to the view of man expressed theologically by Calvin and psychologically by Hobbes, the view that defined him either as a sink of iniquity or as an inescapably selfish, aggressive and mistrusting animal. When Bolingbroke condemned the *Travels* for depreciating human nature, he sounded a note that was to become increasingly shrill as the century progressed. Isaac Barrow denounced 'the monstrous paradox . . . that all men naturally are enemies one to another'[6] – a clear vote for the Lockean model of the state of nature as against the more pessimistic analysis upon which *Leviathan* is predicated. Shaftesbury, so crucial as a shaper of the new sensibility, attacked the Church for its emphasis on original sin; in its anxiety to con-vince men of sin, the Church had become the foe of virtue. The older view of man, whether Hobbesian or Augustinian, was a calumny – on this, whatever their other differences, the men of the new age were unanimous. Voltaire's chief complaint against Pascal and La Rochefoucauld was that they had erroneously and mis-chievously persuaded the public to interpret self-love always in a bad sense and he credits his own century for the revolutionary change whereby ideas of vice and pride were no longer inevitably attached to the word. A revolution in ethical thought is, if we can trust Brunetière, precisely what had taken place: 'rarely, if ever, has so profound a transformation occurred more swiftly. Everything has changed.'[7] From the pessimism of Pascal to the optimism of Leibniz, from the self-love of La Rochefoucauld to the benevolence of Hutcheson, from the scepticism of Montaigne to the rationalism of Locke, Toland and Clarke – surely revolution is not too strong a term for such an alteration.

It is easy to see why Swift's book provoked the wrath of these lovers of humanity, the party to which Gulliver himself had belonged before his defection to the rational horses – how else could they interpret his behaviour than treason, depravity or madness? Swift took, of course, a very different view. He found himself surrounded by men who thought themselves emancipated and who were proud of their superiority, prepared at most to concede that the lower classes often behaved disgracefully, but rejecting indignantly any suggestion of kinship with such creatures. Sin was either obsolete or the prerogative of the lower orders, and the cultivated no more admitted the presence of sin in their hearts than they did the *canaille* in their drawing-rooms. The candour of the Duchess of Buckingham's stinging rebuke to John Wesley makes this splendidly clear: 'It is monstrous to be told that you have a heart as sinful as the common wretches that crawl on the earth.'[8] When Swift used a similar imagery, he put it in the mouth of the Giant King where it functioned to condemn the whole human race, not divide it into sheep and goats according to the demarcations of social class. People who shared the Duchess's complacency were understandably outraged when Swift, with Gulliver as mouthpiece, brutally told them that their fine clothes, language, sentiments and practices were simply refinements of Yahoo nastiness, that the beau and the Yahoo were brothers in the flesh. *Gulliver's Travels* struck them as an offensive attempt to return them to the prison of original sin from which they had broken free, and, as Cassirer points out, they were unanimously resolved never again to suffer that captivity. 'Man is at present in disgrace among all those who think; they heap upon him all manner of vices. Perhaps he is soon to awake and to demand the restitution of his virtues.'[9] But already in 1726, before Vauvenargues wrote these words, many men were wide-awake and spoiling for a fight with anyone who dared to question the dignity of human nature.

Swift, for his part, invited such an attack. He surveyed what the enlightened were pleased to call civilisation with a contempt that matched their complacency. It was precisely the materialist, progressivist era that he regarded as both imminent and degenerate. In a tradition of Old Testament pessimism he was convinced that man was still the vehicle of original sin and that man's weakness showed itself most flagrantly and infuriatingly in his pride in a false innocence:

> Their deeds they all on Satan lay;
> The Devil did the deed, not they.[10]

Swift's worst contempt was reserved for the doublethink in man that permitted him to be one thing and think himself another, committing abominations while denying responsibility for them. Reinhold Niebuhr in our own time expresses a like puzzlement in face of the same paradox:

> No cumulation of contradictory evidence seems to disturb modern man's good opinion of himself. He considers himself the victim of corrupting institutions which he is about to destroy or reconstruct or the confusions of ignorance which an adequate education is about to overcome. Yet he continues to regard himself as essentially harmless and virtuous.[11]

For Swift, as for Niebuhr, man's absorption in the myth of his own innocence is his greatest liability and worst affront.

The myth of human goodness is Swift's prime target. 'What has sunk my spirits more than even years and sickness, is reflecting on the most execrable corruptions that run through every branch of public management.'[12] He enjoyed the role of Alecto, found relief for his indignation in lashing offenders, and refused to abide by the Duchess of Buckingham's social categories when wielding the whip; the Duchess of Kendal, fine lady though she is, is really a she-Yahoo, the Duke of Marlborough shows an avidity for the shining stones as great as any of his brethren in Houyhnhnmland. The Academy of Lagado was scarcely calculated to flatter the savants of the Royal Society or their European colleagues. One by one Swift investigates the prized institutions of European civilisation – church, army, law, learning, science, monarchy, aristocracy, all those cherished cultural achievements that allegedly raise man's life above the beasts – and one by one he exposes them as a mixture of filth and folly.

His book succeeded brilliantly in being the offence it was meant to be. Men who thought themselves innocent were convicted of guilt; men who boasted of being *animal rationale* were shown to be Yahoos; above all, men complacently happy were denied the right to be so. It is always, for Swift, better to be sadly wise than deludedly self-deceived. The proof that Swift's sortie had hurt is there in the cries of the wounded. The attack upon him for libelling man mounted in intensity as the century advanced. Bolingbroke's restrained reprimand is mildness itself compared with Thomas Warton's censure of the *Travels* as expressing 'a sentiment that dishonours [Swift] as a man, a Christian and a philosopher',[13] and this in turn sounds tame when set beside Young's passionate outburst: 'What a monster hast thou made of the Human face divine!'[14] There was to be no let up in the next century. Hazlitt is a lone voice as he defends Swift against the now standard charge of misanthropy and derides those who bridle at not finding their own deluded estimate of human nature in *Gulliver's Travels*[15] But after Hazlitt the floodgates open as criticism cedes to censure and abuse. Scott cannot justify on moral grounds 'the nakedness with which Swift has sketched this horrible outline of mankind degraded to a bestial state', and speculates that it may well be the 'first impressions of . . . incipient mental disease'.[16] By the end of the century Lecky feels qualified to diagnose Swift's misanthropy as a constitutional melancholy 'mainly due to a physical malady which had long acted upon his brain'.[17] The ease with which literary critics and biographers moved into the fields of pathology and neurology indicates the strength of the assumption that the fourth voyage could only be the work of a madman, since only a madman could hold such a low view of human nature. No one, of course, can compete with Thackeray when it comes to anti-Swift hysteria – it is startling to reflect that the following account of the *Travels* occurs in a study of the English *humourists*: 'horrible, shameful, unmanly, blasphemous . . . Yahoo language, a monster gibbering shrieks and gnashing imprecations against mankind . . . filthy in word, filthy in thought, furious, raging, obscene'.[18] Edmund Gosse, as Thackeray's disciple, demands the banishment of Swift's foul book from every decent household in the land.[19] It is a massive indictment and a formidable array of witnesses, and it provokes an irresistible question: how can these men be talking about the same book that Eliot hailed as one of the greatest triumphs ever achieved by the human soul?

It is worth noting that Eliot's tribute is specifically directed towards the fourth voyage rather than towards the *Travels* as a whole, the very voyage that made Swift's detractors regard him as depraved or mad or both. The fourth voyage is, clearly, the crux. That Swift knew very well what he was doing is plain from the 'Letter to Sympson' when Gulliver, very perceptively for someone supposed to have lost his wits, observes that Houyhnhnmland is the provocation the benevolists choke on. Nobody, he points out, disputes the truth of Lilliput or Brobdingnag: 'I have never yet heard of any Yahoo so presumptuous as to dispute their being, or the facts I have related concerning them; because the truth immediately strikes every reader with conviction'.[20] Despite the strategic exaggeration, this does nevertheless highlight the essential fact that the other voyages do not offend, and are not meant to offend, in the way that the final voyage does, that it *is* the truth of Houyhnhnmland that we cannot abide. Even when we learn that the third voyage was in fact the last to be written, we recognise that the sojourn among the rational horses is the deliberately culminating insult of the book – that Swift, with unerring artistic instinct, placed it last is all the proof we need. Two conclusions are undeniable: first, that Swift meant to hurt someone, and, second, that he succeeded brilliantly in doing so. All that remains is to establish Swift's target and his strategy for drawing blood.

The protests from Bolingbroke onwards readily reveal this target as the myth of human goodness so dear to the liberal mentality. Swift despised it as the product of pride and pursued it even when it took cover within traditional religion. The man who exclaimed, 'Miserable mortals! can we contribute to the honour and glory of God?', and went on to express the wish that the prayer might be struck from the prayer-book, was clearly no candidate for membership of the human nature admiration society.[21] For Swift, not the luminous intellect but dark instincts govern man and society, and the sooner we admit this, the quicker we might do something about it. The *philosophes*, thinking themselves the friends of man, are, in truth, his worst enemies, much as a doctor who does not see a patient's illness endangers his life. The 'Voyage to the Houyhnhnms' has, accordingly, a twofold purpose: to show the patient his true condition and to lash the charlatans who tell him that he is well.

To achieve this dual aim, Swift took certain traditional themes, most notably *le mythe animal* and the voyage of discovery, and re-shaped them to his own brilliantly original ends.

Le mythe animal is, for Swift, not just a rhetorical device – in 'A Modest Proposal', for example, it expresses a point of view integral to his judgement of Ireland. Ireland, however, became for Swift a kind of laboratory for testing and verifying general theories of human nature; if he first found the Yahoo in Ireland, it was merely as a prelude to finding him everywhere else. Ireland was his window on the world and its green-tinted glass coloured all that he saw. Hence *le mythe animal* is, we shall see, just as decisive for the 'Voyage to the Houyhnhnms' as it is for 'A Modest Proposal'. Gulliver, however, had to go voyaging before he could recognize the Yahoo, and so logic supports chronology in advising us to begin with Swift's innovative use of the voyage of discovery as the quickest way to the core of his scandalous book.

We know from his own mouth that, to prepare for its writing, he had been saturating himself in travel literature, no doubt most of it the standard humdrum catalogue of marvels to be found in these generally tall tales.[22] But at this level Swift's interest was only marginally engaged. Intent on making a devastating critique of his own civilisation, he ingeniously adapted the *libertin* tradition of the voyage of discovery as the instrument for achieving this aim. The delicious irony was that in turning this tradition on its head, he caught the *libertins* and their followers in a trap of their own making. *Sapientiam sapientiae perdam*: for Swift there was no higher pleasure. *Gulliver's Travels* uses the voyage of discovery to reassert the view of man discredited by the *libertins* and their eighteenth-century descendants, and it is easy to imagine the relish with which Swift went to work.

The *libertins* employed the voyage to undermine Christian civilisation, and the extent of their influence can be gauged when we hear even Dryden ecstatically recounting how Columbus in the New World found

> guiltless men, who danc'd away their time,
> Fresh as their groves, and happy as their clime.[23]

The Noble Savage was conscripted as a cold warrior against Christian ideology, and the voyage, by contrasting a neurotic Europe, victim of a religion designed to induce misery, with sunny, carefree paganism, became a weapon in the anti-Christian arsenal. The virtuous Chinese, the noble Huron, the happy Polynesian, however different, had one thing in common: they were not Christians, i.e. not hag-ridden, deformed, culturally-corrupted creatures. The *libertin* writers reinterpreted the fall as *into* Christian civilisation – man fell out of Eden into the Church. Jesus was either the morose Galilean who had disastrously conquered or a gentle humanitarian whose pure ethical teachings had been perverted by a pack of life-hating priests. The voyage of discovery, in *libertin* hands, was clearly not just an entertainment, but an important instrument of propaganda. Certainly this is what Diderot strove to do in his philosophic fairy tale, the *Supplement to the Voyage of Admiral Bougainville*. The book is only superficially travel literature; it is fable rather than anthropology, with Tahiti a mythical rather than a geographical construct, an island existing in a doctrinaire imagination rather than situated in the sea. It is not science but indoctrination: come and join us, cries Diderot, see how happy your lives would be if only you rejected the priests' lies – this is his message to his fellow-Europeans. The book's real aim is to change Europe, not describe Tahiti. The island is a teaching aid in a *philosophe's* moral lesson: our surprise is to lead to envy and our envy to emulation.

The journey is just as integral to the meaning of *Gulliver's Travels*, with Swift, in a very different way, just as much a propagandist as Diderot. To appreciate this we need only contrast the travels of Gulliver with those of his contemporary, Crusoe. Crusoe's journeys leave him unchanged, the same person he was before he undertook them. In a very real sense Crusoe *has* no experience, is immune to it – he is the same restless entrepreneur at the end as at the beginning. On the final page he marries, has three children, loses his wife through death, and goes adventuring again, all in one sentence. Crusoe cannot wait to get back to the life he loves and always has loved from the moment he defied his father's wishes to go to sea. Nothing has changed; all these voyages have merely confirmed Crusoe's identity, have, if anything, made him more Crusoe than ever.

With Gulliver things are very different; if the travels are Gulliver's, he is likewise theirs – he belongs to them and they mould and alter him, making him successively a Lilliputian and a Brobdingnagian, if not physically, certainly mentally. He hotly denies the charge of adultery with the Lilliputian lady instead of hooting at its absurdity; he loses patience at the dilatoriness of his rescuers after his stay in Brobdingnag – why doesn't someone simply hook a finger though the ring of his box and lift it out of the water? A Brobdingnagian could do it and Gulliver has forgotten that ordinary people are not Brobdingnagians. Gulliver has, one might almost say, too much experience, lacks certain vital antibodies that might help him to resist it – he is the prisoner of experience where Crusoe is so breathtakingly above it.

Gulliver's extreme amenability to change, his almost chameleon-like receptivity towards it, is evidenced above all in the last voyage which effects so profound a transformation in him, thus making it so paradigmatic of a major theme in twentieth-century literature. The contrast with the use of the journey in nineteenth-century fiction is instructive. The journey in the *Travels*, as in *Heart of Darkness* or *Death in Venice*, is a metaphor, the objective correlative of an internal dislocation, of the kind of dramatic alteration which an older terminology would have described as salvation or damnation. It is in this sense that the *Travels* belong with *The Pilgrim's Progress* rather than with *Martin Chuzzlewit*. Bunyan sends his hero travelling because he is the true wayfaring Christian and the road he walks is a metaphor for the search after salvation. Dickens sends *his* hero to America because sales are flagging, and Dickens calls in the New World to restore commercially the failure of the old; the voyage is not indispensable to Martin's growth as a character, but is simply a bright idea for stimulating consumer interest. Dickens, very amusingly, grasps the opportunity to ridicule America, but Martin's journey is, finally, incidental to the book's meaning. By contrast, the journey *is* the meaning of *Gulliver's Travels* and *The Pilgrim's Progress*, just as it is of *Heart of Darkness* and *Death in Venice*.

The journey in *Martin Chuzzlewit* is representative of the journey in nineteenth-century fiction as a whole – there are no journeys of the metaphorical kind, merely changes of scene, different locales; people travel, but the movement is strictly topographical, never metaphorical or internal. There is no journey *into* the self as there is in Bunyan and Swift, Conrad and Mann. Sydney Carton goes to Paris to lay down his life for Lucy, an opportunity which London does not supply. Mr Dorrit goes to Italy to find out that nothing has changed, that he's the same as ever, as much a prisoner in Venice as he ever was in the Marshalsea. *Bleak House* shuttles between London and Leicestershire, but not to expose any radical discontinuity such as exists between Houyhnhnmland and England, or

Bavaria and Venice. London is one place, Leicestershire another, with Lady Dedlock linking them at the level of plot; the contrast is used skilfully by Dickens for variety and narrative suspense, but not to produce any conversion of character in those who travel from one place to the other. Only in *Daniel Deronda* is there a hint of the Damascus Road experience, but the novel ends with Palestine still in the future tense and the life-transforming journey still to be made.

The 'Voyage to the Houyhnhnms' is, by contrast, such a journey, superficially from England to Houyhnhnmland, essentially from Pelagius to Augustine, from cosy domesticity to radical alienation, from benevolism to misanthropy, from an assumption of innocence to a conviction of sin. Gulliver is changed, changed utterly, and the book describes and explains the transformation. Crusoe lists as one of the greatest evils pressing upon him the fact that he is divided from mankind, a *solitaire*, one banished from human society; the alienated Gulliver celebrates this separation from humanity as his greatest blessing.[24] There is no hint of the impending change in the astonishing opening sentence of the last voyage. Astonishing, of course, only in retrospect, for Swift's artistry conceals from us the shocking disclosure so guardedly withheld till the climax, namely, that the man who sits down in his house at Redriff to write his story is a misanthrope. Gulliver tells it as it happens, so that events are interpreted as they presented themselves at the time, emotions described as initially experienced, not mediated through the much-altered sensibility of the alienated man. It is a remarkable feat on Swift's part, for we tend to forget the beginning by the time we reach the end, an end which is in such devastating contrast to the beginning:

> I continued at home with my wife and children about five months in a very happy condition, if I could have learned the lesson of knowing when I was well. I left my poor wife big with child, and accepted an advantageous offer . . . .[25]

Only in hindsight does it strike us as a bafflingly intriguing statement. The speaker is a born-again man who now repudiates human existence as irredeemable Yahoo filth, who regards his wife as a female Yahoo, a breeder of vermin, and his children as the fruits of a nasty trick by nature upon him to perpetuate Yahoo existence. Yet the opening sounds like a lament for lost happiness, regret for a false step taken. The lost happiness is inseparable from a lost innocence; back home in Yahoo England (before he knew it *was* Yahoo) he had been 'in a very happy condition'. Unfortunately, he had failed to learn 'the lesson of knowing when I was well' and had regrettably, as he now sees it, 'left my poor wife big with child' to go wandering again. Pascal declared that all our troubles stem from an inability to sit still in one room, and Gulliver's self-reproaches make him sound like another example of that tragic unrest.[26]

Houyhnhnmland is at once both education and disillusion; at the same time as Gulliver stops being a fool he stops being a happy man. It is, of course, essential that he should begin the voyage as fool, since the voyage is the record of his education. The opening pages present a series of mistakes beginning with Gulliver's unfortunate decision not to stay put in England and so remain a good Englishman, citizen, family man, happily accepting the social roles prepared for him by the society into which he was born. Next, Captain Pocock is briefly introduced as a warning about what happens to those who will neither take advice nor let well alone, a pointer to Gulliver's own fate. 'An honest man and a good sailor' – like Gulliver himself – Pocock was regrettably 'a little too positive in his own opinions, which was the cause of his destruction, as it hath been of several others. For if he had followed my advice, he might at this time have been safe at home with his family as well as myself.'[27]

Pocock, clearly, is to Gulliver as Captain Fresleven in *Heart of Darkness* is to Marlow – a hint of what's to come, a forerunner who suffers a similar catastrophe. But, in addition to the irony of Gulliver's deploring anyone's destruction for being too sure of himself, there is, in retrospect, the problem of deciding the identity of the person who criticises the obstinacy of his lost colleague. 'At this time' clearly refers to the moment of writing – these are the words of the man busy with his memoirs. The man dragged back protesting to his wife and children by Don Pedro is reprimanding the headstrong Pocock for not being 'safe at home with his family as well as myself'. The reader at this point cannot, of course, foresee the alienated Gulliver, jumping overboard from Don Pedro's ship, preferring death in the sea or at the hands of savages to returning to his Yahoo home. Five years after that return Gulliver is still disgusted with England – 'home' is precisely where he does *not* feel safe, and, in his view, with good cause, for he regards the Yahoos he lives with as dangerous and treacherous animals. Swift's narrative technique requires, of course, that the bombshell of

Gulliver's misanthropy should be held back for the final pages, so that, reading the book for the first time, we do not puzzle over these contradictions, for we do not see them. What we do know is that Gulliver, unlike Pocock, is a survivor, who, for that reason, feels himself superior to his lost colleague; but, equally, we are entitled to assume that the fourth voyage has been a bad experience which Gulliver would have done well to avoid. Otherwise why the lamenting opening sentence? Whatever has happened to him and whatever he has learned, it has not made him a happy man. If the truth sets you free, it is a bleak liberation.

His own mistake in leaving home and Pocock's suicidal resistance to good advice are followed by another misjudgement which is the immediate cause of the Hoyhnhnm exile. He is forced through sickness among his crew to take on new recruits at the Barbadoes and Leeward Islands and they turn out to be buccaneers who later mutiny and put him ashore on an unknown island. It is the third mistake within one page, surely too many to be just coincidence. Is the voyage to reveal a catalogue of blunders? This suspicion is reinforced when we recall that the illness which killed off some of his crew, thus compelling him to recruit the future mutineers, was calentures – a disease incident to sailors within the tropics, characterised by delirium in which they fancy the sea to be green fields and try to leap into it. It intensifies the theme of self-destruction resulting from self-deception, of men rushing to embrace a ruin which they misinterpret as liberation. Is the physical fever of calentures a proleptic annunciation of the mental fever that will possess the deluded hero at the end of his adventures? Yet, come the end, we are compelled, unless we wish to regard the whole experience as an unmitigated disaster, to join Gulliver in reassessing his mistakes as belonging to the *felix culpa* variety, since it is thanks to them that he meets the wise horses and learns the sad truth of his own condition. This knowledge makes it impossible to continue the good husband, father, citizen and patriot who set out from home, but the happiness of these roles now appears as an Epicurean folly which the hero of truth must sternly renounce.

The problem of reconciling the contradictions between the voyage's beginning and end has led to the spinning of elaborately sophisticated theories about the *Travels*, concentrating upon the devious character of the narrator. Why does the misanthrope lament his lost family and homeland? Why doesn't he proclaim

triumphantly from the start the boon of his Houyhnhnm enlightenment? One answer is to divide Gulliver into two, Gulliver-author
and Gulliver-character. Gulliver-character has the adventures
while Gulliver-author writes them down. Although a raging misanthrope, Gulliver-author, with a detachment that Flaubert or
Joyce might have envied and with a reticence worthy of a Jamesian
narrator, holds back his present mature point of view until the
climax. With breathtaking skill he projects himself as he once was,
as Gulliver-character, holding views which his present self must
regard with contempt. Gulliver-author is, we perceive, a consummate literary artist, brilliantly able to create the illusion of the
immediacy of his former self's experience.[28]

Yet the truth is that the Jamesian approach to the *Travels* is
completely inappropriate, creating more problems than it solves.
Swift is not a novelist at all, far less a Jamesian one, but a satirist
whose paramount aim is not the presentation of character but the
devastation of pride. Gulliver is not a character, much less a
complex 'compositional centre', but a tool in Swift's hands for
subverting human dignity. Sometimes he is an *ingénu* as when he
watches uncomprehendingly the rope-dancers of Lilliput, sometimes corrupt as when he attempts to bribe the Giant King with the
secret of gunpowder, sometimes he denounces England as a cesspool, sometimes he boasts about the ingenuity with which we blow
our enemies to bits – he has, in fact, no psychological consistency
because he is forever at Swift's disposal, to be used in whichever
opportunist way Swift decides. Swift does not create characters, he
savages pride. How to do the maximum damage to human vanity:
this is the key to his narrative method, and sophisticated distinctions between Gulliver-author and Gulliver-character, however
ingenious, are really irrelevant to the text.

The maximum harassment of man – this was the problem that
Swift set himself to solve at the outset of the last voyage. He decided
that reader and narrator should both enter Houyhnhnmland in the
same deluded condition, sharing the same foolish hubris of
western man, equipped with the same fatal set of assumptions
concerning his own superiority. We accompany Gulliver on a
journey from innocence to experience, from complacency to demoralisation, and are made to participate in the same process of in-
crimination. It is the journey that *vous autres*, the misguided
champions of *animal rationale*, must be inveigled into making, and
the last thing Swift wants is to put them on their guard too soon.

First get them into Houhnhnmland in the company of a lover of humanity, one of their own kind, and then spring the various traps that leave them in the end demoralised and dismayed. It would have been counterproductive to expose Gulliver from the outset as an alienated man, because we are to follow him as he reluctantly reaches his depressing conclusions about man, England and home. To show him straight off as a raging misanthrope would have jeopardised the sense of identification upon which the success of the book depends. Gulliver enters Houyhnhnmland as author as he entered it as character, not because *he's* a brilliant literary artist, but because Swift is. Swift needs a normal, everyday, unimaginative Englishman, thoroughly conformist, blindly obedient to the beliefs of the society from which he comes – *our* society, which we, too, unthinkingly revere and obey – because what happens to him is to have profoundly disturbing consequences for us. To present him too precipitately as a hater of our society would have made us distrust him from the start – even with the book as written there is still a massive resistance on our part to its unnerving discoveries.

Gulliver, then, enters Houyhnhnmland like any ordinary European traveller, with the standard set of assumptions, prejudices and preconceptions. He does not expect to meet equal, far less superior beings, but savages, childish primitives, whom he can cajole, bribe or overawe by dint of the superior cultural inheritance he possesses. How could a man like Gulliver believe otherwise? He is *homo sapiens, animal rationale,* the crown of creation; better still, he is European man, and, best and most conclusive of all, he is English man, the highest conceivable production of culture and the Everest of anthropological excellence. That this is his implicit credo is evident from his conduct. Even although he is marooned on Houyhnhnmland, an unwilling visitor, he still arrives, in the best European tradition, fully equipped with a supply of 'toys', trinkets and knicknacks to beguile the simple natives. All western sailors, he tells us, carry such items for just such emergencies, and his attitude is that of a whole civilisation at a moment of colonialist expansion, a civilisation which regards its own superiority as axiomatic. It is the attitude unwaveringly held by Crusoe throughout his adventures and reflects the established European – savage relationship of the time. It is the attitude which Gulliver holds on his entry into Houyhnhnmland but which the experiences of the last voyage will stunningly reverse.

This reversal is brought about through a series of parallels and

contrasts in whicn Gulliver, Houyhnhnm and Yahoo are played off
against each other. Within a couple of pages Gulliver meets and
misunderstands the two creatures that will so profoundly alter his
life. Yahoo and Houyhnhnm are similarly startled when they first
encounter the newcomer and each reacts by preventing him from
going on his uninterrupted way, but there the resemblance ends.
Their modes of detaining him are worlds apart, the one belonging
to the order of nature at its filthiest, the other to the order of culture
at its most dignified and authoritative. It is the astonished Yahoo
who makes the first overture towards Gulliver and who gets beaten
with the flat of a sword for his loathsome familiarity. His roar of
pain summons a herd of supporters and produces the assault which
places Gulliver in danger of death by excremental suffocation –
their method of attack is faithful to the sensation of disgust provoked in Gulliver as he first surveys them. Only the arrival of the
horse saves Gulliver by causing the filthy creatures to flee.

The horse is equally puzzled at the sight of Gulliver but otherwise
there is a significant transposition of roles which has the effect
straight from the outset, long before there is the slightest suspicion
of brainwashing, of aligning Gulliver with Yahoo rather than with
Houyhnhnm. Gulliver, in a way that comes naturally to man by
virtue of his cultural conditioning, attempts to stroke the horse as a
means of keeping it docile and friendly; he is politely but very
firmly rebuffed for presuming to take such a liberty. The assumption of superiority implicit in Gulliver's gesture is at once ques-
tioned in this tiny hint of the far more shocking *bouleversement* to
come. The horse's civilised but distinctly disdainful snub is the first
minor shock that Gulliver will sustain in a programme of re-educa-
tion that necessitates unlearning as a prelude to learning. The horse
puts Gulliver in his decidedly inferior place, much as Swift himself,
darkening at Sheridan's forwardness, might have reproved him for
overshooting the mark.

But, of course, far from there being any excremental onslaught,
there is not even the slightest violence, as befits the rational
creature that the Houyhnhnm will prove to be. The horse relies
upon moral authority, not excrement, to defend itself against impertinence. Even in rejecting Gulliver's condescending advance,
the horse continues to be mild and dignified – it is simply that the
interloper, however puzzling, must be made to understand from
the start that in Houyhnhnmland the horse rules and that Arch-
bishop Marsh's logic-manual has no authority within this country.

Homo est animal rationale, equus est animal irrationale; stick to such breathtakingly arrogant assumptions and you will go hopelessly astray in Houyhnhnmland. The impression of equine authority is reinforced by the arrival of the second horse and the conference that follows; after the politely formal greeting, the two animals go aside and converse 'like persons deliberating upon some affair of weight'.[29] So the young Swift might have watched from a distance while Sir William Temple walked with some important visitor in the garden at Moor Park discussing the fate of Europe. The horses are clearly superior from the outset, long before there is any hint that Gulliver has fallen victim to the Houyhnhnm propaganda machine and been brainwashed into accepting their ascendancy. Their superiority plainly resides in themselves and not in Gulliver's deluded, disordered mind.

The idea of trying to cajole such superior beings with the trashy trinkets aimed at dazzling primitive simpletons is preposterous, though not as yet to the brainwashed Gulliver. For Gulliver *is* brainwashed, has been so long before he reaches Houyhnhnmland – he has an unfaltering certitude that his own species, man, is the perfection of nature; this explains his astonishment as he watches the two horses. 'I was amazed to see such actions and behaviour in brute beasts.'[30] The underlying assumption is glaringly obvious: since, alone in creation, man has a monopoly of reason, one of two things must be true. Either the horses belong to a race of rational supermen who have communicated to these beasts a portion of their own vast intelligence; or they really are men after all, magicians in disguise, which would account for their being so orderly, rational, acute and judicious. The unquestioned axiom of human superiority, the hubristic hauteur of the anthropocentric delusion, could not be more visibly demonstrated. Swift, who had as an undergraduate studied Marsh's logic but who had over the years grown away from its arrogantly facile premises, is determined that Gulliver shall do likewise. Before the mind can play host to truth, it has to be cleared of cant; Gulliver has to shed false learning before he can acquire true. His attitude to the horse is crucial for this process. At the start he expects to be carried on its back; at the end he is boasting with provocative humility of the breathtaking privilege which the Houyhnhnm permitted at parting, the kiss on the hoof so graciously granted and so reverently performed.

But already in the first meeting of man and horse, anticipations of the future transformation, clues for the watchful, have been provided. It is the Yahoo who tries to touch Gulliver, just as it is Gulliver who tries to touch the Houyhnhnm, and in each case the superior being indignantly rejects the presumptuous advance. It is the Yahoo who roars with pain when Gulliver strikes him, just as Gulliver similarly roars with pain when the puzzled horses, investigating the mystery of his clothing, squeeze so much that they inadvertently hurt him. In each situation it is Gulliver's affinity to the Yahoo, the inferior partner, that is being emphasised. Burke calls conduct 'the only language that rarely lies'. On that reliable criterion we can safely assume Gulliver's inferiority. He obeys the horse; without any need for force he quietly does what he is told to do. Peremptorily commanded to stop when, during the horses' discussion, he starts to walk away, he immediately, unprotestingly, does so. The Yahoos try and fail to subdue him with dung, but the moral authority of the Houyhnhnms, the neigh of command, is in itself enough to stop him in his tracks. When the horses move off, Gulliver dutifully walks behind as instructed. Pizarro's mounted men seemed like celestial beings to the ignorant Indians and in *Heart of Darkness* the white men are like gods. But right from the start, even though there is much about Gulliver that baffles them, the horses treat him as an inferior creature. Their attitude never alters; the great change is to occur within Gulliver as he gradually comes to accept the justice of their judgement. There may be, to begin with, mutual incomprehension – theirs at his un-Yahoo like 'capacity', his at their astonishingly 'human' reason – but there is never any doubt as to which in the end will emerge as the commanding creature.

Nor is there any doubt that from the start Gulliver recognises the dignity of the one, and the filth of the other, animal. The horses strike him as neat, clean and attractive – significantly, the first female he meets is a 'very comely mare'. The Yahoos, by contrast, are ugly and revolting, filthy from first to last, without one single redeeming quality. To describe them as evil is to flatter them, for they are so only in a peculiarly Swiftian sense. They are odiously banal, and, pondering this, we touch upon one of the major differences between Swift and our modern investigators of the dark epiphany. It is too facile to explain this difference by pointing to the Romantic Revolution intervening between us and the great Augustan. Long before that the idea of evil as dangerously and attractively glamorous, of the greatness and hence the seductiveness of diabolism, is present in our culture – Milton's ruined archangel is all the proof we need. But the commentary of Blake and Shelley on *Paradise Lost* and the evolution of the damned hero from Byron and the Brontës onward shows how Romanticism intensified the temptation to flirt with the grandeur of evil. Macbeth so easily modulates into Raskolnikov and the commission of a crime becomes with Nietzsche the test of daring and the proof of greatness. Evil is what the timid condemn because it is beyond them; the hero has the courage to step over the prohibitions imposed on petty souls.

Of this attitude there is not the slightest speck or scintilla in Swift. We scour his pages in vain for a glimpse of the romantic malefactor, of Macbeth or Milton's Satan, Manfred or Cain, Ahab or Peter Quint. Swift denies man the romantic satisfaction of imagining himself a great sinner when he is merely vermin; nobody ever secretly hankered to be a Yahoo or his equally disgusting brother the beau as some do dream of being Melville's Ahab or Milton's Satan. The demonic is noticeably absent from his work, is invoked at all only to be derided as a shabby trick by ignoble man to shift blame on to someone else's shoulders. The idea that either heaven or hell is faintly interested in such nasty nonsense strikes Swift as simply another token of man's intolerable conceit.[31] Surveying the whole gamut of human folly from a little boy playing truant to a lost maidenhead and a highwayman dying on the gallows, Swift derides the human tendency to magnify our mean misdemeanours by attributing to them an infernal inspiration – 'the Devil did the deed, not they!'[32]

We will find no great criminals or demonic heroes in Swift; what we will find in abundance is a squalid, glamourless filth – not diabolic supermen, but unclean animals, beaux and Yahoos. Swift is the master of disgust, lord of the latrines, and the *cloaca* is his domain. The great criminal is essentially no different from the petty culprit; it is the same effluence, only more of it and causing a greater stink. His 'Satirical Elegy on the Death of a Late Famous General', in which he bitterly inverts the elegy genre, is designed to strip the glory from Marlborough and show him for the contemptible miscreant he is:

> How very mean a thing's a Duke;
> From all his ill-got honours flung,
> Turned to that dirt from whence he sprung.[33]

Swift's strategy of satiric reduction aims at demolishing all human pretensions to any kind of greatness, including satanic: Henry IV is merely a Yahoo whose erection has almost caused a European conflagration, Louis XIV's diseased rectum has governed history for a lifetime – man is forever cut down to his contemptible size.[34] Since evil for Swift is always associated with disgust, Gulliver's description of the Yahoo should not surprise us: 'I never beheld in all my travels so disagreeable an animal, nor one against which I naturally conceived so strong an antipathy.'[35] And, as always in Swift, if the male is repulsive, the female is even more noisome. Instead of the 'very comely mare', there is the female Yahoo, anus, pudenda, dugs and all, guaranteed to castrate the erotic imagination. In Dutch law to lie with a Hottentot woman was an offence punishable by death, but from the disgusted accounts of the travellers such prohibition was redundant – 'they need not have laid that restriction upon them, the very smell and looks of such creatures being a sufficient antidote against lechery.'[36] Gulliver is protected against the attractions of evil by an advanced capacity for disgust.

The disgust is, in fact, so intense that it interferes with his vision. It is ironical that Gulliver, who at first mistakes the Houyhnhnms for men in disguise, fails to see that the Yahoos really are men in disguise. Certainly the 'very comely mare' does not return Gulliver's compliment when, after the briefest of inspections, she contemptuously dismisses him as a Yahoo. She, unlike Gulliver, spots the resemblance immediately. When Gulliver is taken out to the yard and placed beside the Yahoo, he, too, is forced to admit the justice of the identification, even if it is to his 'everlasting mortification'. He knows, in fact, that the identification would be even more complete and convincing but for the blessed camouflage of clothes – the Houyhnhnms think that Gulliver looks very like a Yahoo despite the unsolved mystery of his dress, but Gulliver knows that, underneath the disguise, he is much more shockingly a Yahoo than the horses suspect.

But even if he is mortified, he is still not brainwashed. Admitting to himself the physical resemblance, he does his best to keep his secret and stay disguised. He is not the kind of devout convert who rushes to parade his iniquities in a mood of exhibitionist contrition. He resists the identification and begs his master not to insult and distress him by calling him a Yahoo, a creature for which he has a total detestation. Even if in the yard line-up he is compelled to acknowledge 'a perfect human figure' in the Yahoo, he continues to find it repulsive, 'although there were few greater lovers of mankind, at that time, than myself'.[37] That strategically situated 'although' is, of course, deliberately provocative and advertises the future misanthrope, but for the rest the words are those of a man resolved to refute the Yahoo charge. Three months into Houyhnhnmland and almost four chapters into the voyage, he is still declining any essential affinity with the Yahoo. Far from being brainwashed, he is telling the Houyhnhnm that once back home in England nobody will believe his story about rational horses. His shipwreck is, like Crusoe's, still strictly literal – he is in Houyhnhnmland only because he doesn't know how to get home. Nor does he feel any need to flatter the Houyhnhnm by pretending that he prefers Houyhnhnmland to England – 'if good fortune ever restored me to my native country' is a statement that betrays no disaffection with his homeland;[38] Gulliver is still a patriot.

This, of course, contrasts vividly with the end when, having implored and been refused political asylum, he laments the catastrophe of his expulsion from Houyhnhnmland and blames it all on 'Fortune, my perpetual enemy'. But the change is gradual and is resisted. Even as late as Chapter 7, more than half-way through the voyage, at a point when evidence of a radical disloyalty is becoming visible, he still nevertheless shows, in a revealing parenthesis, an unease with the man-Yahoo identification. He is reporting the Houyhnhnm on the shortcomings of man, as represented by Gulliver, in contrast with the Yahoo – 'I could neither run with speed, nor climb trees like my brethren (as he called them) the Yahoos in this country.'[39] The interpolation clearly shows that Gulliver resents the identification – its tetchy attribution to the Houyhnhnm makes it plain that he has still not appropriated it himself. Before he does appropriate it, a long course of Houyhnhnm education is necessary.

There is, however, some justification in the objection that the education we witness in the fourth voyage is not just a one-way process, for if the horse teaches Gulliver, it is equally true that Gulliver teaches the horse. They learn from each other, and if Gulliver is amazed at the rational horses, they are just as astounded at the wonderful Yahoo. From the start he confounds them with his linguistic ability. Just as Gulliver initially assumed that the horses must be sorcerers disguised, so they assume, equally erroneously, that Gulliver must have been taught to imitate a rational creature. Nobody, clearly, is safe from cultural conditioning and the shackles of ingrained assumptions. The horse simply cannot credit Gulliver's tall story about crossing the sea in a ship crewed by Yahoos, for he knows that no Yahoo could do this, just as he knows that no Houyhnhnm could build such a vessel – Gulliver cannot be telling the truth. Yet Gulliver *is* telling the truth as even the Houyhnhnm Master is gradually forced to admit. The fact that the Houyhnhnm listens and learns is proved, in rather chilling fashion, when he recommends to the grand representative council as a means of solving the Yahoo problem the castration technique first brought to his attention by his wonderful Yahoo.

It is true, then, that the Houyhnhnm has much to learn from Gulliver just as Gulliver has much to learn from him. But it is vital to distinguish between what each has to teach the other. It is essentially a difference between the indicative and the imperative moods, between science and morality, is and ought – the horse has to learn certain facts, whereas Gulliver has to learn certain values, and values shockingly at odds with the cultural baggage he has carried from England. We, as readers, already know what Gulliver knows; there is nothing he can teach us, at least in his pre-Houyhnhnm state of mind, about England and Europe, lawyers and war, and all the rest – in these subjects we are all graduates of the same university. Does Gulliver have to go to Houyhnhnmland for us to discover that war is hell and lawyers are crooks? The crucial importance for us of the fourth voyage is not what Gulliver has to teach but what he has to learn. What he learns is surely what we, too, must learn – for what other reason was the book written? We are taken to Houyhnhnmland to unlearn what we already know, to surrender the assumptions that flatter us, and learn from the Houyhnhnm our true condition. It is nothing less than a question of how we are to live, since the way we live now is so appallingly wrong. The Houyhnhnm Master, having listened carefully to Gulliver, tells us so, and the Houyhnhnm Master is right. On matters of fact he is often mistaken but his value judgements are always *ex cathedra*; the horse has spoken and the case is finished. *Vous autres* will not like it, but where in all Swift is there the slightest hint that he wrote to please *vous autres*?

There can, accordingly, be no greater distortion of the book's purpose than to concentrate too closely upon the mistakes of the Houyhnhnms, many and obvious though they be. They go on making these mistakes to the very end – on the eve of his expulsion, Gulliver, looking from a hilltop with his pocket-glass to spy the nearest land, sees about five leagues away a small island which the sorrel nag, lacking all conception of any country but his own, mistakes for a blue cloud. *Quantum sumus, scimus:* we know what we have been programmed to know and the sorrel nag knows there is no land but Houyhnhnmland. But Gulliver knows better and islands are not clouds, however much one venerates those who say they are. We all, Houyhnhnms included, live in perceptual prisons, slaves to the arbitrary norms which we deludedly elevate into unchallengeable truths, arrogantly taking as cognition what is no better than mere custom. Nobody is immune: Lilliputians, Brobdingnagians, Laputans, Houyhnhnms – and Englishmen – exhibit the same proneness to mistake conditioning for truth.

But it would be a strangely redundant voyage if its main purpose was to expose the false views of the Houyhnhnms by telling us what we already know: that men can build ships and sail them, that in Europe men rule horses and not the converse, that countries exist other than Houyhnhnmland, and so on. Not the 'scientific', factual blunders of the horses but the sins of men – this is what the book exists to expose and condemn. The very ignorance of the Houyhnhnm, even in its most complacently erroneous form, becomes for Swift the means to highlight human depravity. The horse shakes his head reprovingly over Gulliver's tall tales of European massacre – he knows that such horrors are a fiction, an invention, the thing which is not, Gulliver telling his outrageous fibs like a little boy bent upon creating an impression; and he knows this simply by looking, since the mere appearance of Gulliver shows that his species has not been equipped by nature to wreak such bloody destruction. What the horse doesn't know, of course, and what we do, is a fact, namely, the invention of gunpowder – it is this invention and not Gulliver's genius for telling lies that explains the catalogue of atrocities just recounted. The scientific ignorance of the horse is the sign of his moral innocence and it would be well for man if he were so blessedly obtuse. Such, at least, is surely Swift's conclusion. He wrote his book not to make fools of the virtuous horses but to launch an attack upon vicious men.

Sophisticated Yahoos who prefer to focus on Houyhnhnm errors, thus deflecting attention from themselves, will have little trouble in finding the placatory evidence. Even Gulliver's clothes are a conundrum beyond the horses' solving, preventing them from making a complete identification of Gulliver as 'a right Yahoo'. Gulliver clings to his disguise 'in order to distinguish myself as much as possible, from that cursed race of Yahoos',[40] even though he knows that he can, at best, only postpone discovery – clothes must wear out and need to be replaced, and whatever can be divested is not integral to us. It is Lear's recognition on the heath as the mad king throws off his 'lendings' to become the bare, forked, unaccommodated thing, the reality beneath the trappings. Clothes are not, Gulliver's efforts to preserve them notwithstanding, a distinction but merely a screen, and, for him as for Lear, stripping is the precondition of self-knowledge. Swift's mode is, of course, the comic, but the underlying meaning is no less serious here than in Shakespeare – the implications for us as human beings are as disturbing in the satire as in the tragedy.

Clothes become a kind of synecdoche, standing for culture itself, for all those things once considered integral to us, indivisible from our essence, which are now shown to be so easily discardable. Throughout the *Travels* the problem of the conditioned reflex, of what taken to an extreme today would be called brainwashing and which Swift would have called the power of habit, is continually present; the final voyage merely carries it to a climax at once comic and shocking. Perhaps, finally, when all inessentials have been stripped away and all accretions removed, the one remaining, inalienable reality that man can call his own will be the nastiness he shares with the Yahoo. If this is the *Travels'* final destination, then the clothes incident, the initial evasion and subsequent disclosure, signals the far more radical disrobing that is to come. In fact, Swift is unwilling to wait for the clothes to wear out; Gulliver's secret is calamitously exposed when the sorrel nag catches him asleep and undressed, and rushes to the master horse with the news that the intruder 'was not the same thing when I slept as I appeared to be at other times'.[41] Sleep, as Freud will announce nearly two centuries later, is precisely the time when the watch is absent and the guards are down. Swift's is, however, a far more shocking suggestion than Freud's, or than Goya's when he called his painting 'The Sleep of Reason'; do we delude ourselves, Swift asks, when we imply that reason was ever awake and in control?

The master, having insisted on seeing Gulliver naked, concludes that he 'must be a perfect Yahoo', perfect, that is, in the sense of complete or total. Gulliver is distressed at being classed with so odious an animal and begs that the mystery of his clothes should not be published any further. He still resists the identification, conceding likeness but not sameness; he admits his 'resemblance in every part but could not account for their degenerate and brutal nature'.[42] He looks like but isn't a Yahoo; appearances are against him, but how many innocent men have been tragically condemned due to misleading appearances, circumstantial evidence and mistaken identity? The stage is set for the trial of Gulliver on the charge of being a Yahoo, a Gulliver whom Swift has very deliberately selected to appear as the universal human representative, a normal, everyday man, good husband, good father, good citizen. From the outset Gulliver presents his credentials to speak on our behalf – when the case begins, 'there were few greater lovers of mankind, at that time, than myself'.[43] As much as Winston Smith in Oceania, Gulliver is the last man in Houyhnhnmland; he is, in his own estimation, as much above the Yahoos as Winston believed himself above the proles. Each of these characters, in his fall, pulls down mankind with him as irretrievably as ever Adam did. In neither case is religion any help; Orwell does not believe, and Swift will only countenance a religion that takes as its premise the idea of human corruption. He deliberately goes out of his way to attack the new, milder form of Christianity, predicated upon the contrary idea of human goodness, that was fast conquering Europe. How else can we explain Gulliver's provocative remark that he still will not allow his wife or children 'to touch my bread, or drink out of the same cup'?[44] Is it at all conceivable that any Anglican clergyman, let alone Swift, could have used these words without realising that he was making an almost explicit repudiation of the Communion service? Clearly, Swift was resolved to go to the limit in his assault upon the new optimism. Know thyself, he advises his contemporaries; it is for Swift the beginning of Christian as well as of pagan wisdom.

The trial of Gulliver hinges accordingly upon a question of identity: is he *animal rationale* or Yahoo, the virtuous being he presumes to be or the odious creature to which he will at first admit no more than a superficial physical resemblance? Gulliver assembles his evidence and tells the Houyhnhnm all about home; the latter listens, nauseated, bewildered, appalled at our perverse ingenuity, so far ahead of anything that the Yahoos of Houyhnhnmland can perform. In presenting his case, the horse, in his turn, establishes a series of convincing parallels between European practices and Yahoo misdemeanours. Finally, the dismayed Gulliver, turning ethologist, does some practical fieldwork among the Yahoos which ends in his accepting the charge of Yahoo as a true bill of indictment. The satire requires, of course, that the as yet unenlightened Gulliver should, in the course of his narration, describe European iniquities as normal, everyday behaviour, or even, in still deeper ignorance, crow over our depravities. He accepts wickedness as normal, hence must be re-educated to see the wickedness of normalcy in a process the exact converse of that which he has long since undergone: we are all trained by the culture into which we are born to sin with equanimity and even self-satisfaction. 'I never wonder to see men wicked but I wonder to see them not ashamed'.[45] Swift battles to restore the sense of shame, in his view deplorably lost from the economy of human emotions. The 'Voyage to the Houyhnhnms' is an education into shame; Swift, repeating the Bible and anticipating Freud, finds in the capacity for guilt the unique spoor of the human being. Will Gulliver learn to become ashamed of himself or will he continue the deluded champion of human dignity that he was on entry to Houyhnhnmland? This is what the book is about.

Even the complacently uncomprehending Gulliver is gradually brought, via the Houyhnhnm's questioning, to see that all is not as well with man as he had thought. The horse hears with puzzled dismay the tale of Gulliver's maritime misadventures, the number and variety of the dangers to which seamen expose themselves, and puts the obvious but seldom-asked question: how does any captain persuade a crew to follow him into such perils? In answering, Gulliver tells the truth as much to himself as to the horse. The men he recruits are almost all fugitives and criminals, murderers and thieves, who prefer the unpredictable hazards of the sea to the certain gallows that awaits them on land. Given that this is the calibre of the colonisers, we should not be surprised at the devastating critique of empire-building that comes in the concluding pages. What other than rape, pillage and murder could we expect from such a gang of thugs as Gulliver's or any other ship's-crew is certain to be? The squalid fiction that these colonisers are really emissaries of Christian civilisation merely adds humbug to infamy; behind the fraud of the cultural mission is the unchecked rapacity of Pizarro and Cortez. Nor does Swift's mordant irony permit us to flatter ourselves, as Conrad seems inclined to allow in *Heart of Darkness*, that the English are, colonially speaking, an immaculate conception, blessedly preserved from the sins of other sea-going rascals – there is no hint in Swift of a 'lesser-breeds-without-the-law' mentality.

And so we proceed through the charge-sheet until every institution to which we point in proof of our civilisation – church, law, army, education, and so on – is exposed as the filthy sham it is. Clothed, it might just escape detection; stripped naked, each is like Duessa unmasked. Gulliver may cling to the myth of virtue and extol 'the dear place of my nativity', may even be so sottishly corrupt as to smile at the horse's scepticism concerning the exterminating power of European man, but gradually the weight of the evidence begins to tell and the balance to tip. Gulliver learns as he unlearns. The Houyhnhnm is first 'wholly at a loss' to comprehend human depravity and then expresses 'amazement and indignation'. Gulliver has to learn to experience these same emotions towards behaviour which he had regarded as normal or even laudable when he set out on his final voyage.

What he learns is that the dear place of his nativity is a sewer, his continent a cesspool. Gulliver's description of western medicine shows Swift capitalising to the full on his genius for disgust. Purges and clysters abound; we float in a sea of vomit and excrement, of evacuations from every possible orifice. The prescriptions rival the ailments in their loathsomeness, made up as they are of toads, frogs, spiders, dead men's flesh and bones. It is a society that is decomposing even as we inspect it, and the images of the flayed woman and the beau's body are its appropriate emblems.[46] As in medicine so in politics – prostitution and power are inextricable: decayed wenches, favourite footmen, these are the significantly named 'tunnels through which all graces are conveyed'.[47] Predictably in so promiscuous a society disease is rampant, and the luxury and lewdness of the upper classes joined to the brutality of the lower are a recipe for national degeneration, ruined fortunes and ruined bodies, 'scrofulous, rickety or deformed children'.[48] It is a society barren of virtue, decency and hope.

This is the truth, and Gulliver, under the influence of the Houyhnhnm, has come to prize truth above all else; why should he tell lies to please *vous autres*, the foolish flatterers of mankind? Pleading guilty to the charge of Yahoo, Gulliver conceives 'a firm resolution never to return to human kind', but to stay with the virtuous horses for ever.[49] It is a resolution thoroughly excusable within the context of the *Travels*, foolish only in the extra-textual sense that we all, Swift included, know that there *is* no Houyhnhnmland to retreat to, *are* no rational horses to revere or to seek asylum from. Gulliver has to come home because home is real and Houyhnhnmland is fantasy, but it is the Houyhnhnms, not the Yahoos, that are fantastic. Gulliver, indisputably speaking with Swift's approval, makes it clear in the 'Letter to Sympson' that the Yahoos are real enough. The fallacy of *vous autres*, reading the book, is to assume that because the Houyhnhnms are an impossible dream, the Yahoos must be an equally impossible nightmare: the first is true but the second isn't. When Gulliver is denied asylum and forced back to the sewer, he writes his *Travels*, not to entertain his fellow-Yahoos, but to hurt them with the truth. Gulliver's is a harsh and revolting medicine, but his master had told him that the best way to cure Yahoo defects is to make a mixture of their own dung and urine, and force it down their throats – the 'Voyage to the Houyhnhnms' is this nauseous potion in literary form, retaliation for that excremental assault suffered by Gulliver at the start of his adventures, an assault which is, in turn, Swift's metaphor for the injuries inflicted upon himself in Dublin and London. 'My taste was me': Hopkins, sick of himself, utters his cry of lyrical despair. Swift, the merciless satirist, rams the dose into our mouths and asks us how we like the taste of ourselves.

Not taste, however, but sight is the sense primarily involved. Swift had already described satire as a sort of glass in which we perversely contrive to see everyone else's face but our own.[50] There are to be no such optical shenanigans in the glass of the *Travels*. We are to see what is there, without prevarication or evasion. Hence the importance of the mirror, of the reflection, of water, in the final voyage. Sight is always the cardinal sense in Swift; the exhortation to look again and see the truth has been rightly described as his persistently recurring message.[51] We should not, accordingly, be surprised to find ocular demonstration playing so large a part in the final voyage. Gulliver has reached the point where he is now convinced that man is simply a Yahoo with clothes, a sort of jabber and a *soupçon* of depraved culture – appearance and reality are one and not, as he had initially insisted, two. The mirrors of Houyhnhnmland, the pools of water, are there to reflect the painful truth:

> When I happened to behold the reflection of my own form in a lake or fountain, I turned away my face in horror and detestation of myself, and could better endure the sight of a common Yahoo, than of my own person.[52]

It is the final lesson in Gulliver's curriculum, the moment of self-recognition, the dark epiphany towards which the whole voyage moves.

Mirrors are the cure for complacency – use them honestly and you will speedily forsake the folly of loving yourself. There is a similar demoralisation in Oceania when O'Brien, having heard the claim that the spirit of man will, in the end, somehow defeat Big Brother, pushes the ruined Winston before the mirror to contemplate the last man in Europe. Back in England, removed from Houyhnhnm virtue, Gulliver goes on using the mirror to keep the fact of his Yahoo nature in the forefront of his consciousness – he has resolved 'to behold my figure often in a glass, and thus if possible habituate myself by time to tolerate the sight of a human creature'.[53] Nothing could be further removed from the spirit of Narcissus or the use to which he put his mirror: Narcissus so loved what he saw that he would not be parted from it. Gulliver, by contrast, uses the mirror to prevent the self-love he has unlearned from ever returning.

Only the fool blames the mirror for what he sees there and only the fop censors it to placate his conceit. Gulliver, renouncing folly and foppery together, looks and accepts the depressing truth. The evidence has become too strong to go on protesting innocence. This is the meaning of that 'odd adventure' which, far from being odd, is perfectly natural, the incident when Gulliver, bathing in the river, is sexually molested by the young she-Yahoo. Hitherto he has clung to the myth of his differentiation, although the Yahoos clearly think otherwise – when they see his naked arms and breast, they claim him for their own. The sight of the naked Gulliver so inflames the she-Yahoo that she leaps hungrily upon him in the ultimate, undeniable act of consanguinity. Only the sorrel nag's timely intervention saves him by forcing her to withdraw: 'she quitted her grasp with the utmost reluctancy' and 'stood gazing and howling all the time I was putting on my clothes'.[54] For the she-Yahoo it is a tragedy of unrequited love, for the Houyhnhnm it is high comedy, the ultimate comic stripping, but for Gulliver it is the end of the line and the *finis* to self-deception. He must be a real Yahoo 'since the females had a natural propensity to me as one of their own species'.[55] The lovesick she-Yahoo becomes for Gulliver a kind of mirror in whose ungovernable appetite he sees the image of his own Yahoo self. Like is attracted to like: it is the law of nature.

These irrefutable reflections lead to the final alienation. Everything is now topsy-turvy. The once longed-for return home has become 'this desperate voyage'. When he sees the Portuguese ship, he paddles furiously in the opposite direction; what we call rescue he calls captivity. His behaviour strikes his rescuers as crazy: 'they all conjectured that my misfortunes had impaired my reason'[56] – the instinctive assumption of *vous autres* whenever their rational superiority is challenged. Had not the nineteenth-century critics declared Swift a madman for daring to disagree with their optimistic appraisal of man? And yet, it must be admitted, Gulliver's behaviour is outrageously abnormal – deliberately so, as Swift intends. The erstwhile lover of humanity is now scandalously misanthropic, but the comedy of his antics should not deceive us into thinking that it's all a joke. The manner of his revulsion from his fellows is certainly ludicrous. Don Pedro, with the tiniest success, tries to restore him to his pre-Houyhnhnm self. Back in Lisbon, after much coaxing, Gulliver 'ventured to look out of the back window' and even reached the point where he 'peeped into the street, but drew my head back in a fright'. Within a week Don Pedro had 'seduced' him down to the street, and, terror lessening, 'I was at last bold enough to walk the street in his company, but kept my nose well stopped with rue, or sometimes with tobacco.'[57] A fool, undoubtedly – but, to judge externally, not much more so than the almost equally alienated narrator of *Heart of Darkness*, back in Brussels from his Congo experience, stalking gloomily the streets of that sepulchral city, and frightening its placid inhabitants with a countenance in which ferocity, hostility and mistrustfulness compete for precedence. It would be unwise to reject what either book tells us simply because of the disordered conduct of their protagonists at the end; that they are disturbed and we are not is not necessarily to our credit.

Nor should Gulliver's concluding protestations of innocence take us in. He may address us as 'gentle reader' as the last chapter opens and bid farewell to his 'courteous readers' near its close, but only a pachyderm could fail to feel the malice with which the conclusion palpably bristles. We should greet with a similar scepticism the disingenuous claim that no one could possibly be offended with his book, since 'I meddle not the least with any party'.[58] 'The party of humanity' certainly did not agree, and that they were sorely hurt is plain from the squeals of protest that have continued to be heard from 1726 to the present day. The genius to induce shock and dismay; the journey from a spurious goodness to appalling truth; the dark epiphany in which the self is forced, through a radical dislocation of experience, to contemplate aspects of its own nature formerly suppressed or ignored: all these make Swift's masterpiece the appropriate template against which to align the modern texts about to be considered.

3

Heart of Darkness: a Choice of Nightmares

Heart of Darkness is a text organised around certain major concepts and the relationships and tensions between them: civilisation and darkness, the mystery of restraint, the salvationary nature of work, the status and cost of knowledge. What follows is an attempt, with *Gulliver's Travels* as template, to trace these ideas as they interact with each other through the book in the belief that the meaning will thereby reveal itself.

Almost three centuries separate the two books, yet, despite this long interval and their many dissimilarities, there is an unmistakable unity of intention that binds them together. The resemblance is, of course, most obvious in the searing indictment of colonialism that fills the concluding pages of Swift's satire. The travels into several remote nations of the world are really an investigation of European society, with the voyage of discovery used to carry complacent European man into the heart of his own filthy civilisation to confront the disgusting truth beneath the imposing façade. Conrad similarly used his own personal experience of the Congo to make an equally radical critique of European civilisation and to expose the sham of its masquerading philanthropy. In each case the protagonists are carefully chosen to be representative of their cultures in certain important respects. Gulliver is a simple seaman, indistinguishably average and unimaginative, the more reliable in that he is not clever – the last man to deceive us with a pack of tall stories. He fumes whenever any doubt is cast upon his character as truthteller. There is no evidence to indicate any tendency to lying before the final voyage and his sojourn among the virtuous horses has sharpened a reverence for the truth to which these creatures are so instinctively devoted. Gulliver can be trusted to tell the truth as he sees it; we may, of course, dispute his interpretation, but only on the ground that he is a dupe, not a liar, Alceste rather than Tartuffe, the gull that some readers find in his name. There is, likewise, an

46

honest soul in *Heart of Darkness* – Marlow, teller of the tale, who, his antipathy to lying notwithstanding, tells, finally, a deliberate lie to Kurtz's Intended. But if the truth is, apparently, too appalling for female ears, this merely confirms that what Marlow tells the men on the *Nellie* is the truth as he sees it.

Heart of Darkness, however, poses a double problem of identity where the *Travels* present only one. Swift needs only one character to launch his attack upon European pride: Lemuel Gulliver, the simple seaman, erstwhile jingo patriot and lover of humanity, who, exposed in a strange land to the tuition of the Houyhnhnms, turns raging recreant to the whole humanist tradition. Conrad, by contrast, uses two characters, sending a good man to a savage place to meet a great man whose greatness includes a genius for philanthropy. Marlow is a decent English gentleman whose calling has developed in him the solid, unspectacular virtues of diligence and fidelity. Kurtz is *l'uomo singolare* whom no one nation can claim: 'all Europe contributed to the making of Kurtz', and the product is a universal genius.[1] 'Tell me, pray . . . who is this Mr Kurtz?'[2] Marlow's intrigued inquiry turns out to be the key question of the book. The identity of Kurtz, made the more problematic because we have to rely entirely upon Marlow in reaching a decision, turns out to have significance not just for Conrad's book but for a major movement in twentieth-century literature. 'In the interior you will no doubt meet Mr Kurtz.'[3] It is a promise that is abundantly and fearfully kept as the century advances.

Certainly, his *curriculum vitae* is most impressive: head of the gang of virtue, musician, painter, writer, orator, philanthropist and the Company's best agent. Given Europe's mission to civilise the dark places of the earth, Kurtz must be acknowledged as our best emissary. He goes out to Africa as the standard-bearer of the west and Marlow follows to report upon the success of his quest. We have sent our best and may confidently expect our best to be good enough. We learn instead of the débâcle suffered by Kurtz and the civilisation he represents. The final lesson is not the excellence of the west but its hubristic enslavement to twin delusions: that it has conquered the darkness within itself and is, accordingly, qualified to dispel it in others.

Swift is equally dismissive of western man's pose as a light-bearer, finding in such pretensions all the effrontery of a bald-headed man peddling hair restorer – that the man may not realise his impertinence merely compounds the offence. How can ignorance excuse presumption when it is its cause? Gulliver rejects the charge that he had been unpatriotic in not annexing for England the countries he has discovered. Lilliput doesn't merit an expedition, Brobdingnag might pose problems even for Marlborough's veterans; as for the Houyhnhnms, far from presuming to dream of civilising them, our felicity would be for them to cross the sea to civilise us. But, as Swift well knows, there *are* no Houyhnhnms, hence no miraculous help arriving from without. Swift despised the device of the *deus ex machina* in life as in art; we are driven back upon our own meagre resources, and, however grim this realisation, it should at least prevent the folly of thinking ourselves superior or secure.

Marlow, speaking for his creator, strives to inculcate a similar uneasiness in his complacently secure auditors upon the *Nellie*. The terror of the wilderness – an 'utter solitude without a policeman'[4] – is that it forces you to face the truth. We have only ourselves to trust in and the nightmare is that this self may be totally inadequate. Anyone who is not simply a complete fool, 'too dull even to know you are being assaulted by the powers of darkness',[5] discovers that Lear is right, that all our 'lendings', all those external trappings and additions, are straw in the wind, with culture itself a fragile membrane stretched over darkness: 'you must fall back upon your own innate strength, upon your capacity for faithfulness'.[6] There is, however, no guarantee that these will be enough; in the interior you may meet Mr Kurtz. Marlow's auditors understandably find this hard to understand, for it contradicts the conventional wisdom about a decisive severance between the totally discontinuous states of savagery and civilisation, darkness and light – either Kurtz belongs to the one or he belongs to the other, but he cannot belong to both. No wonder, believing this, they react irritably to what must seem to them extravagance and even hysteria. Yet the unity of the world, the seamless garment of experience, are the key doctrines of the book, the harvest of Marlow's Congo adventure. His empathy with Kurtz comes from feeling the pull of the same attraction and he is saved from a similar destruction only by the blessed preoccupation of keeping his craft afloat. Kurtz, without such mundane protection, is caught and exposed by the jungle as a man 'hollow at the core'. Marlow struggles to communicate to those listening a sense of human vulnerability; below the deceptively secure surface lies chaos.

Swift likewise anguished over unprotected man; the problem of

Heart of Darkness is the one that vexed Swift throughout his life – how to procure and where to locate the protective discipline, the self-restraint, without which man's life reverts to unbridled appetite and jungle darkness. Swift preferred Christianity to the great pagan philosophers because he believed that the guarantees of heaven and hell make the moral life a feasible programme and not simply a pious aspiration.[7] How to persuade selfish men to behave decently: this is, for Swift, the only real social problem and it cannot be solved without a cast-iron system of rewards, deterrents and punishments. Natural man, released from the pinfold of religion, will inevitably stray, and the greater his licence and the surer his immunity, the more flagrant will his aberration be. Gyges in *The Republic* embodies this fearfully indemnified freedom. Acquiring a ring that confers invisibility, Gyges, immunity guaranteed, kills the king, seduces the queen, and makes himself tyrant. Plato, far from legitimising Gyges, presents him as the unjust man who cannot see that virtue is to be embraced regardless of its penalties and vice shunned regardless of its rewards – we are to love virtue, not for its prizes but for itself, even when, as with Cordelia, it brings only destruction.

It would be unjust to say that Swift regards such disinterested virtue as moonshine – the sextumvirate extolled by Gulliver in Part III clearly indicated how much Swift valued heroic self-sacrifice.[8] But what is equally plain is that he no more expected to find such heroes among ordinary men than he did a phoenix among pigeons. Ordinary people inhabit a far less exalted realm than Cordelia, and only a judicious combination of carrot and stick keeps the unheroic mass even waveringly attached to virtue. Such realism turns a virtuous Gyges into an oxymoron; the tiny heroic elite apart, a man with the opportunities and guarantees of Gyges will act as Gyges does – to expect otherwise is like asking water to run uphill or wolves to turn vegetarian. The sole hope of restraining Gyges is to convince him that he cannot avoid retribution, very probably in this world, infallibly in the next. Hell is Swift's trump card, the sinner's inescapable destination; if it did not exist Swift would invent it because it has no rival as a deterrent. He knows, of course, that people avoid wrongdoing for other, commendable reasons, but none of these has the attractive inexorability of hell.

The justice of this world is vulnerable to the bribery of the rich and the intimidation of the powerful; people fear the police, but the police are sometimes corrupt and sometimes mistaken. Again, people behave well because they court public opinion and know that a reputation for wrongdoing is a social hindrance. But since, as Glaucon in *The Republic* argues, the most accomplished form of injustice is to seem just when one is not, what must we expect from a man clever enough to combine the greatest crimes with a spotless reputation? Swift is unhesitant:

> But let it consist with such a man's interest and safety to wrong you, and then it will be impossible you can have any hold upon him; because there is nothing left to give him a check, or to put in the balance against his profit. For, if he hath nothing to govern himself by, but the opinion of the world, as long as he can conceal his injustice from the world, he thinks he is safe.[9]

The atheist Wharton, contemptuously indifferent to public opinion, is a monster fit only for extermination; Gyges is a Yahoo licensed to bestiality without risk of retribution. Only if they can be induced to believe in hell will society be safe. Hence Swift's absolute commitment to Christianity as the one hope of restraining the jungle.

Conrad shares Swift's belief in human depravity but not his trust in religion as the answer to it – on the contrary, he dismisses Christianity as originating in an absurd oriental tale and of causing an infinity of anguish to innumerable souls on this earth. In 'An Outpost of Progress' Kayerts hangs himself, significantly, from a cross: the alleged instrument of salvation is really a weapon of self-destruction. To look there for the salutary discipline is the grossest of errors. Conrad prefers instead to seek salvation in the work of this world. In the preface to *Chance* he reveals that 'what I always feared most was drifting unconsciously into the position of a writer for a limited coterie';[10] he found the antidote in work structured by a deliberate act of will. The therapeutic, indeed redemptive, function of work is vital to an understanding of *Heart of Darkness* – where work is absent, man becomes derelict. 'Work will overcome all evil . . . . A man is a worker. If he is not that he is nothing.' Leonardo da Vinci is enlisted to prove that 'work is the law' and that 'without action the spirit of man turns to a dead thing'.[11]

The dread of drifting manifests itself in Marlow's praise of his dead helmsman: 'he had done something, he had steered'.[12] What saves us is a work ethic, an unremitting devotion to the task, and

Marlow's regard for the handy legionaires, those admirably competent invaders of Britain, links up with his enthusiasm for the red areas of the contemporary map – for him this colour is emblematic of exemplary imperialism, of real work manfully tackled and intelligently done. All the other colours signify a moral inferiority, an exploitation as wasteful as it is wicked. It is the inane shelling of the jungle by the French gunboat that bewilders Marlow; it is the mess, even more than the malice, of the grove of death that makes Marlow turn back to work as the only way to 'keep my hold on the redeeming facts of life'.[13] In *Under Western Eyes* Razumov comforts himself with the reflection that 'the trivialities of daily existence were an armour for the soul'.[14] The 'miracle' of the chief accountant is the greater because he preserves himself by an act of will against the surrounding demoralisation. When Marlow overhears the manager scornfully dismissing Kurtz as an ass on account of his missionary dreams, we are to place the derider as one of the flabby devils, come to Africa in a vile scramble for loot – Kurtz is a fallen angel but the manager has always grovelled in the mud.

Work is always invested with a redemptive power. Hearing of Kurtz's sudden change of mind when he decides, after a three hundred mile journey, to return to his station, Marlow instinctively interprets this in his most favourable light: 'Perhaps he was just simply a fine fellow who stuck to his work for its own sake'.[15] In a similar disposition Marlow contemplates the young Russian's book on seamanship; its humble, unenthralling pages are made luminous by reflecting 'a singleness of intention, an honest concern for the right way of going to work'.[16] The case for work is not simply that it is good for us – without it we are lost. Travelling up the river, Marlow becomes aware of the brooding, vengeful jungle and might easily have succumbed to its atmosphere but for one blessed deficiency: 'I had no time'.[17] He is so busy keeping his old craft afloat that the darkness is held at bay. The sulky devil within the old boiler is giving Marlow and the fireman such trouble that neither 'had any time to peer into our creepy thoughts'.[18] If only Kurtz had been harassed in taming an external devil, he might never have capitulated to the devil within. Keep busy and you keep the darkness out.

The most explicit avowal of the value of unremitting toil occurs when Marlow truculently explains to his exasperated auditors why he had not gone overboard to join in the forest savagery that he found so seductively appealing: 'Who's that grunting? You wonder

I didn't go ashore for a howl and a dance? Well, no – I didn't. Fine sentiments, you say? Fine sentiments, be hanged! I had no time'.[19] Employment is the defence against Dionysos. Kurtz's misfortune is that he had too much time, and the proverb tells us what the devil contrives for those over-endowed with this commodity. Only once in the book is there a hint that work, too, has its occupational hazards. There is something chilling in the miraculous chief accountant as he complains that the groans of the dying are distracting him from his figures – efficiency may mean inhumanity and devotion to work may be bought at too steep a price. But, this single instance apart, work in *Heart of Darkness* is the boon that saves us.

It is this insistence that we, as much as anyone else, need saving that is the chief scandal of Conrad's book. Marlow's hearers, like Marlow himself before he entered the heart of darkness, live in the happy delusion that they are already irrevocably saved; the world is two, divided between those who live in the light and those who stumble in darkness. We in the civilised west live in the light. Today it has been argued that the most unnerving phenomenon of our century has been the growth of barbarism in a surrounding matrix of high civilisation – it is even suggested that this barbarism is not inimical but intimately related to the culture within which it throve.[20] Why did our shining humanist tradition prove so fragile a guard against political bestiality? Was it indeed a guard at all or was it not precisely here that we were most vulnerable to the solicitations of sadism? Conrad's is a prophetic work because it confronts in 1902 the problem that challenges us today: the darkness at the heart of our civilisation. Even when they go too far, it is easy to see why some readers, impatient with the thesis of Marlow's inner journey, the descent into the self, brusquely insist that Conrad's book is really about the tenuousness of civilisation.

The central assumption of nineteenth-century thought was that light and darkness were discontinuous, mutually exclusive states – where the one advanced, the other, perforce, retreated. Intellect, science, the arts, culture, were all necessarily on the side of progress; where they flourished, all savagery, moral included, withered. Even Freud, so wary in his estimate of human possibilities and so conscious of the animal in man, assures us that the threat to culture does not come from the educated or the brainworkers.[21] In such people the atavistic, aggressive impulses have been sublimated into intellectually productive channels, and the risk to them is minimal because of the cultural shield around them. *Heart of Darkness* challenges this axiom of cultural superiority by refuting the conventional division into backward and advanced, savage and civilised, dark and light, insisting instead upon a single world and a unified experience. What irritated Marlow's auditors as hysterical exaggeration strikes us today, the ambiguous privilege of twentieth-century history behind us, as a grimly irrefutable report of the way things are. Just a short stroll from Weimar stands Buchenwald and many who revered the first supported the second. Conrad would not have been confounded; it is, after all, Kurtz, the heir of all the ages, the knight of civilisation, who scrawls on his own noble manuscript the exhortation to exterminate the brutes – the same piece of paper exhibits simultaneously light and darkness. The jungle is in the interior, the real darkness is the heart of man. Conrad gives Kurtz the outstanding cultural endowment that makes him the star pupil of western civilisation in order to smash the delusion that culture and darkness are incompatible: Kurtz is a fallen master to prove that no one is secure.

The problem of restraint, Macaulay and Freud notwithstanding, is universal, restricted neither geographically to the dark places of the earth nor sociologically to the lower strata of the populace. Even in ostensibly civilised lands where the earth seems a shackled monster, the problem, so Marlow insists, still exists, albeit in a disguised form.[22] The urgency with which he attempts to impress this upon his nonchalantly secure auditors helps to explain the linguistic stridency which has continued to exasperate hearers of the tale down to our own day. Marlow strains to make them see and loses his patience when they don't – the policeman and the two good addresses shelter them from the terror of being. The radical freedom, at once exalting and revolting, which Kurtz lays claim to is as troublesome to communicate as the descent into hell that Marlow is trying to describe. How to create an image of hell credible to modern man as represented by the cosy coterie on board the *Nellie*, how to transform a tale which is a travelogue of contemporary economic exploitation into a quest story with a profound theme of initiation and moral education – Conrad knew the difficulty of his task. To succeed he has to become Marlow: 'You must search the darkest corners of your heart . . . for the image' – 'The artist descends within himself.'[23] The manner of this search and descent have not pleased all of Conrad's readers.

Yet all those critics who complain about Conrad's language as he strives to communicate the mystery of evil have already been anti-cipated within the text in their grumbles concerning linguistic mysticism and adjectival insistence. That Conrad knew he was provoking such irritation and consciously accepted this as a risk inseparable from what he was attempting should be plain to any reader of the book. More than half way through his tale Marlow stops to defend himself against a grunt of impatient incompre-hension from one of his friends, driven beyond good manners by a particularly outrageous part of the narrative. The impoliteness is, Marlow sees at once, both justified and obtuse – justified because, to a man with a butcher round one corner and a policeman round the other, that is, to a sensible, middle-class Englishman with his emotions firmly under control, Marlow is simply talking embar-rassing and undisciplined rot. Having made a fool of himself at the time, he is doing it all over again in the hysterical way he tells his tale. But Marlow also sees how misplaced, even if pardonably so, his friend's irritation is. Men like the lawyer and the company director are bound to go wrong when they insist upon interpreting Marlow's Congo experience within the context of their own tidy English existence. Marlow, losing patience, goes on the offensive: they do not know and will not learn; how dare they, therefore, criticise his behaviour? What upsets them is his un-English lack of sang-froid, his confession of the intense grief he experiences when, believing Kurtz to be dead, he laments that he will never hear that voice. Marlow aggressively denies that he has either surrendered to emotional extravagance or behaved absurdly: 'Absurd! Absurd be – exploded!', before proceeding to the provocatively offensive claim: 'Now I think of it, it is amazing I did not shed tears. I am, upon the whole, proud of my fortitude'.[24] The reversal is breath-taking; they are embarrassed because he has behaved like a cry-baby – he retorts that he has in fact borne himself like a hero.

One is reminded of Clive who, when impeached, defended him-self against his accusers, not by denying their charges but by reminding them of what he had refrained from doing. His cen-surers were angry and shocked at what seemed to them his rapa-city; his reply was that, considering his opportunities, his acquisitions had been breathtakingly modest: 'By God, Mr Chair-man, at this moment I stand astonished at my own moderation.' When everything is permitted, any degree of self-restraint is a marvel. Those who have not been in Clive's position are incapable of appreciating the modesty of his conduct, for the truly surprising thing is not his extortions but his abstentions. And so, even in his exasperation, Marlow sees how difficult it is for his friends to understand what happened without first experiencing it themselves. Only as a result of his Congo education does Marlow perceive the hitherto unsuspected unity of experience – that the Thames flows into the Congo and that the howling savage is a brother, not some alien being from another world. Nature is a continuum, a single, interpenetrating whole, and the water imagery further reinforces this theme of indissolubility.

Conrad's personal stake in all this is reflected in his disclosure that 'before the Congo I was only a simple animal'[25] and that the breakdown he afterwards suffered was crucial for his artistic and intellectual maturation. In both cases, Conrad's and Marlow's, there is a sense of initiation into a fuller scale of human being – of growth which is at once a radical discomposure of the self and an education in reality. (Again, the parallel with Gulliver is unmistakable.) In *Heart of Darkness* this education is a process of coming to realise that restraint is a kind of miracle that we casually take for granted whenever it is blessedly present; without it we cease to be human, yet, in Conrad's pessimistic view, its provenance is a mystery. At best we have it fortuitously, yet we delude ourselves that it is inalienably ours. Conrad's fear is that restraint is not natural to us and that civilisation fosters a lazy and dangerous assumption that we possess by right what is ours only by accident. Bertrand Russell tells us that Conrad 'thought of civilised and morally tolerable human life as a dangerous walk on a thin crust of barely cooled lava which at any moment might break and let the unwary sink into fiery depths'.[26] Doubtless it was this suspicion of the fragile filaments of liberal civilisation that drew Orwell to Conrad when Orwell was composing his own critique of liberal delusions in *Nineteen Eighty-Four*.

The precariousness of restraint is what strikes us once we have exposed the fallacy of a world decisively segregated into civilised and savage spheres. The world is one. No later than the second paragraph we are told that the Thames is the 'beginning of an interminable waterway'; all waters are one just as all history is one – the Thames ultimately flows into the Congo just as the decent young Roman in a toga mending his fortunes in savage Britain rehearses Marlow in darkest Africa. Time is a trick which should not blind us to the essential ahistorical unity of human nature – nineteen hundred years ago, properly understood, is simply 'the other day'. What is true of time holds good for space: the biggest, greatest town on earth, the centre of civilisation, has a 'mournful gloom' brooding over it anticipatory of the jungle where Kurtz lost (or found) himself. The Congo, psychologically speaking, is a step away, the death camp neighbours the concert hall and lecture room.

That Conrad means to establish this sense of unity is plain from the series of connections, thematic and imagist, that he weaves throughout the book. The grass that grows through Fresleven's ribs is there to remind Marlow of the grass sprouting between the stones in the city of the whited sepulchre, and the reader remarks the association the more in that he, unlike Marlow, sees the dead Dane before he visits Brussels. As he travels through a deserted land from which the people have fled in terror of the white intruders, Marlow hears 'the tremor of far-off drums', and the sound, far from impressing him as alien or remote, is linked in his mind with the ringing of bells in a Christian country;[27] we are not so far from the wild as we like to imagine. Our first view of the lofty frontal bone of Kurtz, 'like a ball – an ivory ball', prepares us for those carved balls outside the station, at first mistaken as ornaments, later revealed as the heads of those sacrificed to the despot Kurtz has become.[28] This network of images linking civilisation and darkness demolishes the delusion of a dual world. As the book opens Marlow sits like an idol; its epiphany reveals that the emissary of light is a Moloch to whom human sacrifice is made.

In minor detail and largescale significance alike, the links between the two delusively disparate realms of experience are repeatedly forged. Kurtz's cousin carries off the report on the suppression of savagery as though it were 'plunder'; the exalted eloquence belongs in the end to the same world as the ivory and the grove of death. Even at the one moment in the book when we might legitimately demand contrast, we get likeness instead. Just before the final darkness (the book ends with that word), the etherial girl of Brussels, fair-haired, pale-faced, with 'pure brow' and 'ashy halo', indisputably a creature of the light, holds out her arms in a vain attempt to recall her lost hero. The action reminds Marlow of the dark, savage woman, 'tragic also, and bedecked with powerless charms, stretching bare brown arms over the glitter of the infernal stream'.[29] The two different women are in identical case, helpless, despite their attractions, to detain the departed man. When the link between such thoroughly dissimilar beings is demonstrated, it is time to abandon the fallacy of divided and distinguished worlds;

what Conrad has put together, let no one put asunder.

Metaphor and theme reinforce this idea of an integrated world; as we penetrate the book there is a continual process of accreted and retrospective significance. On the opening page we learn that the five men on the *Nellie* are all united, despite their different vocations, by the bond of the sea. The cliché is to be redeemed from banality when we come to realise that the story is about the chaos that ensues when all bonds and restraints are cancelled. The image of the pilot, the man who can be trusted to steer, similarly lends itself to the interpretation of a tale of moral shipwreck. When Marlow introduces his Congo voyage as 'the farthest point of navigation and the culminating point of my experience',[30] the symbolic significance of the river journey is as unmistakable as that of the road in Bunyan. Conrad's book has, in fact, been described as 'a Pilgrim's Progress for our pessimistic and psychologizing age . . . Conrad's longest journey into self'.[31] When the accountant assures Marlow that Kurtz 'will go far, very far', he is simply referring to career prospects; only at the inner station are we to appreciate in full what going far really means. Everything is permitted; the moral Pillars of Hercules are no more – *ne plus ultra* is, for Kurtz, an obsolete expression. Kurtz is, indeed, a hero because of this navigational audacity – the other pilgrims are equally amoral but lack his daring. The manager is angry at the heads on the fence but only because of the unsoundness of the method; Kurtz's conduct has for the time closed the district to trade and profit. If heads on poles can advance these things, the manager will not shrink from decapitation. Marlow overhears the two rogues discussing the troublesome Russian interloper and the possibility of getting him hanged; the problem is a purely practical one: 'Why not? Anything – anything can be done in this country'.[32] Kurtz simply carries this to its appalling extreme. In the Congo Gyges rules.

Yet not absolutely. Marlow encounters two miracles in the heart of darkness: that of the chief accountant, heroically keeping his books and himself in the grove of death; and the even more astounding miracle of the abstemious cannibals. The accountant's achievement is an ambiguous one, for the self he preserves is less than human and the triumph over squalor is itself compromised, but there is a shining transcendence, a stunning imcomprehensibility, about the cannibals' renunciation – it seems so far above what we might reasonably expect from human beings. That Conrad knew the compulsion of appetite and the weakness of will is plain from the most cursory reading of his work. Dr Monygham in *Nostromo*, anticipating Orwell's Winston Smith, despises himself for having cracked under torture, for having failed to resist the irresistible pain which at the time makes every other consideration of truth and honour fade into insignificance.[33] He cannot help what he did then nor what he feels now – nature is, in each case, too strong for control. But this simply makes the cannibals' discipline all the more astounding. 'Restraint! What possible restraint?' Nevertheless, the miracle has occurred and Marlow meditates 'one of those human secrets that baffle probability'.[34] The paradox is the more perplexing, for, while civilisers succumb, cannibals resist.

The jungle is a place with no external checks, an utter solitude without a policeman, traversed by untrammelled feet, where the only salvation comes from two related things: devotion to external duty and dependence upon an inner strength. The allegedly civilised white men completely flunk the test, Kurtz in the grand style, the others in their sordid fashion. They are hollow men. Kurtz 'lacked restraint in the gratification of his various lusts'; 'there was something wanting in him – some small matter which, when the pressing need arose, could not be found under his magnificent eloquence'.[35] He is 'a tree swayed by the wind'. His Russian admirer sees this too, though he characteristically tries to turn it into a further proof of greatness: Kurtz could shoot him simply because he 'had a fancy for it, and there was nothing on earth to prevent him from killing whom he jolly well pleased'.[36] On earth is inclusive and refers to what is inside Kurtz as well as outside. Kurtz is Gyges: for both, inclination, opportunity and act are identical. The Russian's slangy formulation should not disguise the terror of the unrestrained self. 'The pressing need' finds Kurtz inadequate. Yet the cannibals restrain the greatest need of all. Marlow tells us the sad but true fact that nothing on earth, neither bereavement nor dishonour nor spiritual perdition, is harder to confront than prolonged hunger. To expect the cannibals to abstain is as likely as finding a fasting hyena among the corpses on a battlefield. Yet the impossible is a fact. The miracle of restraint occurs in the unlikeliest place of all, among the darkest inhabitants of the heart of darkness. The white men do what they dare according to the limits of their audacity; it is the cannibals who, paradoxically, display the self-discipline that is the hallmark of the human. A major irony of Conrad's book is that it seeks the secret of self-restraint and yet, on finally finding it, cannot explain it. This mystery, too, is left in darkness.

The choice forced upon Marlow is, however, not between Kurtz and the cannibals but between Kurtz and the faithless pilgrims, between, that is, the two contrasting styles of moral indiscipline presented by the book. Marlow as newcomer is not permitted to be an indifferent spectator of this conflict but is compelled to commit himself. It is increasingly recognised that the story is not primarily about Kurtz or the brutality of colonial exploitation; it is about Marlow and the terrible illumination that, paradoxically, comes to him as, in his quest for Kurtz, he descends into darkness. Once accept Marlow as the central figure and the epic machinery of the tale is plain to see. Whether the source be Virgil or Dante or Milton, whether the parallel be with Bunyan's pilgrim or Faust or the grail hero, the focus is Marlow and the change effected in him.[37] Kurtz enters the picture, as it were, only incidentally at the end as an agent in Marlow's acquisition of knowledge. If the story is not about Marlow's self-discovery, its length is quite indefensible. As much as *Gulliver's Travels, Heart of Darkness* is about what happens to its narrator – Kurtz is no more the centre of this tale than are the Houyhnhnms of theirs.

The squalid atrocities of the company station are decisive as Marlow makes his choice of nightmares. The grove of death is an entropic hell inhabited by flabby and foolishly rapacious devils. It is a scene of such mean apathy that Marlow turns for relief to the other kind of devil who sometimes possesses mankind – the strong, red-eyed devil of violent lusts. The deplorable state of the station makes it plain that 'the flabby devil was running that show',[38] and Marlow seeks solace from this vileness in work. It is the vulgarity of the evil that sickens him, the despicable manager and his mean machinations, the sordid Eldorado Expedition with not one redeeming sin among its myriad vices. For Marlow a taint of imbecile rapacity hangs over the whole enterprise, and Kurtz, by contrast, seems positively heroic in the audacious uniqueness of his wrongdoing. He has, in Marlow's eyes, one insuperable advantage over his rivals: 'He won't be forgotten. Whatever he was, he was not common.' *Was uns alle bändigt, das Gemeine:* Goethe's lament is not applicable to Kurtz.[39] Alongside the petty pilgrims with their petty souls, Kurtz is a giant, and this is to his credit even when the stature is satanic. Kurtz himself condemns his Lilliputian opponents in his dying denunciation of the manager: 'You with your little piddling notions – you are interfering with me.'[40] On this issue Marlow sides with Kurtz – he turns in disgust from the manager towards the wilderness, grateful for at least having a choice of nightmares.

As the tale approaches its climax, Marlow increasingly emphasises the satanic grandeur of the exceptional man. When the young Russian refuses to let Kurtz be judged by ordinary moral criteria, insisting that 'this man has enlarged my mind', Marlow is provoked to deny that Kurtz was 'any idol of mine'.[41] He comes, nevertheless, to share, at least in part, the Russian's admiration. He agrees when Kurtz declares that he had 'immense plans' and was 'on the threshold of great things'[42] – Kurtz's sins are clearly not of the huckstering Eldorado kind. His is an exalted, almost dignified, evil that raises him to that bad eminence occupied by Satan. In contrast to the grovelling insects of the company, Kurtz 'had kicked himself loose of the earth . . . had kicked the very earth to pieces'.[43] He is a demon elevated above the petty concerns of little men, and there is gain as well as damnation in this transcendence. Marlow sees 'on that ivory face the expression of sombre pride, of ruthless power, of craven terror – of an intense and hopeless despair'.[44] It is the face of Satan who was once Lucifer, the lightbearer who became the prince of darkness. Damned, certainly, yet in liberating himself from earth and renouncing all restraint, Kurtz simultaneously becomes a hero of psychological navigation and reaps the harvest of this cognitive audacity when, just before death, he experiences 'that supreme moment of complete knowledge'. The untrammelled exploration ends in an apprehension of horror, but Marlow is convinced that only a very special kind of man is capable of such an insight, so far beyond both ordinary man and squalid scoundrel alike. 'The most you can hope for is some knowledge of yourself';[45] only the hero can go all the way. Marlow's own dull struggle with death contrasts sharply with Kurtz's intensely dramatic demise. Intensity of experience is made the assay of greatness. Kurtz is 'the remarkable man who had pronounced a judgement upon the adventures of his soul on this earth', a hero because 'he had something to say. He said it'.[46] This emphasis upon the word (it is the calamity of never hearing Kurtz *speak* that so dispirits Marlow when he mistakenly thinks Kurtz dead) associates Kurtz with the artist, that is, with Conrad himself – the artist who 'is so much of a voice that, for him, silence is like death'.[47] Marlow, by contrast, discovers humiliatingly when the time comes that he has nothing to say. 'Better his cry – much better. It was an affirmation, a moral victory.'[48]

When we inquire more closely into the nature of this victory or ask how Kurtz's death could ever be regarded as any kind of victory, far less a moral one, we find ourselves on the other side of the chasm that separates us from a man like Swift; underlying Marlow's assertion is a set of attitudes that Swift would have denounced as pernicious folly. The epiphanic moment in Swift is always a sickening awareness of the self's enthralment to filth: the beau's carcass, the flayed woman, Strephon in the nauseating bedroom, Gulliver confronting his Yahoo nature – all are deeply implicated in the shock of the sordid without the slightest hint of any romantic exaltation. There are, as has been seen, no concessions to glamorous evil in Swift. Hence there can never be any choice of nightmares for Swift, because for him *all* evil is indistinguishably sordid; great sinners simply mean a greater stench. Swift's reductionist purpose is to destroy the romantic myth of the great sinner. The Duchess of Kendal is just a she-Yahoo with a large wardrobe; the Duke of Marlborough, imposing reputation notwithstanding, is merely a sophisticated version of his Yahoo brethren lusting after the shining stones. Swift would have found nothing to admire in Kurtz and would probably have condemned Conrad's book as an ingenious Yahoo apologia for sin.

There has been, evidently, a sea-change, a whole cultural shift, between Swift's age and our own, and this new way of evaluating experience is explicable in part to a very different attitude to the doctrine of the mean. In so far as Swift's work is not simply an expression of despair, it exhorts us to adopt a realistic appraisal of our position. We cannot become Houyhnhnms and we must not become Yahoos; we are not pure intellect but neither should we be irremediably animal. There is a human mean between these extremes and we must strive to find it – salvation is to be sought in the middle place. The middle place is, however, according to the Romantics, precisely where we should avoid if we would be saved – one need only glance at the proverbs of 'The Marriage of Heaven and Hell' to see the essential link between wisdom and excess, authenticity and extremism, in the Romantic mind.

From the outset the word 'mean' has had two meanings: the average, the moderate course of action, the midpoint between extremes; and what is petty, despicable and squalid. There is an etymological pressure upon us to regard the mean as mean, to feel guiltily that the middle position is an evasion, a shrinking from commitment. This has spilled over into politics and twentieth-century history has been shaped by the conviction, shared by an increasing number, that fainéant and liberal are synonyms. Important elements of our cultural inheritance insist that salvation is *not* to be found in the middle place. The longing for the absolute, the seduction of the extreme, is honoured in our art even when it is prudently eschewed in our lives. A moral superman like Brand is just as terrifying as an amoral superman like Tamburlaine – his virtue causes more suffering than the most talented sinner would have produced with twice his opportunities. Yet Ibsen claimed that 'Brand is myself in my best moments', and clearly does not intend us to prefer the moderate mayor and provost, tepidly corrupt in themselves and catering to our own tepid corruption. Total commitment fascinates, regardless of its final goal, whether it be Aucassin rejecting paradise in favour of Nicolette and hell, or Bunyan's hero abandoning the world to go questing after eternal life. We admire the wholehoggers, those who go all the way even when we do not approve the way they go.

Religion joins art in exalting this idea of total, extreme commitment. 'You are neither hot nor cold. How I wish you were either hot or cold! But because you are lukewarm, neither hot nor cold, I will spit you out of my mouth.' The words of Christ as recorded in John's Gospel find an echo in Blake's celebration of energy in 'The Marriage of Heaven and Hell', as also in his portrait of the young subversive in 'The Everlasting Gospel'. In scripture and poem alike the target is a temporising prudence which thinks it is foolish to take no thought of the morrow and crazy to save one's life by losing it. Such people are too dismally prudent to surrender themselves to anything, including evil – they are like Leon Bloy's bourgeoisie, incapable of mortal sin, and if they are not evil it is because they are not even alive. The real sin in Browning's 'The Statue and the Bust' is a procrastinating timidity which frustrates the redemptive adultery:

> I hear you reproach, 'But delay was best,
> For their end was a crime.' Oh, a crime will do
> As well, I reply, to serve for a test,
> As a virtue golden through and through.

Cowardly conformity is not virtue, for there can be no virtue without courage:

> And the sin I impute to each frustrate ghost
> Is – the unlit lamp and the ungirt loin,
> Though the end in sight was a vice, I say.

The language of parable is employed to commend what conventional Christianity would abhor, but increasingly as the century progresses and the revulsion against bourgeois values intensifies, it is only a crime that will do to serve for a test of freedom from mediocrity – from Raskolnikov to Conrad's Kurtz and Thomas Mann's Adrian Leverkühn the line is both clear and unbroken. Christ's endorsement of violent extreme over Laodicean tepidity is reaffirmed by certain twentieth-century Christian writers. Eliot, facing waste land and hollow men, provides his own variation on the theme when assessing Baudelaire: 'So far as we are human, what we do must be either good or evil; so far as we do evil or good, we are human; and it is better, in a paradoxical way, to do evil than to do nothing; at least, we exist'.[49] In *Brighton Rock* it is because Pinkie is so dedicatedly evil that we are to prefer him to the hollow woman who pursues him. When Rose asks him if Ida is good, he laughs contemptuously: 'She? . . . She's just nothing'.[50] This is Greene's judgement as well as Pinkie's. Ida *is* nothing, neither hot nor cold, and Greene invites us to join with him in spewing her out. Be good, be evil, but be something.

The assertion of Kurtz's heroism becomes both intelligible and defensible in the light of such an injunction, for if, as Eliot says, it is better to be evil than to be nothing, then Kurtz surely qualifies. This explains why the respective endings of *Heart of Darkness* and *Gulliver's Travels* are at once so alike and so different. Gulliver and Marlow both return from their travels in a mood of dark misanthropy, but Gulliver's disaffection stems from his encounter with Houyhnhnm perfection, while Marlow's comes from his complicity with Kurtz's diabolism. Marlow's attachment to Kurtz becomes the stronger back in the city of the whited sepulchre as, disdainfully, he watches 'people hurrying through the streets to filch a little money from each other'[51] – mean European equivalents of the faithless pilgrims and the Eldorado hucksters. Whatever else he may have done, Kurtz did not filch. The misanthropic intensity of Marlow's

contempt extends to the way they 'devour their infamous cookery
. . . gulp their unwholesome beer . . . dream their insignificant
and silly dreams'.[52] Their very existence is an affront, what they are
even more than what they do; at least Kurtz was a great criminal
and it is better to be wanted for murder than wanted for nothing.
Sophia Antonovna's preference in *Under Western Eyes* for those
who burn rather than rot is relevant here:[53] Kurtz burns while the
others rot, and the fire is the proof of his distinction.

Marlow's sweepingly inclusive dismissal of these mean medio-
crities recalls the Giant King's contemptuous condemnation of
European man: 'And yet, said he, I dare engage, these creatures
have their titles and distinctions of honour; they contrive little nests
and burrows, that they call houses and cities; they make a figure in
dress and equipage; they love, they fight, they dispute, they cheat,
they betray.'[54] No wonder Gulliver is indignant; not just our misdemeanours but everything we do is the target of this nonchalant
contempt. Marlow does not follow the finally alienated Gulliver to
the point of stuffing his nose with tobacco, but the same revulsion
from noisome man is patently present. These ordinary people
pursuing their routine chores are worthless beings, close to un-
persons, to use the terminology of Orwell's last book. Depressingly, they exist, but with no right to existence: 'they trespassed
upon my thoughts'.[55] The vindictively aggressive Marlow decides
that trespassers shall be prosecuted and the twentieth century will
sanction this policy even up to gas chambers and gulags. From the
great height of Kurtz, who had kicked himself free of earth, Marlow
surveys like some misanthropic star-warrior a tiny, contemptible
world which he has already mentally vaporised. We remember the
Olympian callousness of the Giant King contemplating 'the most
pernicious race of little odious vermin that nature ever suffered to
crawl upon the surface of the earth'.[56]

Marlow in Brussels recalls Gulliver in Lisbon and anticipates
Jean-Baptiste Clamence in Amsterdam. In all three the anger is
directed as much at human ignorance as at human iniquity: men do
not know how vile they are. Christ pleads for pardon on the ground
that the sinner does not know; Swift, Conrad and Camus make this
the chief accusation. Unlike Gulliver and Clamence, Marlow feels
no sense of mission to make these blind men see, but what inescapably emerges from *Heart of Darkness* is that the man who sees,
whether directly and to his destruction like Kurtz, or mediately and
less catastrophically like Marlow, is somehow superior to the dull

fools who live in darkness without suspecting it. Only an élite is capable of the truth and each member pays heavily for the privilege – knowledge is a costly and painful mystery, which is why its devotees compensate themselves by looking down upon the mass of happy, uninitiated ignoramuses. Two classes of men are immune to the darkness: the dullards who elude diabolism because they lack the capacity for it, and those thunderingly exalted creatures who are altogether deaf and blind to anything but heavenly sights and sounds – men for whom the earth is only 'a standing place' and not our sole habitation. Marlow despises the first and dismisses the second as irrelevant. Kurtz's greatness is related to the fact that he had something to say and said it. The unremarkable inhabitants of Brussels are, by contrast, voiceless nonenties, while the language spoken by the etherial beings is a private dialect irrelevant to human concerns. Marlow does not explicitly condemn such other-worldliness – 'whether to be like this is your loss or your gain I won't pretend to say'[57] – but the tone of jaunty unconcern is in itself a dismissal. 'The earth for us is a place to live in';[58] on this criterion Kurtz is superior both to the etherial beings and to the inhabitants of Brussels – the former live, but not on earth, while the latter, though on earth, are, in a very real sense, scarcely alive.

To live is to know, and by that token Kurtz's life has been intensely significant. The futile dunces of Brussels are, conversely, guilty of the unforgivable sin of not knowing what they live for: 'They were intruders whose knowledge of life was to me an irri-tating pretence, because I felt so sure they could not possibly know the things I knew.'[59] Marlow's is a gnostic superiority and his master has been Kurtz – as much as the Russian, Marlow can claim that 'that man has enlarged my mind'.[60] Hence his disdain for those dolts still stuck in pre-Kurtz stupidity and his fury that they continue to pursue their inane business in blithe disregard of the surrounding darkness. The peculiar distinction of Swift is a rage at the imbeciles who will not be saved: 'I cannot but warn you once more of the manifest destruction before your eyes, if you do not behave yourselves as you ought.'[61] Marlow has the Swiftian contempt without the compulsion to save: 'I had no particular desire to enlighten them, but I had some difficulty in restraining myself from laughing in their faces, so full of stupid importance.'[62] The Marlow who 'totters' about the streets of Brussels, 'grinning bitterly at perfectly respectable persons', is, from one perspective, clearly deranged, a madman in the mode of Gulliver. But *Heart of*

Darkness was no more written to arraign Marlow and justify Brussels than the *Travels* were written to ridicule Gulliver and uphold England. The tale on the *Nellie* is told to us all, and we, too, must measure our own lives against the life of Kurtz, that strangely ambiguous hero. Great sinner or nonentity: that is the choice of nightmares offered us; that this choice produced appalling consequences as the century advanced makes it the more important that we recognise it in one of its earliest, most artistically significant manifestations.

Heart of Darkness is a text about gnosis, about initiation into the mysteries, about how they are transmitted, cherished and concealed. Marlow despises the pompous old fool who claims to be Kurtz's cousin and who, even in speaking the truth, blunders upon it. He declares Kurtz a universal genius before blowing his nose and withdrawing in senile agitation. It is the wrong time to use one's handkerchief and still expect to be taken seriously. Marlow appropriately surveys him with all the contempt of the insider for the bumptious ignoramus. Kurtz *is* a universal genius but only the privileged Marlow knows the secret of that greatness: the power to look at the darkness. It is a secret to be jealously guarded, naturally enough, since it is what raises Marlow above the dullards around him. Such élitism forbids the secret's being published to the world, though it may be divulged to tiny groups judged capable of the appreciative sympathy that such a revelation demands. The men on the *Nellie* must be made to realise the high compliment Marlow pays them when he decides that they, too, are man enough to face the darkness. This is the importance of Marlow's meeting with Kurtz's Intended at the story's close.

The initiate must not betray the mystery to outsiders, and for *Heart of Darkness* the outsider is preeminently the woman, at least in her protected, western form. The girl is not, of course, crassly mediocre like her Brussels compatriots; *her* inadequacy for the mystery is that she is too etherial, one of those idealistic beings who will break upon the bitter knowledge that Marlow has brought home from the heart of darkness. It is a forbidden knowledge, knowledge of unholy things, the kind that must be withheld from the pure woman if she is to stay immaculate. It is so clearly a knowledge of hell – 'horned shapes . . . . the glow of fires . . . the colossal scale of his vile desires'[63] – and in Conrad hell is for the men who are man enough to face it, but is strictly off limits for women. Marlow respects this prohibition, stonewalling the girl's questions,

agreeing with grim irony that Kurtz was 'a remarkable man'. Gnos-
ticism entails irony – if the many cannot know, they must go
ironically astray, as Kurtz's Intended does. At the tale's climax (as
throughout *The Secret Agent*) irony is transformed from a tactic into
a total perspective. The girl is so sure, while Marlow knows how
cruelly mistaken she is. He keeps resolutely quiet, letting her stay
within her protective illusions until she is left the only thing of light
in a room dominated by darkness. Hideous truth versus beautiful
delusion: it is the characteristic Swiftian antithesis, sustaining all of
his work and given classic expression in the 'Digression on
Madness'.

Marlow's misanthropy is accordingly modified by the need to
exclude the girl from the knowledge which simultaneously elevates
and incriminates, making its possessor an accomplice of the darkness he discovers. When the girl ironically demands her fiancé's
last words because she wants 'something to live with', we confront
the Swiftian alternatives: the terrible, crippling truth or the beautiful lie that promotes survival. Marlow's response is, however, not
the Swiftian one; he supplies the lie by telling her that Kurtz's last
words were her name. Her ensuing exultation merely deepens the
cruelty, much as Lear's joyful delusion that Cordelia lives sharpens
the play's pessimism. For *we* are not deluded, but continue to
inhabit an imbecile universe where rats live and Cordelia dies.
Lear's happiness is not for us, because what we know we cannot
unknow. The same is true of *Heart of Darkness:* Marlow spares the
girl but is implacable towards us – *we* know Kurtz's last words, and
the truth which is too dark for the Intended is apparently not too
dark for us.

The story ends in darkness, with the reader made initiate of the
mystery. Ambiguity is, of course, present throughout – deliberately so, in accordance with Conrad's conviction that 'nothing is
more clear than the utter insignificance of explicit statement'.[64] He
had told Blackwood during the writing that although its title was
Heart of Darkness, 'the narrative is not gloomy'.[65] The story may be a
modern rendition of the fall from innocence, with Kurtz as the man
driven from the Garden, but, damned though he is, Kurtz is also a
hero – a hero, indeed, because of his damnation. *Heart of Darkness*
demands our consent to the insight that a vision downward and
dark may be just as true and tonic as a vision upward into the light.
To refuse this consent is to risk joining the listeners on the yawl in
their self-condemning incomprehension. The ambiguity of the end

accords perfectly, therefore, with the tale we have heard; there is loss as well as knowledge. We have learned and would not willingly surrender this dark knowledge for all our previous comforting ignorance. That incurable itch to know which is the distinguishing mark of western man, urging him on, regardless of discomfort or even anguish, to penetrate the truth of things, is validated by the book – Kurtz's cognitive daring is what makes him the book's ambivalent hero. The need to attend to leaky boilers and procure the indispensable rivets saves the ordinary man, but life is more than surface-truth, and it is the Promethean criminal who extends the range of human experience, even if he perishes in the enterprise. For such audacity is shown, too, as having its price, and the cost does not stop with Kurtz and Marlow. *Heart of Darkness* has been squandered upon the reader who still feels secure after reading it; the dark epiphany must be ours or it might just as well have never taken place.

4

Death in Venice: the Boons of Chaos

Conrad's fallen hero had been an artist, but there is nothing in the text that would entitle us to ascribe his fall to his artistic gifts. The most we can say is that his art was in the end no guard against the darkness, but not that it was its accomplice; he falls despite being an artist, not because he is one. The hero of *Death in Venice* is in very different case, for his destruction is inseparably linked to his vocation, and we are to see in this particular catastrophe a demonstration, however extreme, of the hazards of art and the perils of its practitioners. Art and darkness as insidiously allied, art as disease or crime, the artist as carrier or criminal, the foe of morality: these are the Nietzschean theses which Mann's tale is designed to uphold.

Again the reaction against nineteenth-century orthodoxy is plainly perceptible. Despite Nietzsche's insistence that art rather than ethics constitutes the essential metaphysical activity of man, despite the aesthetes' repudiation of the claims of morality over art, there was still consensus as to the essential underlying harmony between the two activities – beauty is truth, truth beauty, and whatever is truly beautiful must also be sensible, rational, ordered. Arnold's celebration of poetry as an interpretation of life, his prophecy that poetry would replace religion as the answer to doubts and perplexities, implies some such reconciliation. In *Tonio Kröger* the hero's friend rebukes him for depreciating his own profession by reminding him in Arnoldian terms of the moral and educative greatness of literature: 'the purifying and healing influence of letters, the subduing of the passions by knowledge and eloquence; literature as the guide to understanding, forgiveness and love, the redeeming power of the word, literary art as the noblest manifestation of the human mind, the poet as the most highly developed of human beings, the poet as saint'.[1] But nobility and saintliness are scarcely the words that come to mind as we watch the demoralised boy-stalker of *Death in Venice*, reckless of reputation, honour and life itself, as he hunts his prey through the contaminated streets of the stricken city. Not the subduing of the passions but their shameful unleashing is demonstrated in the subversive art of Mann's story. What, we ask in consternation, has happened to poetry and the poet in the passage from the last century to our own?

Mann's preoccupation with disease and death, with the abnormal and pathological, against all that is healthy, robust and normal (product of his own divided legacy of *Künstler* and *Bürger*) makes him a key figure for understanding this transition. Already in the nineteenth century there is evidence that the artist had stopped supporting culture unequivocally and was leaning towards a new barbarism. Gautier supplies the rationale for this transfer of loyalties: *'La barbarie vaut mieux que la platitude . . . plutôt la barbarie que l'ennui'*.[2] The artist moves to the dubious periphery of society to live as pariah or criminal. *Death in Venice* is the supreme artistic representation of this emigration, but it is not platitude or boredom that drives Aschenbach towards his alliance with crime or disease. It is the strain of being civilised, the sapping toll of the civilised life and its cruel cost in neurosis and nervous exhaustion as computed by Freud, that tempts Aschenbach to relax and let go, to unclench the knotted fist and enjoy the sweet abandon of the hanging, open palm. In *Doctor Faustus* Mann will push on to a position where the discipline of art is enrolled in the service of the demon; in *Death in Venice* he depicts that prior situation when discipline and demon clash.

The paradox is that the artist is finally undone by a vision of beauty, but it is a paradox that will perplex no one familiar with Nietzsche's central argument in *The Birth of Tragedy*. Conversely, those who either ignore or dismiss the Nietzschean thesis will find it difficult, if not impossible, to accept *Death in Venice* as a coherent and artistic whole. Aschenbach's story, deprived of its Nietzschean key, will simply admit the reader into the outer chamber of its almost anecdotal simplicity. A distinguished and ascetic German writer, baulked in the literary work he has in mind, decides on impulse to go south to Italy. He reaches Venice, is first attracted to and then obsessed by a beautiful Polish boy. Finally, after an abortive and half-hearted attempt to leave the city which he now knows to be in the grip of the plague, he is forced to admit to himself that he loves the boy to the total disregard of every other consideration, decency, honour and life itself. He is chained to Venice by a disreputable passion even when the cholera epidemic, still denied by the city authorities, becomes an open secret. After a frenzied pursuit of his lover through the infested streets, he eats contaminated strawberries to allay his feverish thirst, sickens and dies.

Viewed from the outside, it is not an implausible story, but neither is it a necessary one. Aschenbach's death might be construed as simply the last accident in a haphazard chain of misadventures. If only he had not got the notion of travelling from the sight of the portico pilgrim at the Munich cemetery; if only he had not met the shameless young-old man who dismayingly anticipates Aschenbach's future self in the barber's chair in Venice; if only his luggage had been sent in the right direction, when, with a last faltering spurt of will-power, he tries to leave the place of temptation. *Wenn das Wörtchen, wenn' nicht wär', wär' mein Vater Millionär.* Doubtless Mann knew the old saw – certainly his story makes it clear that he saw through it. If only Macbeth had not met the witches or Duncan had not so obligingly and provocatively made himself his murderer's house-guest. But it is no accident that the witches comes to Macbeth in the first place and the will to evil can always contrive its own opportunities. To think otherwise is to mistake symptoms for causes. The same is true of *Death in Venice.* Aschenbach's misdirected luggage goes in the *right* direction, and all those messengers appear to him because that is what they are – messengers, not casual or adventitious acquaintances. The portico pilgrim comes to call him south as the witches come to call Macbeth to kingship – that is the pilgrim's whole reason for existing and, his mission accomplished, he can disappear as eerily and mysteriously as he arrived. Aschenbach does not become a painted dandy because he meets one on the boat; he meets one because that's what he is to become. His arrival in Venice may seem accidental, but Venice is the one place on earth that can tempt him to relax and relish the boons of chaos. What seems impulse is really destiny, and accident is simply the misnomer that our myopia applies to design. Not the caprice of the catastrophe but its inexorability is what impresses the reader of Aschenbach's tale.

It is in accounting for this sense of inexorability that *The Birth of Tragedy* becomes not just helpful but indispensable. There are no necessary connections, viewed from without, between Aschenbach's flagging creativity and his death, between homosexuality and cholera, between the writer's way of life and his dangerous exposure to youthful beauty. The lesser, naturalistic achievement of *Death in Venice* is the plausibility of the events it recounts – the outer chamber of the story is a perfectly satisfactory habitation in that the mind easily accepts that all this could have happened. But the real and deeper achievement is the matching of surface event to symbolic significance, the creation of a coherent pattern of meanings in which every single thing, from the moment Aschenbach forsakes his desk in Munich to the moment he dies in his deckchair in Venice, is connected in a single process with an inner necessity – all this, the mind concludes serenely, *must* have happened. Only Nietzsche enables us to penetrate to this inner chamber where what might seem arbitrary or at best probable is recognised as inevitable.

The chapter entitled 'Snow' in *The Magic Mountain* helps to explain why Aschenbach's fate is so inseparably linked with his vocation. Hans Castorp, caught in a snowstorm, has a vision of a beautiful, happy people (clearly idealised Athenians) enjoying life round a temple within the deepest recesses of which horrors are being perpetrated.[3] This presents in ideogrammatic form the key argument of *The Birth of Tragedy* – that art, especially tragic art, proceeds from the creative conflict between Apollo and Dionysos, from the Apollonian transfiguration of the Dionysian tumult, from the imposition of form and measure upon primitive emotions. Apollo holds Dionysos in check and the result is a species of 'illusion' masking the fearful truth; the terror of the world is made beautiful. If the power of Dionysos over a people is very great – if they are, as Nietzsche says the ancient Greeks were, a ferocious and barbaric people – then the adversarial, controlling Apollonian power must be all the greater. Nietzsche describes the Dionysiac rapture as a state wherein the individual became 'so stirred' as to forget himself completely; what followed was 'a complete sexual promiscuity overriding every form of established tribal law; all the savage urges of the mind were unleashed on those occasions until they reached that paroxysm of lust and cruelty'. He concludes that 'what kept Greece safe was the proud, imposing image of Apollo'.[4] If Dionysos is controlled, the result will be the highest kind of art, for only the most consummately developed sense of form will be enough to tame the initial chaos.

When Arnold rebuked his fellow Englishmen for being too Hebraic and insufficiently Greek, and asked them to adjust the balance of these elements within themselves, the Greeks he had in mind were clearly those who adhered to the Socratic tradition of luminous intellect and civilised discourse. If he thought of Dionysos, of the goat-god, at all, we can be sure it was with suspicion and disapproval. The Greeks that Aschenbach dreams of shortly before his death belong to a very different tradition indeed – to the orgiastic rapture and madness uncovered and extolled by Nietzsche in *The Birth of Tragedy*. Far from being a part of our nature that we should try to eradicate or a tradition that we should disavow, all this is the necessary precondition of art: 'Apollo found it impossible to live without Dionysos'.[5] But to live with him entails resisting him. Mann's tale shows what happens when the will to resist crumbles and Dionysos triumphs. It is, accordingly, crucial that the life-transforming journey in *Death in Venice* should be undertaken by an artist, for it is very much a journey from Apollo to Dionysos, from the officially sanctioned view of art to its subversive opposite, from its decorous appearance to its shocking origin. Beauty is as dangerous a substance as asbestos, with the artist as much at risk from the occupational hazards of his trade as the miner or the diver from his. 'Verily it is well for the world that it sees only the beauty of the completed work and not its origins nor the conditions whence it sprang; since knowledge of the artist's inspiration might often but confuse and alarm and so prevent the full effect of its excellence'.[6] But if the world is safe, the artist is not.

On the beach the grave, middle-aged German contemplates the beautiful Polish boy: 'the elder's dignified and cultured mien let nothing appear of his inward state'.[7] It is the mere semblance, soon to be shattered, of Apollonian control. Nietzsche's account of art is very similar to Swift's view of existence: the surface is sunny and deceptively secure, while underneath are dark forces and loathsome faults, shocking but undeniable. Repression and sublimated reproduction are the aesthetic secret; art, like civilisation in Freud's analysis, is the reward for instinctual renunciation. The Aschenbach to whom we are first introduced is such an artist, a hero of the categorical imperative, the poet according to Kant. The limpid grace of his work is a deception, for his art is unnatural in the sense that it has been wrested from life, a victory achieved only by dourly fighting every inch of the way, a service over which he toils as painfully as any slave in field or mine. He has made himself what he is by an unceasing act of will and his story opens at a moment when the burn-out point is dangerously imminent. Apollo, exhausted, is about to drop out, and Dionysos, still within, is poised to take revenge for all those years of confinement and control.

Tadzio's beauty can still inspire the disintegrating artist to create; with that perfection in view, sitting on his deckchair, Aschenbach composes his last piece of work when news reaches him of that key question troubling Europe which he is so supremely qualified to answer. It is still the work of a master, but it is, significantly, only one and a half pages long – sustained creation is now beyond him, as, very soon, any kind of creation will be. Art comes from the conflict between Dionysos and Apollo; when Apollo retires from the contest, passion inundates everything and art is impossible. Aschenbach abandons art for action, sublimation for stalking; instead of being impelled by Tadzio's beauty to create, he is driven to pursue the boy through the streets of the city – almost as if Dante, instead of writing *La Vita Nuova*, had become a peeping-tom lurking outside Beatrice's apartment. Tonio Kröger feels that he pays for his art in the ascetic exclusion of his life.[8] The artist records life by not living it. Aschenbach begins by observing Tadzio, but the dispassionate detachment ends in frenzied involvement, as he moves from noticing to observing to waiting and on to stalking. His destructive obsession takes him away from art and into life. *Death in Venice* shows what happens when the artist leaves the haven of form to confront beauty head-on – he is destroyed like Semele in the arms of Zeus.

Yet the tale's symbolism is never so obtrusive as to deflect us from the thoroughly realistic, almost sordid, matter of its surface. Mann's achievement, like Bunyan's, is to locate his journey in a world simultaneously faithful to psychology and myth. He moves in the opposite direction to Bunyan but to the same impressively successful end. Bunyan's hero flees from the City of Destruction to search for the Celestial City, but he also journeys through Lincolnshire and many of those he meets en route are everyday English people. Mann's artist sets out from Munich to arrive at Venice, but these geographical realities are also symbolic states and the characters he encounters are all emissaries from a mythological world. From the beginning the novel as a form has exhibited a propensity towards realism, social documentation, an interrelation with historical event, a delight in social fact, but the novel is also a fiction, a fable, an instrument for expressing our pleasure in tale. Mann is especially gifted at fusing the mythopoeic power of fiction with its socio-referential relevance, fable and fact, into one aesthetic whole.

This combination of outer realism with inner symbol is the distinguishing characteristic of Mann's fiction as demonstrated in the dense detail of *The Magic Mountain* where every character functions at a dual level. The soul of Hans Castorp is the prize of the contending forces in this modern rendition of the Everyman morality tale. Claudia Chauchat is thus simultaneously a slovenly yet excitingly attractive woman who bites her nails and slams doors, *and* another manifestation of that Slavic disorder and formlessness which are so menacing to the German spirit. The bosom which allures Joachim Ziemssen is both literally and spiritually diseased;[9] Claudia Chauchat is at once a realistic character and a symbol of what threatens the young hero as he moves through a story in which the ancient demons and goblins reappear in modern form. Carelessness, enervation, disease and death are as palpably present on the *Zauberberg* as they are in Spenser's Bower of Bliss; the disciplined life is as much demanded of Aschenbach and Castorp as it is of Guyon, while Venice resembles Acrasia in the fatal lure which each emits.

Aschenbach's surface journey is from the library to the lido, the desk to the deckchair, but these ordinary, everyday objects are invested with intense symbolic significance and are made to stand for opposing life-styles: discipline versus indulgence, repression versus unconstraint, form versus dissolution – man as mind, in Settembrini's nobly humanist formulation, or man as water, in Behren's reductive analysis, unstable and fluid, without fixed limits.[10] Munich, which Aschenbach leaves, is the city of service and duty, where the Kantian artist, descendant of officers, judges and civil functionaries, conscientiously toils to produce masterpieces that seem effortless in their perfection. His whole tradition excludes 'the sweet idleness and blithe *laissez aller* that belongs to youth';[11] he lives like a clenched fist, tense in achievement, the exemplification of Luther's secularised *Beruf*. *Durchhalten* is his motto, Frederick the Great his model, fortitude under suffering his recipe for greatness, for all greatness comes from mastering weakness, from labour accomplished at the edge of exhaustion. It is fitting that Aschenbach's day should begin with a cold shower, for his art, outwardly so serene, is the internal equivalent of gritted teeth.

But if Munich is the city of mind, Venice is the city of water, home of art, disease and immorality, where the firm lines of the disciplined life turn fluid and definition cedes to promiscuity. It is a place to play rather than work, even when the gamester should really know better, as in the case of the young-old man, so sickeningly askew among his young companions. Every aspect and item of Venice undermines the life of effort and challenges the *Beruf*; even to sit in a gondola is to capitulate to lawlessness in the softest, most luxurious, most relaxing seat in the world. That a gondola resembles a coffin and is also used for sexually illicit adventures links death, immorality and luxurious abandonment in a single object.[12] Water is, of course, crucially significant as 'the yielding element' in which one can give up struggling and drift instead with the current, embracing sweet *far niente* – even at the mercy of a potentially psychotic boatman, Aschenbach prefers the irresponsible bliss of acquiescence to the strenuous exertion of self-defence. In Munich one makes things happen, in Venice one lets it be. It is a lotus-land where even the naturally industrious can slip into ruinous ease, the one spot on earth with the charm to undo Aschenbach, as fatal to the ascetic life as the Bower of Bliss.

The two life-styles, with their associated mythologies of North and South, contend with each other, and the Mediterranean gods prevail. In Venice Aschenbach thinks of his mountain home, the theatre of his summer labours, where the clouds hang low and where, amid violent storms, the ravens he fed swung in the tops of the fir trees.[13] It is perhaps the one moment in the tale when realism seems outraged and we withhold belief – did Aschenbach really feed ravens in Munich? The ravens implausibly enter the story as the companions of the Scandinavian gods whom Mann is proposing as symbols of energy and icy exertion. It is this Nordic inheritance that Aschenbach repudiates in favour of the classical Elysium, that very different paradise of the southern imagination, 'where no snow is and no winter, no storms or downpours of rain; where Oceanus sends a mild and cooling breath, and days flow on in blissful idleness, without effort or struggle, entirely dedicate to the sun and the feasts of the sun'.[14] This reasserts, even in its individual words, the promise of ultimate rest given by Proteus, associated like Venice with the sea, to Menelaus in Book IV of *The Odyssey*. Munich and Venice, mountain and sea, storm and sun, Nordic vitality and Mediterranean indolence – the symbolic antagonisms could not be more explicit, and so determined is Mann to present them that he is even prepared, with his questionable ravens, to risk the surface realism otherwise so faithfully achieved.

For what could be more realistic than the opening sentences of the tale? A man exhausted by long, unremitting, academic labour, finding his imagination flagging, puts down his pen and leaves his desk one day to go for a walk in a highly specific locale which is still there today for our inspection. He sets out from his house in Prince Regent Street, walks through the English Gardens towards Aumeister, reaches the North Cemetery, where, noting black clouds gathering over Föhring, he decides to wait for a tram to carry him back to the city. The circumstances, the detail, are thoroughly convincing, and this realism is sustained in the minutiae of trains, boats and timetables in his later journey to the South. Yet the walk he decides to take in Munich is prelude to that subsequent journey so decisive for his destiny, and he steps through the front door in Prince Regent Street into a mythological realm as well as into a Bavarian city. It is a decision as fateful as Gulliver's for that fourth voyage or Marlow's when he sailed for Africa, and Aschenbach's journey is similarly invested with a significance transcending his own individual lot. The second sentence tells us that his adventure coincides with a moment of crisis for Europe itself. The opening sentence has already presented him as an 'official' man, a representative figure, honoured by his country for his services to culture. Like Europe, he, too, now teeters on the edge of a breakdown and the imminent journey will end in releasing the inner, authentic man so long and so rigorously suppressed by the official self.

Outer realism dovetails perfectly with inner symbol. There is something ominous and eerie about the 'quite empty' neighbourhood of the graveyard and mortuary chapel where Aschenbach waits for his tram.[15] Even when that emptiness is ended by the appearance of the pilgrim-figure in the portico, it intensifies rather than dissipates the sense of mystery and unease. The man's arrival is so sudden and inexplicable that his presence is a riddle rather than a reassurance. It provides the narrator with the opportunity to employ a device which he will use with dramatic effect throughout, the offer of competing interpretations of the same event: 'Whether he had come out of the hall through the bronze doors or mounted unnoticed from outside, it was impossible to tell. Aschenbach casually inclined to the first idea'.[16] The alert reader, however, sensitive to the atmosphere of eeriness evoked by the writing, far from being casual, ponders the significance of this unexplained appearance.

Mann is, of course, far more subtle and less insistent in his use of the alternative explanation than, for example, Hawthorne. The

description of the mysterious stranger only hints at a diabolic or
deathly association – the 'two pronounced perpendicular furrows'
on his forehead are only vaguely reminiscent of the devil's horns,
but even the suggestion, slight as it is, is sufficient to fuel the
reader's unease.[17] When this facial characteristic recurs in the description of the street-musician later in the story, our suspicions are
confirmed and our apprehensions justified as the furrows assume,
retrospectively, a more precise menace than at their first mention.[18]
Nevertheless, from the first there is something sinister about the
portico pilgrim, something domineering and ruthless, 'and his lips
completed the picture by seeming to curl back, either by reason of
some deformity or else because he grimaced, being blinded by the
sun in his face; they laid bare the long, white glistening teeth to the
gums'.[19] In retrospect, this is plainly the death's-head, the first of
the messengers who prepare Aschenbach for that climax when,
dying, he sees the Summoner beckon him to come. But the full
sense of this first bidding only reveals itself in the light of the
subsequent encounters; for the present Mann is happy to permit
the double explanation, realist and mythic, the grimace caused
either by the sun or by the death-spasm, so long as he can establish
a mood of uncertainty and threat.

What is not uncertain is the effect of the pilgrim's apparition
upon Aschenbach. It induces so sudden and transforming a medi-
tation that when this is broken by the tram's arrival, he just as
suddenly realises that the man is no longer there. Having completed his mission, the stranger disappears as inexplicably as he
arrived. Aschenbach, who had hitherto regarded travel as a necessary evil, now feels an impulse to wander – the first step in a
complete reversal of values. The 'vaulting unrest' he experiences,
the 'youthfully ardent thirst for distant scenes', are clearly connected with a resurgence of long-suppressed instincts.[20] Again we
have a choice of explanations as Mann first tells us that all Aschenbach felt was no more than a longing to travel, but then contradicts
this by describing it as 'a seizure, almost a hallucination'. Certainly
there is nothing normal about the vision that comes to him of the
mephitic swamp, of nature in that monstrous, menacing form that
attracts Marlow and destroys Kurtz.[21] There is, simultaneously, the
first announcement of the disease theme, as the new, sudden
craving for indiscipline and flight is described as a 'contagion' – the
ascetic hero, the man of iron will, succumbs to the spiritual equivalent of Asiatic cholera. The very points of the compass take sides in

a geographical confrontation of values: North and West stand for discipline and duty, South and East for disease and abandonment.

This symbolic conflict of values, this mythic infrastructure of gods and demons, is evident almost from the beginning. The ancient hulk, the hunchbacked sailor, the goat-bearded captain sitting below decks with the Faustian contract that will take Aschenbach to degradation and death, all play a similar role to those queer, disturbing people that Marlow meets in Brussels before starting out for the heart of darkness; even as they fulfil the requirements of realism, they just as incontrovertibly belong to another realm of experience. The strange, threatening gondolier who tells the weakly blustering Aschenbach that he *will* pay, is clearly modelled upon Charon, the despotic boatman of Hades, carrying his charges to their appointed destinations, with or without their consent. Tadzio, swimming in the sea, is just a Polish boy on holiday, but, to Aschenbach's ecstatic gaze, he is a young god emerging from the waves, and the stronger Aschenbach's homosexual obsession becomes, the more Venice resembles 'a world possessed, peopled by Pan',[22] where Poseidon is present on the beach and Hyacinthus in the dining-room. The impudently obsequious street-entertainer, recalling and combining elements of earlier characters – the portico pilgrim, the young-old man, the strange gondolier – thereby becomes a figure of composite menace, carrying at once the smell of carbolic and the whiff of crime and corruption. No reader could deny that we have been well prepared for Aschenbach's final dream of the stranger god and the delicious ritual of orgiastic surrender. Yet neither can anyone say that the real world of everyday objects, of desks, tramcars and deckchairs, is in any way devalued or slighted to accommodate the world of myth and symbolism. It is after his final visit to the barber that the berouged Aschenbach walks in a wind that recalls the sounds made by 'unhallowed ocean harpies who follow those devoted to destruction';[23] the doomed sinner of Christianity merges with the fugitive of classical mythology, and the strength of Mann's art is that it can sustain the weight of these differing elements, realism and myth, psychology and symbolism, fact and fable. Even the final mythic image of Tadzio as the pale and lovely Summoner can include as one of its components an abandoned camera standing on a tripod near the water's edge, its black cloth snapping in the wind.

The ease with which the tale connects disparate dimensions and experiences is its most obvious characteristic. Thus the link between art and lawlessness is established from the start, long before Aschenbach arrives in Venice; not Venice but art is the danger – Venice simply removes the protective shield. The paradox of art is that it is simultaneously moral and immoral – moral in that form is the expression of discipline, and discipline is on the side of morality, immoral in that form, caring only for itself, subjects the moral world to its own requirements. The chameleon poet delights as much in a Iago as in an Imogen. Moreover, art is a dangerous pursuit for the reason that Plato alleges: it undermines the self and tempts the singer to become what he sings. Maupassant is perhaps the most fearful nineteenth-century instance of this transformation – *Monsieur Maupassant va s'animaliser'* – but his is merely an extreme example of a general occupational hazard. Aschenbach can depict the horrors of the Seven Years' War in his study of the great Frederick only by descending mentally into that inferno: 'art heightens life', but the price is that 'she consumes more swiftly'.[24] Outwardly the poet is calm and austere, inwardly he is as ravaged by his spiritual adventures as any libertine by his carnal ones. The chameleon poet is also the criminal poet.

The world, which is so entranced by the beauty of the work of art, would be disgusted if it saw the source from which that beauty came. The rose blooms in the dung, and the flower is lovely though its birth is foul. It is, similarly, in the foul rag and bone shop of the heart that the ladder of poetic inspiration is grounded. When Aschenbach, inspired by the beauty of Tadzio to write, finally puts his perfect work aside, he feels exhausted and broken: 'conscience reproached him, as it were after a debauch'.[25] Criminal passion and aesthetic triumph are inseparably linked and achievement is accompanied by a sense of guilt. Mann explicitly calls attention to this paradox of the artistic nature when he refers to 'that mingling of discipline and licence in which it stands so deeply rooted'.[26] *Death in Venice* presents the catastrophe that occurs when this precarious balance collapses and the artist becomes the full accomplice of unreason in its assault upon the social order. When Aschenbach deliberately keeps hidden the city's secret corruption because to publish it would mean losing Tadzio, he reveals himself as the criminal artist, preferring beauty to order and pleasure to morality: the two hidden iniquities, the city's plague and the artist's infatuation, are shown as one. When near the end Aschenbach sits with his fevered forehead pressed to the stone well, his conclusions on the hazards of the life of art are the more irrefutable because they are visibly proved in his own flesh – the pursuit of beauty is 'a path of perilous sweetness, a way of transgression'.[27] Art is finally as incompatible with citizenship as sin with salvation: 'we poets can be neither wise nor worthy citizens'.[28] The artist, his imposing magisterial style notwithstanding, is similarly disqualified as a teacher, for how can he save others who cannot save himself? – 'for what good can an artist be as a teacher, when from his birth up he is headed direct for the pit?'[29] However austere the poet, the abyss is his destination.

Nietzsche treats with withering scorn the assumption that the artist can contemplate with immunity and equanimity the nude female body – for him this stems from the foolish arrogance of believing that the artist has somehow ceased to be a man. The trap set for the artist in *Death in Venice* is an even more insidious one in that the threat comes from a boy rather than a woman, reinforcing the artist in his delusion of security. The first time Aschenbach sees Tadzio he 'noted with astonishment the lad's perfect beauty'.[30] With a connoisseur's instinctive delight, he naturally proceeds to contemplation and sits 'absorbed'. Next morning he experiences a Joycean epiphany when he is startled at 'the godlike beauty of the human being'.[31] It is the artist's eye that perceives 'the head . . . poised like a flower in incomparable loveliness', and the cultured man who makes the identification with Eros.[32]

The similarity to Stephen Dedalus on Howth strand, ecstatically grateful for the beauty of the wading girl, is, however, finally misleading, for the pure, detached exultation of the young Irish artist is beyond the power of the ageing German one. There is something suspicious in the flat phrases chosen by Aschenbach to disguise the turmoil within – one need only contrast his 'very good indeed!' with Stephen's elated cry – and, disconcertingly, even already, Aschenbach is aware of 'the watchful eye of the functionaries',[33] namely, the various guardians appointed to protect the boy from harm. Tadzio is, it seems, from the first a prize to be won rather than an object to be looked at – Aschenbach resembles the aroused lover rather than the detached observer; not Stephen Dedalus, but the hero of *The Romance of the Rose* or, at a less elevated level, Leopold Bloom looking up Gerty MacDowell's skirt, is where we must finally locate Aschenbach. In *Death in Venice* detachment is a delusion and a snare; contemplation becomes an obsession which compels its victim to shameful activity. From a Dedalean standpoint Aschenbach has surrendered to kinesis and pornography, an impulse to be one with the beloved object rather than, like the god of creation, remain separate from it. The creator must not be a possessor, since, for Joyce, to own is to run the risk of being owned, and involvement can lead to a loss of self, as so clearly happens to Mann's distraught hero. Even when Aschenbach seems to be a Joycean figure, his inner state is too dangerously unstable for the mandatory detachment to be sustained. His devotion to beauty leads him into humiliating activity; instead of writing a poem, he rouges his cheeks or rests his desperate head on the beloved's bedroom door. Art, the reward for renunciation, for disciplining Dionysos, is now impossible, and chaos and cholera together destroy him.

It follows that Aschenbach can no more attribute his misfortune to accident than a miner regard his emphysema as a piece of bad luck – in each case the damage inflicted is easily predictable. Neither is ignorance or even heedlessness an available excuse, since Aschenbach very quickly knows what's happening and consents to it. He sees the beauty of Venice but sees simultaneously its foulness and duplicity – 'half fairy-tale, half snare'[34]; if he is trapped, he has only himself to blame. He is hardly in the city when he smells 'the stagnant odour of the lagoons', and the 'hateful sultriness' of the narrow streets, the exhalations hanging low over the place, are objective reminders of the spiritual threat.[35] Resting in the quiet, forsaken square, he 'wiped his brow, and admitted to himself that he must be gone'.[36] The admission is wrung from him despite his obsession with Tadzio; Venice and what it stands for are bad for him, physically and morally, and he knows it. He knows what he ought to do but lacks the resolve to do it. His very decision to leave Venice is characterised by indecision and even reluctance; he quarrels with the porter who tells him when it's time to go, he deliberately loiters over his meal in the unconfessed hope of seeing the charmer for the last time. When he finally tears himself away, it is in the mood of a broken-hearted lover: 'his bosom was torn'. Grief overwhelms him at 'the thought that he should never more see Venice again'.[37] Yet it is so clearly a diseased love, the recurrence of an old, familiar addiction, for this is the second time that the place has made him ill and forced him 'to flee for his life'. He knows that Venice is 'a forbidden spot, to be forever shunned';[38] like any other addict, he knows his fix is killing him, but cannot break free.

When the news of the misdirected luggage breaks, 'a reckless joy,

a deep incredible mirthfulness shook him almost as with a spasm
. . . the unbelievable thing came to pass . . . all he had thought to
have left forever was his own once more'[39] – so might a man rejoice
on learning that he still possessed a tumour; what is really a death-
sentence is ecstatically embraced as though it were a last-minute
reprieve. He sits in the returning gondola, outwardly so dignified
and self-possessed, inwardly convulsed with illicit delight like a
truant schoolboy – he has regressed beyond the festive irresponsi-
bility of the painted dandy he met on ship to reach boyhood itself. It
is one of a series of minor epiphanies leading to the final shocking
revelation of the totally demoralised man. Honesty grows with
abandonment. Deciding to break Tadzio's spell by laying a friendly
hand on his shoulder, he first recoils in excited fear and then reflects
that it might have led to 'a sane recovery from his folly'.[40] Mann
takes the opportunity to reveal Aschenbach's honest confrontation
of his situation: 'the ageing man did not want to be cured . . . his
illusion was far too dear to him'.[41] He still shrinks at this stage from
exhibiting his folly – he wants to be sick but in secret. At the end,
the sickness at its zenith, he recklessly forsakes all circumspection
and tracks Tadzio, heedless of observation.

In doing so he fulfils the Nietzschean prescription in becoming
'the opposite of the esthetic, contemplative, un-willing disposition';[42] he also becomes the opposite of Socratic man. In his shocking revaluation of Greek civilisation Nietzsche had identified
Socrates as the enemy of myth and tragedy; not Apollonian control
but Socratic ethics is fatal to tragedy, and in the nineteenth century
Nietzsche exhorts his contemporaries to end this rational bondage:
'Socratic man has run his course . . . . Dare to lead the life of tragic
man, and you will be redeemed'.[43] Socrates is, for Nietzsche, the
sworn enemy of tragic art and the Dionysiac spirit because of his
insistence that whatever is true must be rational, whatever beautiful ordered. Virtue is knowledge, all sins arise from ignorance,
only the virtuous are happy: Nietzsche identifies these as the basic
Socratic maxims and judges their shallow optimism to be hostile to
tragedy.

Aschenbach's case clearly poses a problem for the whole Socratic
outlook. How is it possible for someone to love his disease or
deliberately refuse to be cured? Socrates says that a man is ill only
because he does not know how to be well; *Death in Venice* shows us
a man who is ill because he does not *want* to be well. Mann himself
was preoccupied with disease, collapse and death. *Buddenbrooks* is

subtitled *der Verfall einer Familie, Death in Venice* portrays the disintegration of Aschenbach, *Doctor Faustus* records not only the
destruction of Adrian Leverkühn but also the fall of Germany and
the tragedy of European culture. *The Magic Mountain* deals with the
baffling phenomenon – it would be outrageous were it not also
indisputable – that some people want to be sick. 'I have been half in
love with easeful death'. Freud, in his concept of the death-wish,
attempted to raise Keats's mournful yearning to the level of a
universal law, and Mann was clearly attracted by the Freudian view
of man as a wilfully sick animal. Naphta in *The Magic Mountain* is
eager to correct Hans Castorp's erroneous belief that disease is
unhuman: 'Disease was very human indeed. For to be man was to
be ailing. Man was essentially ailing, his state of unhealthiness was
what made him man'.[44] To be human is to be sick. It is the same
insight in different terminology that we find in Camus's *The Plague*,
though Camus insists that to be human also entails struggling
against the disease. Hans Castorp, to Settembrini's dismay,
consents to become 'one of us', that is, he surrenders to the spirit of
disease and deserts the profession of engineer in the Flatland to
become an invalid on the mountain. But *The Magic Mountain* is,
finally, a comedy in which the hero makes his escape by electing
health above disease. *Death in Venice*, by contrast, is a tragedy in
which the hero is destroyed because he chooses disease rather than
health, the boons of chaos rather than the responsibilities of order.

It is a choice which the Socratic analysis cannot comprehend. No
man does evil knowingly; if we do find him pursuing evil, it is only
because he has mistaken it for good. There is a rational solution to
every problem and our salvation is merely a matter of increased
enlightenment. Ovid and St Paul are less sanguine: *video meliora
proboque, deteriora sequor;* for I do not the good that I wish, but the
evil that I do not wish, that I perform. Aschenbach, too, contradicts
the wholesome simplicity of the Socratic analysis. Not only does he
know that what he's doing is dishonourable – he does it for that
very reason. After his meeting with the candid young Englishman
in the travel bureau, Aschenbach has absolute, irrefutable verifi-
cation of his suspicions about the plague – what is so shocking is
the effect of this discovery upon him. It is not unlike the reaction of
Conrad's Kurtz to his jungle revelation; Aschenbach is 'feverishly
excited, triumphant in possession of the truth at last, but with a
sickening taste in his mouth and a fantastic horror at his heart'.[45]
Now that he knows Venice to be in the grip of pestilence, he

automatically knows that 'one decent, expiatory course lay open to him; he considered it'.[46]

Mann makes it clear that Aschenbach's is a deliberate, pondered choice and not the impulsive reflex of the moment. And, having considered, he decides *not* to do the decent thing, the thing that 'would restore him, would give him back himself once more'. The truly staggering fact is that he does not *want* the restoration of his former, lost self, for 'he who is beside himself revolts at the idea of self-possession'.[47] Such a restoration means a re-acquisition of reason and self-mastery, the return to an ordered existence and to the old life of effort. The very thought of this restitution makes him wince. Far from warning Tadzio's mother to take her son from the stricken city, he fiercely resolves upon silence: 'It must be kept quiet . . . I will not speak.'[48] He becomes the plague's ally, preserver of the city's guilty secret, colluding jubilantly with the disease because it matches the pollution in himself. It is a momentous, life-shaping decision, and it is fitting that on the night of this delinquent silence the dream comes that 'left the whole cultural structure of a life-time trampled on, ravaged, and destroyed'.[49] The followers of Socrates can protest all they wish, but Mann's tale shows us a human being deliberately and knowingly willing his own destruction.

Hence the final dark epiphany as the painted, fevered boy-stalker sits exhausted in the same desolate square where he had recently planned his involuntary escape, eating the contaminated fruit that will kill him, the fruit as forbidden now as it was in Eden and which he devours just as heedless of the risk he runs: 'there he sat, the master'.[50] The word is heavily ironic, for it describes his lost self and not the abject slave he now is. The man once officially ennobled by an admiring established order in tribute to the classic restraint of his art is now the thrall of subversion and chaos, as degraded and revolting a spectacle as the pitiful Winston Smith after his dehumanisation by the Thought Police.

But Mann's tale, unlike Orwell's prophecy, does not end with an image of degradation holding us in fascinated loathing. There is not much doubt as to what Orwell intends when he shows us the last man in Europe crushed beyond all reprieve and loving his humiliation. We have witnessed a catastrophe of the human spirit, an unmitigated disaster which touches the sadistic in its stern refusal of the slightest consolation. Orwell's book is itself a kind of Room 101 in which the author immures us to confront the worst thing in the world. *Death in Venice*, by contrast, does not end in the woe-begone square but on the beach, and no one who attends to the closing paragraphs can miss the sense of victory as well as downfall, of breakthrough as well as breakdown. The world of myth is summoned to refute any reductive distortion that a simplistic realism might promote, and the outcome is the final triumph of that bi-focalism, that ambiguity of interpretation, which the tale has throughout sustained. Aschenbach is, like every other tragic figure, hero as well as victim, and, as such, more akin to Kurtz than to Orwell's failure. *Death in Venice* and *Heart of Darkness* adopt a similar romantic stance towards the illicit and forbidden; at the core of each is a celebration of the lawbreaker, of the man who dares to go the whole distance. It is a characteristic that separates Conrad and Mann not only from Swift but also from their successors, Camus, Orwell and Golding, when, in the altered moral landscape of the advancing century, they, too, came to grapple with the problem of evil.

One of the devices used by Mann to support the doubleness of his tale is, as has been noted, that of the dual explanation, the offer of competing exegeses; another, parallel technique is that of the shift-ing narrator. Sometimes Mann adopts a mimetic narrative mode in which the mood of the hero determines the presentation of events – it is a kind of inverted ventriloquism where the narrator provides a voice for the character's views. The description of Aschenbach watching daybreak from his bedroom window illustrates this per-fectly. Nature becomes a lover and dawn a sexual exhibition: Eos, rising from her spouse's side, approaches as the 'ravisher of youth', seducer of young men, the sea 'heaves forward on its welling waves', while 'from horizon to zenith went quivering thrusts like golden lances'.[51] Such explicit imagery makes it clear that this is much more a rendition of Aschenbach's internal passional turmoil than a description of a Mediterranean dawn; the nature presented has been filtered through the heightened consciousness of the lovestruck man.

The same is true when the episode of the misdirected luggage leads to the surprising conclusion of the 'guest detained by so happy a mischance'[52] – is, we object, 'happy' the appropriate word in view of the catastrophic consequences that the accident has for Aschenbach? Surely this is how the unbalanced man felt at the time, but that *he* rejoices merely intensifies the tragic irony, for *we* know better. Because the narrator has surreptitiously handed over his pen to the self-destroyer does not oblige us to join in the latter's delusion. That Mann does not mean us to be caught in so blatant a trap seems borne out when Aschenbach is later described as 'the fond fool' who recklessly pursues his charmer into the Sunday mass. We feel more comfortable with this as presumably reflecting the narrator's own considered judgement, not the addict's fond assessment of his conduct but an external appraisal of his folly, and this objective evaluation seems ratified when Aschenbach re-appears as 'the unhappy man' who wakens shattered from his dream of orgiastic excess. It links up with the earlier presentation of 'the spellbound man', in shameful thraldom to his 'doting heart'.[53] This shift of perspective, from Aschenbach's misguided vision to the narrator's censorious revision, is so perfectly done that the picture of 'the master' sitting degraded in the forsaken square strikes the reader as the final, complete truth of the matter to which nothing can be added or taken away.

Yet we would be wrong to see Aschenbach simply as the anti-exemplar of a cautionary tale or to read *Death in Venice* as a morality showing the sinner's comeuppance. The final paragraphs will not permit the neat packaging of *Death in Venice* as a simple story of sin and retribution. From one angle Aschenbach *is* a degraded wretch, fit recipient of our pity or revulsion, and, considering what he once was, our reaction might well be that of the Chorus in Marlowe's *Faustus:*

> Cut is the branch that might have grown full straight,
> And burned is Apollo's laurel bough,
> That sometime grew within this learned man.
> Faustus is gone: regard his hellish fall,
> Whose fiendful fortune may exhort the wise
> Only to wonder at unlawful things

But this is a one-eyed view in a story which calls for double vision. From another angle Aschenbach is a hero of the spirit, who, paying the ultimate price, wins through to an awareness of his real self. Such a view is not only possible but compulsory from a Nietzschean standpoint. 'All that is now called culture, education, civilisation will one day have to appear before the incorruptible judge, Dionysos.'[54] When that day comes archetypal man will be cleansed of the illusion of culture and authentic man will appear, beside whom his cultured self will dwindle to a false cartoon.

Some such displacement occurs in *The Immoralist* as we watch a puritan being re-educated to 'a confused consciousness of untouched treasures somewhere lying covered up, hidden, smothered by culture and decency and morality'.[55] It is the same awakening as Aschenbach experiences, though for Michel the joyful acceptance of his homosexuality also entails abandoning a dying wife. But there is the same sense of a breakthrough to emotional reality: 'at the touch of new sensations, certain portions of me awoke – certain sleeping faculties which . . . had kept all their mysterious freshness'.[56] There is also a conviction of a true self which must at all costs be liberated, whatever the damage to culture and morality in the process. Michel is driven to search for 'that authentic creature, "the old Adam", whom the Gospel had repudiated, whom everything about me . . . had begun by attempting to suppress'.[57] In this quest he comes to despise 'the secondary creature, the creature who was due to teaching, whom education had painted on the surface. These overlays had to be shaken off.'[58] Like the scholar he is, he finds the appropriate metaphor for his condition in the image of a palimpsest and refers to 'the scholar's joy when he discovers under more recent writing and on the same paper, a very ancient and infinitely more precious text';[59] the later writing must be effaced in order to read this older message. Gide's hero is so elated with the discovery of his true self that it would be foolish to include *The Immoralist* in the tradition of the dark epiphany – the triumph of authentic man over false culture leads here, not to the destruction of the hero, but of his wife. A sense of triumph amid desolation is, however, the defining characteristic of the dark epiphany in its earlier twentieth-century manifestations. If the jungle destroys Kurtz and Venice Aschenbach, they simultaneously furnish truths which the heroes would otherwise forever miss. 'The persistent official policy of silence and denial' with which Venice masks the truth of its corruption has its disturbing analogue in the repressive self-censorship by which the official von Aschenbach once lived – but in each case the truth is great and will prevail. Better hell than hypocrisy.

Once again there is a link with Swift, the Swift of the flayed woman and the beau's carcass: the surface is pleasing but false, the interior is loathsome but true, and truth is superior to deception. What separates Conrad and Mann so decisively from Swift is that for him this truth remains a scandal; he insists that we face it but never advocates complicity with it nor proposes for canonisation the man who makes the breakthrough. Gulliver is a hero because he confesses the Yahoo in himself, not because he extenuates, far less celebrates, it. Humiliation is Swift's business, not apotheosis.

The brutal anti-romanticism of Swift makes it easy to imagine how he would have reacted to the heroes of *Heart of Darkness* and *Death in Venice* – the passion-drunk artist and the power-drunk emissary would have provoked in him an icy disdain. For Swift, too, had a mission – to hunt down and destroy the romantic sensibility wherever it presumed to exist. Those enthusiasts, including romantic lovers, who parade their extravagant passions as proof of an exaltation above matter, a liberation of the spirit from its fleshly prison, must be mercilessly dragged back to the foul ditch which is their true and natural habitat. 'Romantic' is, for Swift, always a term of contempt, and the foolish effrontery of romantic passion is cruelly exposed in the woman who marries for love in 'The Progress of Love'; dreaming herself a heroine of romance, she ends up a syphilitic whore whose husband is her pimp. Subtending every romantic dream is a bedrock of physiology – disguise it as you will, it is finally, inextricably enmeshed in Yahoo brutality. Swift feared Dionysos, the exaltation of the non-ethical, sexual energies, the triumph over moral reason. He likewise feared myth as either a deluded attempt to transfigure matter or an excuse for nastiness – in *The Mechanical Operation of the Spirit* the vocabulary of Orphic ritual is used for purposes of degrading deflation and myth is stripped of its highfalutin pretensions to appear as the sordid transaction it is.

There is not much doubt as to how Swift would have regarded Aschenbach – he had not been so merciless towards heterosexual love in order to turn mild towards pederasty. Behind the pretentious Platonic smokescreen, Aschenbach would have struck Swift as merely an ageing pederast, deplorably misconducting himself on a seaside debauch. All those classical and mythological allusions would have been scornfully dismissed as the sophisticated rationalisations of a cultured Yahoo – we know only too well what Swift thought of the impertinence of little paltry mortals conceited enough to believe that either heaven or hell was even faintly interested in their nasty nonsense. Swift is too implacable a de-mythologiser to sit patiently through the final scene of *Death in Venice*; scorning the mythical infrastructure from the beginning, he would surely have been infuriated by the concluding apotheosis. 'Their loads they all on Satan lay: / The Devil did the deed, not they!' Substituting Dionysos for the devil would not have mollified him – why won't these human beings take responsibility for their own shameful transgressions?

At the level of surface realism (the only level that Swift would have accepted) a middle-aged man dies of Asiatic cholera in a deck-chair while taking his last look at the boy who obsesses him wading in the sea. At the deeper, mythic level the boy has become 'the pale and lovely Summoner', the last of all those messengers from a spectral world who have appeared to the privileged, imperilled artist, and this final messenger points towards 'an immensity of richest expectations'.[60] The bifocal demands of the story prevent us from derisively dismissing this as pretentious clap-trap, for by now the mythic occupies the centre of the stage. Aschenbach has not just suffered a sordid collapse, but is also en route to Elysium; a psychological-physical disintegration is alchemised into a dignified and lovely apotheosis, a mythic return to bliss.

The reader must either consent to this transformation or forgo the final revelation of Mann's tale. Suppose that Dante is only half right, that the poet descends into hell, but does not, after all that he endures, come forth to look once more upon the stars; suppose that the price of art is life as the price of salvation is death; Aschenbach might then easily be seen as the hero, the poet as hero. He dies at the height of his powers, overcome by a passion that his ethical reason condemns, but man, certainly artist-man, does not live by ethics alone. Aschenbach's end is at once a defeat and a rebirth, and, dying, he knows a reality that he had hitherto refused to admit to consciousness. Kurtz prefers the horror to the hypocrisy of Brussels, Aschenbach opts for the Dionysian rapture against the bland respectabilities of society – the fact that each dies for his choice is merely the irrevocable certification of heroism. You have to die to be born again: Aschenbach is simply the artistic ratification of the momentous doctrine that the pious daily announce. The shame of the Cross is linked to its glory. Hence in *Death in Venice* the downfall of the hero is not finally presented as a deplorable event, but as the consequence, fearful yet vindicatory, of entering upon a forbidden path which is simultaneously the route to an ultimate self-realisation. Nietzsche declares that tragedy denies ethics. Even if we shrink from this as too extreme, we will surely agree that in tragedy the hero's sin and death are in the end somehow justified, are perhaps even a salvation. There seems no good reason to deny to Kurtz and Aschenbach a similar vindication.

5

Nineteen Eighty-Four: the Insufficient Self

Orwell's debt to Swift is plain even to an inattentive reader – *Animal Farm* is so clearly a levy upon the comic treasury of the *Travels* – but a reading of the essay on Swift reveals the full extent of the reluctant admiration wrested by the genius of the great Augustan from his twentieth-century descendant.[1] While barely willing to allow the *Travels* as a work falling just on the right side of sanity, Orwell nevertheless simultaneously ranked it as one of a handful of irreplaceable masterpieces produced by western man, a test of our trusteeship, to be preserved whatever else we might be forced to relinquish. The Swift connection is by now a commonplace of Orwell criticism; what is still not, however, sufficiently recognised is the degree to which *Nineteen Eighty-Four* is shaped by Swift's great fable; how, specifically, in wrestling with the central problem of *Gulliver's Travels* – the hunt for the human being – Orwell came to create his own dark masterpiece.

Both texts pursue the truth about man, seeking the true self, the authentic person, who will at last be found beneath the accretions of culture and the drapings of mythology; both end in a kind of conversion in which once sacrosanct dogmas about human identity are exposed as totally untenable superstitions. Gulliver travels to all those strange places and meets all those remarkable peoples to confront, not the truth of the external world, but the reality within – he is his own greatest, most appalling discovery. What he finds shatters the complacent assumption enshrined in the logic books: *homo est animal rationale.* The pool in Houyhnhnmland reveals a very different, nauseating reality. Winston is likewise taken to Room 101 not to penetrate the truth of Oceanic society, to add the 'why' to the already mastered 'how', but to be broken with the revelation of his own turpitude; Big Brother remains a mystery, it is Winston himself who is shockingly uncovered. In each case the reaction is the same: after such knowledge, what forgiveness? That the one investigation is conducted in the mode of comic satire while the other, depressingly humourless, confines its reader to a pessimistic prison, should not obscure the basic underlying similarity. The search for the self ends for each in catastrophic success; the chill disclosure of human corruption occurs in Houyhnhnmland and Oceania alike.

It has long been recognised that intimidation is the prime objective of Swift's satire, that the 'Digression on Madness' and Gulliver's last voyage strive to induce in their reader a sense of demoralisation, a fearful questioning of what it means to be human, verging upon a panic-stricken intuition that it may mean nothing at all. No one who reads the *Travels* can miss the theme of conditioning and entrapment that informs the whole fiction. For many centuries we in the west have celebrated the autonomous self as the highest of all our values, so precious that we continue, even yet, to reject solutions to our grievous social problems when such remedies threaten the sanctity of individual rights – the earthly paradise itself come too dear if the cost is the suppression of the self.

Gulliver's Travels shockingly proposes that this exalted idea of the self, self-justifying and inviolable, cornerstone of Christianity and humanism alike, is mere delusion. As Gulliver moves from society to society, to be moulded anew to each fresh set of cultural assumptions, the nihilistic speculation becomes increasingly insistent: perhaps there is ultimately no self at all, no central human core, beyond the reach of manipulation, perhaps there is nothing essentially human to withstand the coercions of culture? Such satire puts on trial the very existence of the self as an entity independent of the social system in which it acquires awareness. What is so unnerving about Gulliver as average, everyday man is that he changes with every change of environment, seems ominously deficient in any fixed or permanent characteristics, is short or tall, clean or unclean, only by comparison; he is a relative creature – giant among Lilliputians, Lilliputian among giants, Yahoo among Houyhnhnms, horse among men. Man, in the sense of some irreducibly human core, some residual quality transcending cultural control, resisting or modifying environmental omnipotence, is shown as fiction and sham, the belief that there is a human *given* exposed as the most pathetic of delusions.

The scandal of Swift is his suggestion that man is merely a mechanism, a function of his environment, imprisoned in a system which he evades, if at all, only to enter another, forever exchanging captivities. All the different peoples of the book live locked into their own structures, unaware or contemptuous of other life-styles, refusing to credit what they have not been programmed to believe. Gulliver moves from culture to culture, demonstrating that the same belief can be invincible or ludicrous depending on its social context and that what we call truth is what others call prejudice; demonstrating, too, just how easily man can be re-conditioned to abhor what he once revered, to regard as normal what was formerly bizarre. But if man is so infinitely malleable, so much a moral and intellectual weather-vane, what becomes of the boasted freedom of the mind, the inviolable sanctity of the self? What makes the *Travels* so chillingly modern is its anticipation of a major theme of structuralism in suggesting that man is simply the sum of his codes, programmed like a computer to follow instructions, incapable of change until reprogramming occurs. There *is* no self apart from society, no nature but only culture, no answer to the question, 'Who is Gulliver?', except in terms of the particular cultural context where he temporarily chances to be.

Yet this is not the whole truth about the *Travels* and can, in fact, taken in isolation, be misleading. Far from putting down the book in the conviction that all is contingent and relative, the reader is only too disturbingly conscious that the search for the self has ended in an absolute fact, namely, the brutal reality of Yahoo man. Only those who believe that Swift's chief target is Gulliver himself, that Gulliver is a gull precisely in falling so foolishly for the Houyhnhnm propaganda that equates man and Yahoo, will be able to treat Gulliver's final disclosures as the delusions of a disordered mind. For such readers Yahoo man is Gulliver's ultimate blunder, *not* Swift's concluding accusation. But those who decline to use Gulliver as a lightning conductor for Swift's contempt have to acknowledge that the Yahoo is a fact of the *Travels* and not just a fool's hallucination. The book which seemed to discredit all truth ends by advancing the hideous truth of Yahoo man. *That* is where Gulliver's search leads, for, back in England, he adheres to the truths of Houyhnhnmland, refusing, as so invariably in the past, to alter his beliefs with the altered environment. We have no right to speculate beyond the book's covers to imagine a new Gulliver, transformed yet again and re-dedicated to the possibility of human goodness. The *Travels* insist that the Yahoo is real; it is the rational qualities we pride ourselves upon that are exposed as spurious.

This is the truth that Swift sends Gulliver travelling to learn. He sets out on his final voyage convinced of certain unimpugnable truths: that England is the queen of nations and man the crown of creation, that society, with all its institutions and artefacts, is the incontestable sign of human excellence. In Houyhnhnmland he is made aware of the frauds that have been practised upon him: man is not *animal rationale* but Yahoo; society exhibits not the glittering evidence of human achievement but the proof of human depravity. Winston Smith is engaged on a similar search which culminates in a similar disaster. Like Gulliver, he, too, strives to fathom the mystery of his own existence – by ransacking his memory, by treasuring every scrap of evidence from the abolished past, by involving old proles in pub conversations in the vain hope of deciphering history. He desperately seeks the evidence that will confirm what he already knows is true: that truth is objective, existing regardless of the fears and wishes of men, that love is stronger than hate, that the skull is an inviolable realm, a no-go area to the strongest conceivable tyrant, that the past is unalterable, with yesterday's event beyond the possibility of recall or revision. These are the adamantine truths upon which Winston relies as he initiates his challenge to Big Brother. From the outset he is prepared for the worst, and the worst is that he will be caught, tortured and executed. But he knows, too, that the truths he cherishes are insuperable and that when his body is dead his ideals will have triumphed.

Nineteen Eighty-Four records an education as Winston is taught, painfully, to discard mistaken views of the world in favour of harsher, more correct ones. His final transformation is as shocking as Gulliver's; Gulliver changes from lover of humanity to misanthrope, Winston from freedom-fighter to power-worshipper, rebel to lickspittle. The full enormity of this metamorphosis can be gauged only by someone familiar with Orwell's political views as expressed repeatedly throughout his essays and reviews. The easiest way to clarify all this is to consider the great change we experience in passing from the world of Conrad to that of Orwell. Much more important than the forty-odd years are the two world wars that separate *Heart of Darkness* from *Nineteen Eighty-Four*. Orwell's dismay in the face of the atrocities left no corner of him where even a scintilla of an earlier romanticism could lodge; consequently, his attitude to evil is closer to Swift's icy disdain than to Conrad's ambivalent fascination confronting Kurtz. If the keynote of *Heart of Darkness* is horror, that of *Nineteen Eighty-Four* is disgust. It is a book dense with disgust, relieved only momentarily by the excursion to the Golden Land or by the brief, anachronistic marital companionship of the room behind the antique shop.

Otherwise there is an atmosphere of terror and tedium, of squalor forever on the brink of nightmare, disgust competing with fear: urine, sour beer, crumbling cigarettes, firewater gin, the reek of sweat, stew like vomit, broken bones, smashed teeth, bloody clots of hair, gorilla-like guards, public executions. Oceania is a dull hell, with O'Brien's elegant apartment the one oasis of beauty in a squalid, crumbling city. Orwell's intense loathing for totalitarianism kept him immune from any tendency to admire, however obliquely, the men of power who had brought such things to pass.

There is at least a hint of hero-worship in Marlow's attitude to Kurtz – it is, after all, Kurtz's diabolism that has made him a significant man as well as a lost soul, raising him above the meanness of the other pilgrims; Marlow feels that it is better to be damned like Satan than dismissed as dross, better to be wanted for murder than wanted for nothing. There is, similarly, more than a trace of admiration in Winston for his torturer, O'Brien, as a being so much greater than himself. Power extorts even from its victims not merely reverence but also gratitude: the Lord giveth and the Lord taketh away – blessed be the name of the Lord; though he slay me, yet will I trust in him. The difference is that while we suspect Conrad as sharing, at least in part, Marlow's romantic view of the great criminal, we know from his own words that Orwell abominated the power-worshipper, especially when he was revealed as lurking, perhaps even unknown to himself, beneath the disguise of freedom-fighter.

Orwell's reaction against the glamorisation of evil that surfaces fitfully in *Heart of Darkness* included a contempt for the cult of the heroic malefactor, the criminal superman who proves his manumission from mediocrity by stepping over the trivial codes of petty men. Repeatedly throughout his writing, in his review of Carlyle, his comments on Stalin, his essays on Burnham and Hadley Chase, he showed his complete antipathy to any element of the Great Man syndrome.[2] Power – his Burma experiences are ample testimony – made Orwell feel ashamed and guilty. When, in *Down and Out in Paris and London*, an old man is humiliated in a pawn-shop and his fellow-victims, waiting their turn to be served, laugh dutifully at his discomfiture, Orwell is sickened more by the sycophancy of the power-worshippers than by the inhumanity of the tyrannical clerk.[3] No other twentieth-century writer has campaigned more strenuously to purge the minds of his fellows of this revolting ailment.

It is all the more shocking that the hero of his last book should end up as the most despicable of power-worshippers, truckling disgustingly to what has unmanned him. It is worse still that Winston should have initially offered himself as Prometheus, defier of unjust power, champion of freedom and individual integrity, the last man in Europe. To choose to be Job is allowable, perhaps even commendable; to suffer unresistingly like Christ or Billy Budd is not necessarily the badge of inferiority. But to be changed into Job after aspiring to be Prometheus is a transformation so great as to provoke unease in the minds of its spectators – it is difficult to believe that the substitution of roles has been achieved by anything other than disgraceful means.

Winston is like Gulliver in that each is finally shown as denying the values once expressed, renegade to all they had previously held dear. The problem is that in each case the writer makes it impossible for us simply to repudiate the renegade as a traitor to the great tradition to which we still unswervingly belong – it would neuter these books to present them as serene affirmations of the values which their protagonists scandalously renounce. If, as we hope, Gulliver and Winston are wrong, they are so in a way that makes it very difficult to eschew their company. The beliefs they reject are ours too, among our most prized possessions, and it is inconceivable that their creators expect us to follow these defectors all the way, abandoning wives for stables and loving our violators. But why, then, do Swift and Orwell impede the reader when he understandably tries to extricate himself from a compromising involvement with the renegade? At what point in these narratives can we, without incurring the charge of Pharisaism or smugness, dissociate ourselves from their heroes' aberrations?

When Gulliver gazes into the pool and sees staring back the face of the Yahoo, he is not just a harmless lunatic inviting our pity or derision – he is clearly commissioned by Swift as our delegate to Houyhnhnmland and it would be altogether too facile to pronounce him insane for daring to call us Yahoos. When Winston cracks so shamefully, yet so inevitably, in Room 101, we witness not just an individual lapse but the fall of man. To jib, however justifiably, at the vulgarity and sensationalism of the rats is beside the point. Not the individual instance but the general psychological law is what concerns Orwell; Room 101 contains the worst thing in the world, represents the unendurable trial. For anyone to claim that he would have overcome Room 101, hence that Winston's capitulation proves only his own personal cravenness, is to make nonsense of Orwell's intention. Our relationship to Gulliver and Winston is far more problematic than a simple rejection of kinship; they are our brothers, even if the relationship gives no cause for celebration. The fact that we are ashamed and discomfited does not entitle us to pretend that they are strangers.

Throughout the *Travels* but especially in Part IV we have only Gulliver to identify with – we know, as does Swift, that there are no rational horses, so that our choice is between Yahoo and human being. When we learn that they are really the same, we feel (and are meant to feel) helpless, for there is nowhere else in the book to go. Our spokesman having deserted to the enemy, we can either follow him across or abuse him as fool. Swift's cunningly contrived trap is that we cannot do the first and should not do the second. Gulliver scores too many hits to be a mere fool. If, within the text, he is unassailable, that is what Swift intends, since it is outside the text, and nowhere else, that he must be proved wrong. Anyone who dislikes being called Yahoo has a simple defence: stop behaving like one.

Nineteen Eighty-Four springs a similar trap. Winston begins as our spokesman, upholding the same pieties that we revere. When, aping Gulliver, he rejects these pieties, his recantation poses a problem. We are not to join him in craven capitulation to Big Brother, but neither, at the risk of being Pharisees, can we dismiss him as a weakling who has fallen miserably below our own high standard. To imply that Big Brother's good fortune was not to have us for opponents smacks of presumption. The book asks us to identify with Winston and to say honestly how we would fare in his place. Orwell's mortifying intention within the text is to extort the humiliating confession that we would do no better. The logic of Oceania is that the last man is doomed to defeat, simply because in such a dark finale any hope of individual resistance has vanished. The book is a grim warning not to let things get so bad or else we are forever lost. Swift wishes his readers to act *outside* and *after* his text, to stop being the Yahoos we are; Orwell wishes his readers to act *outside* and *before* his text, lest we become the slaves of his prophecy. Prevention is Orwell's aim, and not simply because prevention is better than cure, but for the far more terrifyingly urgent reason that there must be prevention because there *is* no cure – Oceania is too late for salvation.

We can, of course, if we wish, dismiss Oceania as a bugaboo, a nightmare existence which our waking state will never countenance, and deny that things can ever become so bad because there are certain inbuilt guarantees – epistemological, psychological, moral – which preclude the possibility of such degradation. But Winston has already said all this and has been shown as disastrously wrong. Not only, liberal protestations notwithstanding, can the worst thing in the world happen, but its probability increases in proportion as it is derided as merely a bad dream – Room 101 is built with the inadvertent planning permission of those who glibly deny its possibility. Orwell was not so foolish as to write a warning against something he believed impossible. Winston's threshold of apprehension at the book's beginning is shown to be far too sanguinely high – he fears capture and death, but not subjugation. But he 'knows', too, that certain other things can never happen, that certain nightmarish speculations cannot survive in the light of day; his punishment is to see the nightmare become fact in the place where there is no darkness.

Winston's dogmas turn out to be delusions, a series of blunders in epistemology and morality. He believes in the existence of truth and the inviolability of love, thereby challenging what Orwell had denounced as the two most monstrous of modern iniquities – the denial of objective truth and the growth of power-worship. Power itself is impotent in the realms of truth and love: $2 + 2 = 4$, whatever Big Brother says to the contrary; Winston loves Julia, and there is nothing Big Brother can do to change it. In mind and heart man is invulnerable. These granite assumptions crumble like clay when put to the test. Winston's root error, the sandy foundation of all his other convictions, is his belief in the sufficiency of the self, his confidence that, however coercive the environment, the individual has it within him to tame experience, to master the external threat and discipline the internal depression. Man is the lord of life and consciousness is his infallible guard against the menace of being.

Nineteen Eighty-Four records the last dispiriting encounter in the conflict between being and consciousness, a problem with which Orwell had had a life-long tussle. What is the relationship between the pressure of external reality and the response of the critical intellect? Does man shape the world or the world man, or is there reciprocal formation with the outcome dependent on which fights harder and endures longer? Orwell clearly rejects the vulgarisation of Marx prevalent in his own time, the view that man is passive before the economic facts of his existence: 'Life is not determined by consciousness but consciousness by life.'[4] Equate life with the productive process and it becomes easy, if not inevitable, to regard human history as essentially the history of changing means of production – the tools that men use are the determinants of human evolution.

'All I know is that I am not a Marxist.'[5] Marx's own words suggest a position more complex than the dogmatic simplicity of some of his followers. He sees man, paradoxically, as at once free and conditioned: 'Men make their own history, but they do not make it just as they please; they do not make it under circumstances chosen by themselves, but under circumstances directly encountered, given and transmitted from the past.'[6] He is not above rebuking crude materialism as a sophomore fallacy: 'The materialist doctrine concerning the changing of circumstances and upbringing forgets that circumstances are made by men and the educator must himself be educated.'[7] Marx's newest exegetes are concerned with promoting the true, original, humanist champion against Kautsky's distortion of the historical fatalist, the iron determinist who saw man's life as just another part of natural history; the oppressive scientific ogre gives way to a man with an open, tentative and inquiring mind, at once provisional and innovative, humanist and fallible. This Marx avoids the twin errors of 'voluntarism' and fatalism: men make themselves but not just as they please; the world is given but not determined; circumstances make man but man makes circumstances; there is a dialectical unity of structural change and changing consciousness.

To rescue Marx from the iron law of History and from a determinism erroneously derived from natural history entailed a more subtle reassessment of the relationship between consciousness and being than the vulgarians of materialism were prepared to allow. Orwell's surprising exegesis of the famous opium allusion shows his own preference for the humanist champion above the infallible scientific realist.[8] In identifying the essence of true Marxism as a refusal to live by bread alone, Orwell deliberately brackets Marx with Christ and praises socialism in the language of traditional religion. Marx is arrestingly ranked alongside Christ as another hero resisting the first satanic temptation: to turn stones into bread, thereby electing man's belly the ruling organ and material welfare the aim of his being.

Orwell's Marx is created in his own image and likeness, manifesting Orwell's own brand of ethical socialism and endorsing his reiterated insistence that man's paramount problem is spiritual rather than material, that a lack of money is minor when set beside a lack of meaning. Bread is important since without it there can be no life, but a sufficiency of bread is not the one thing needful: 'The belly comes before the soul, not in the scale of values but in point of time.'[9] Not every human problem is a derivative of economics. Flory in *Burmese Days* is troubled by a lack of meaning, not a lack of means; the slums imprisoning him are those of the spirit – on any spiritual means test he lines up with the wretched of the earth. Not till Winston Smith will we meet another Orwellian protagonist for whom money counts so little. Flory and Winston are alike in that their difficulties are never financial – they crave significance, not cash, are victims of ontological rather than material deprivation. Flory's problem is not *how* but *why* to stay alive, and his failure to solve it reveals a bankruptcy that is existential rather than financial.

Unlike Flory, Dorothy Hare survives but in a curiously inconclusive way. Materially speaking, the book is a circle, ending where it began: a harassed drudge is once again making costumes for a fête, just as she was when her breakdown occurred. What *has* changed is her consciousness, not her being, for the book enacts an interior journey from Christianity to atheism – Dorothy returns to her father in Suffolk but not to her father in heaven. She starts out confident as to the *why* of life, worried only about the *how*; with enough money to pay the bills she might have staved off breakdown and gone to the grave impervious to doubt. It is the breakdown that takes her to otherwise unknowable worlds where religious faith withers away. She begins the book worrying about money and ends it worrying about meaning – money, she finally perceives, is important but secondary. Her loss of faith notwithstanding, she is still the same earnest, ascetic, industrious puritan she was, simply more lugubrious now that she knows 'the deadly emptiness . . . at the heart of things'.[10] She has learned, crucially, that 'all real happenings are in the mind';[11] concluding, like the rebel Winston, that what truly matters is internal, she espouses consciousness, the primacy of the indomitable mind, as her defence against the wasted world. A bleak stoicism, an almost narcotic absorption in the task to hand, no matter how petty that be: these are the weapons of consciousness against a brutal, inane being. Consciousness holds being at bay, as Dorothy confronts the

world with the stoic assumption that the mind is master of experience, that the resolved intelligence can shape even calamity to its
own requirements. It is a victory when contrasted with Flory's
suicide, though not of a kind to make the heart spring with joy.

Such a triumph over circumstance fails to inspire in us a sense of
human transcendence or pride in man's nobility, for it lacks the
exhilarating ring of Milton's Lady routing the enchanter: 'Fool, do
not boast, thou canst not touch the freedom of my mind'.[12] Dorothy,
by contrast, grits her teeth and soldiers on. Orwell discovers this
sense of exuberant invincibility, paradoxically, among the
apparent deadbeats of Paris and London. He finds, elatedly, that
the slum corrupts but does not denature: man is greater than his
environment, with the power to triumph over his external conditions. The spirit, though shackled to matter, can, nevertheless,
soar free of its chains; being limits consciousness, yet consciousness can overcome being. Material conditions matter, but are not
everything. It is life that shapes economics and not economics life.
To accept the latter is to be an idolator. The English are particularly
prone to economic idolatry in their assumption that money
measures life and that to be poor is to be sinful. That is why Bozo,
the crippled pavement artist, is so bravely nonconformist in rejecting guilt – why should he be ashamed of a beggary he did not
choose and cannot help? Unlike Flory and Winston, he repudiates
the oppressor's degrading valuation. The worst degradation, as the
organisers of the extermination camps realised, is that which is
appropriated and internalised, when the victim sees himself as
vermin. Conversely, no person is completely victimised until he
annuls himself. Bozo will not annul himself. Doubly penalised,
lame and poor, he challenges the sinfulness of poverty, will not
agree that he is worthless because he is poor. Through his interest
in astronomy, he succeeds, though penniless, in maintaining intellectual standards; scorning environmental servitude, he taps his
forehead and insists, 'I'm a free man in here'.[13]

This triumph over the world is the more inspiring when we recall
that it was beyond Flory as it will be beyond Winston. Winston's
belief in the indomitable mind is exposed as a pathetic delusion
that shrivels when tested. Bozo, by contrast, stands out like an
Abdiel in an army of tramps too broken to dispute their manifest
iniquity. 'There was, clearly, no future for him but beggary and
death in the workhouse';[14] he is, nevertheless, the freest man in the
book. Down in the depths Orwell discovers nobility as well as

degradation: the Russian waiter, Boris, the old man who gallantly finds the money for a shave from his meagre weekly income, the little Glasgow tramp who runs after Orwell to pay a debt – each in his own way testifies to the spirit of the unconquerable poor, the nobility of the human being.[15] Even in a prison Orwell finds the free spirit, in the *cloaca* delightedly detects pure crystal. It is a conviction that touches its Everest point in the figure of the Italian soldier in *Homage to Catalonia* – 'no bomb that ever burst shatters the crystal spirit'; nor no slum either.[16]

Man is greater than his environment – hence the obscenity when his environment insults his dignity. But no matter how vile the world, man need not be its helpless victim, far less its accomplice, for resistance is always his privilege. Even in the most unpropitious circumstances – Parisian slum and English dosshouse, the stricken North of England with its poor huddled in apathetic desolation, the nightmare city of Barcelona given over to witch-hunt – Orwell finds the proofs of man's invincible nobility. Even in Spain where the first intimations of totalitarian horror announced themselves, the triumph of consciousness over being is simultaneously present. In the brave little officer and the decent Civil Guard, Orwell pays homage to human transcendence. Man is the master of society, lord of politics and economics, not their helot. And so, despite the atrocities and betrayals, Orwell returns from Spain assured of the unbreakable crystal spirit, 'with not less but more belief in the decency of human beings'. Far from feeling cheated, he is elated: 'I have seen wonderful things and at last really believe in Socialism which I never did before.'[17]

Man is both decent and insuperable; when the world does its worst, he does his best, and his best is always good enough. The decency of ordinary folk is the epiphany that illumines the close of *Keep the Aspidistra Flying*, the blessed permanence of London is the redemptive vision at the end of *Coming Up for Air*. 'The bombs aren't made that could smash it out of existence.'[18] The pool at Lower Binfield is irreprievably polluted but London is reassuringly indestructible. To London add man. Consciousness is the master of being; the self is always sufficient whatever the challenge.

No wonder that Orwell's readers are perplexed and dismayed when they engage *Nineteen Eighty-Four* – how to account for so shocking a recantation of all that had been so previously cherished? The confidence in unconquerable man is as shattered as the shattered paperweight and consciousness is now the terrified thrall of being. The tradition of heroic resisters linking the earlier books finds no successor in the humiliated, failed rebel of Airstrip One. Here is no Flory refusing to tolerate an intolerable existence, no Dorothy stoically measuring reality against her own resolute mind. If, as Boris says, victory goes to him who fights the longest, then it is, scandalously, O'Brien, and not Winston, who has the staying power.[19] If, as Bozo says, external repression is futile against the brave spirit, that spirit is now dismissed as the discredited dogma of an outworn mythology. Gordon Comstock's reverence for the tree of life is an anachronism – the Party is about to abolish the orgasm and commence *in vitro* fertilisation. George Bowling's assurance that human nature is too massively, solidly established to be altered is a delusion; there *is* no human nature, simply a substance malleable as putty in Big Brother's hands.

All Orwell's reiterated rebukes and warnings to the optimists and liberals are now embodied as real, unexorcisable horrors. He had urged the English not to trust the deceptive legacy of liberalism: the empty guarantees that truth must prevail, that persecution must defeat itself, that mental freedom is inviolable – all those beliefs of the nursery which surprise us when still cherished by the political adult.[20] He had identified as a major weakness of English culture the 'sentimental belief that it all comes right in the end and the thing you most fear never happens'.[21] Whatever appals the mind cannot happen: first article of the liberal creed. By contrast, *Nineteen Eighty-Four* nerves itself to imagine the worst and then enacts the horror. From the outset Winston fears that his rebellion is the act of a lunatic and the book verifies his fears. Room 101 is the harsh school where the defects of a liberal education are corrected.

Why, for example, is H. G. Wells so foolish as to believe that only good men can be good scientists?[22] Perhaps science itself, eugenics in particular, might carry the manipulative threat: 'it may be just as possible to product a breed of men who do not wish for liberty as to possible to produce a breed of men who do not wish for liberty as to against brainwashing as it was against bombs? The liberal assumes that the human spirit is a constant throughout history, forever threatened but, like Dryden's hind, destined never to die. It is a belief that rests ultimately upon the anti-historical conviction that human nature is an unalterable datum, unvarying from age to age, superior to history and immune to event. From the Enlightenment assumption of a constant human nature to Bertrand Russell trusting to the spirit of man as an insuperable check to totalitarianism, this belief has been the cornerstone of western optimism, shared, as the crystal allusion shows, by Orwell himself.

But what if it isn't true? What if man is not a constant, what if love of liberty is merely a cultural artefact, a conditioned reflex that fades as the matrix alters? Slavery cannot endure, declares the liberal; Orwell points to the great slave states of antiquity which lasted for millennia and asks how we can be so sure that they cannot return, this time the more permanently because they will have science and technology to support them.[24] Men bred for servitude is a nightmare that an innocent liberalism will not contemplate, but does that mean that it cannot happen? 'What sickens me about left-wing people, especially the intellectuals, is their utter ignorance of the way things actually happen.'[25] Nineteen Eighty-Four rubs the intellectuals' noses in the dirt they will not see, even when it is sometimes of their own making. 'The thing you most fear never happens.' What Orwell most feared was the shattering of the crystal spirit; that the speculation was abhorrent was no reason for banning it.

Hence the deliberate affront to the optimists as Orwell goes to the other extreme: they had said such horrors *cannot* happen; Orwell's text shows that they *must*. Winston as dissident intellectual is defeated and it is a blunder to believe that this is simply due to O'Brien's controlling the dials of torture, for Winston is defeated in the mind, precisely where Milton's Lady, taunting the torturer, denied he could reach. The past is unchangeable, truth is objective, words have fixed meanings, love is invincible – all of these precious axioms are revealed as hanging on the slenderest filaments; the book shocks because in it every one of these propositions is refuted. 'It is quite possible that we are descending into an age in which two and two will make five when the Leader says so.'[26] Suspense comes, if at all, not from wondering whether Winston can elude, far less overthrow, Big Brother, but whether he can sustain defiance to the modest extent of dying for the faith, winning the martyr's crown: 'the object is not to stay alive but to stay human'.[27] Even covert martyrdom, a secret defiance carried to the grave, a purely internal heresy, will be enough to keep a man human. No need for Winston to join Spartacus, More and Bonhoeffer provided he can die, privately hating Big Brother; let being win every argument so long as consciousness has the last word. But even this limited victory is a fantasy, as much a piece of wish-fulfilment as Jack the Giant Killer. The Giant wins; the dissident loses everything except his life in the book's appalling conclusion, the more appalling in that he is still alive.

The privilege of heroic death is as obsolete as Shakespeare and the paperweight, and humanism is denied even a martyr. What Winston most fears as lunatic, heretic, minority of one, is that there *is* no truth to die for, and the book confirms his dread. Relying on the spirit of man, Winston might just as well have trusted in Poseidon or Thor or the exploded God of Christian mythology. The freedom of the mind is as gross a superstition as the flying house of Loreto, excusable in Milton's Lady, blessedly ignorant of Pavlov and brainwashing, but unforgivable in the residents of Oceania. Not the heavens but the cellars of Miniluv testify to the omnipotence of the new god. Man's palimpsest existence deprives him of any irreducible human core, any inviolable consciousness, to defend him against the reality in which he lives, moves and has his being.

Winston's dilemma is the same in ethics as in aesthetics: the things he admires have no place in the life of Oceania. Like diary and paperweight, love and friendship, even tragedy itself, are simply fading memories of a bygone ethos, belong to 'a conception of loyalty that was private and unalterable. Such things, he saw, could not happen today.'[28] Even the traditional gestures of sacrificial love have become a target for realist derision – the nonsensical act of the lifeboat woman in trying to shield the child from the bullets makes the cinema audience laugh. 'We live in an age in which the autonomous individual is ceasing to exist – ceasing to have the illusion of being autonomous.'[29] Once man believed himself a free and separate being; the twentieth century has taught him better. *Nineteen Eighty-Four* rounds off his education by showing that love, generosity and friendship are equally pipe-dreams.

The twin nightmares of *Nineteen Eighty-Four* are verified in the end. The first is the epistemological dread of being locked within the self with no access to objective truth and, consequently, no way of knowing if such truth exists. The associated moral horror is to be walled within the self with no outlet to generosity or love. Winston starts out fearing the epistemological nightmare and ends up trapped in the moral one. 2 + 2 are whatever Big Brother decides and the whole world, Julia included, can perish provided Narcissus lives. There *is* no truth, epistemological or moral, to live or die for. The paradox is that Winston's self-love is yoked to self-contempt. A person sinks to the pit of degradation when he internalises the humiliator's judgement. Such was the strategy pursued in the camps. The aim was not simply to make Auschwitz *das Arschloch der Welt* (the world's arsehole) where human beings were transformed into waste product, but to bring the victims to regard themselves as excrement. The victim's sense of his own value must be destroyed within the citadel of his own mind, since, whoever harbours his own worth, has thwarted the totalitarian enemy. To retain even a scintilla of self-respect is to possess a power to resist which Big Brother cannot tolerate.

Consciousness determines being, despite what the Marxists say; the man who believes in his own value continues to have it – the last man in Europe remains so as long as he wills it. Orwell was intrigued by the snobbish tramp he met in the spike: 'in the sight of God . . . he was not a tramp. His body might be in the spike, but his spirit soared far away, in the pure aether of the middle classes.'[30] The tone is amused, almost derisive; what Swift calls self-deception and Sartre *mauvaise foi* is discernible in this superb exhibition of essence prevailing over existence, consciousness over being. Orwell pokes fun at the self-deceiver, yet there is also something admirable in this no-surrender attitude, this brave resolve not to be submerged in tramphood or permit matter to dictate to spirit.

Winston depressingly fails to match this resolve. In the Ministry of Love spirit cravenly capitulates to matter when Winston finally accepts himself as the bag of filth which the mirror reveals. He cannot sustain the amphibian existence, the ability to inhabit simultaneously the diverse worlds of being and consciousness, which enables the snobbish tramp and the pavement-artist Bozo to live invincibly in degradation. The tramps and deadbeats of Paris and London are filthy *and* generous, foul-mouthed *and* loyal, still, however incredibly, temples of the Holy Ghost, hosts to the crystal spirit. *Nineteen Eighty-Four* appals to the degree that it fulfils O'Brien's vow to drain man of all redemptive nobility. Gone is the sense of comradeship that shines through the vilest environment, the sense of self-respect that exalts the frequenters of gutters; only the Yahoo remains, squalid, mean, lost to all possibility of heroism or self-transcendence. Winston is not the man he thought he was or tried to be, not dissident nor rebel nor lover – what possible bearing could *his* thoughts or strivings have upon his destiny? He is the wretch of O'Brien's deciding, the mere commodity of the system within which he transiently functions. Being rules, O.K., is the dismaying graffito scrawled over Orwell's last communiqué.

The world is barren of truth and love, a dual dispossession which provokes very different reactions. It is shocking to learn that there is no truth because it leaves one feeling cheated; man is mistaken about the universe, but, far from being responsible for its un-reason, he may well feel betrayed by the world's failure to match his rational demands. But it is sickening to learn that there is no love, because, if true, that *is* man's fault and his shame – this time the deficiency is internal, with man compelled to see himself as traitor rather than victim. In an absurd world where he alone has value, man can continue to regard himself as victim or even as tragic hero. Hence the importance of Room 101 as the appropriate climax of Orwell's despondent text; it exists to exhibit man as insufficient, even vile, to reveal him as a bag of filth, thereby denying him the tragic status which has hitherto always been his consolation for defeat. Orwell defined tragedy as a destruction in which man nevertheless shows himself greater than the forces that destroy him; Big Brother refuses Winston the privilege of tragedy, for the defeat in Room 101 is immitigably abject.

Winston is demolished along with his humanist hopes. We can, if we wish, soften this conclusion by treating it as the débâcle of a very flawed individual whose failure leaves the true doctrine intact, thus wrenching the text away from the despair-of-a-dying-man view to that of a cautionary tale for progressives, an optimistic exhortation to those who share the faith not to repeat the blunders. The temptation then is to import into the text a tougher strain of humanism (our own, naturally) which would have sustained Winston if only he had found it. The related fallacy is to pity poor Winston for not being like us and it is the graver because he *is* like us, is intended by Orwell as the universal representative, his defects not those of an individual or a group, but, at crucial points, of humanity itself. The quotation from Lermontov's preface to *A Hero of Our Time*, annexed by Camus to describe his own 'hero' in *The Fall*, could just as appositely precede *Nineteen Eighty-Four*: 'It is in fact a portrait but not of an individual; it is the aggregate of the vices of our whole generation in their fullest expression.' It is much too facile to condemn Gulliver as madman or Winston as coward and think thereby to evade the criticism of ourselves – impossible to believe that Swift and Orwell meant us to escape so easily.

The pool in Houyhnhnmland and the mirror in Miniluv are alike in forcing man to confront his true self, and in each case physical loathing parallels inner corruption. The *philosophes* may prate about *animal rationale* but Yahoo is the revolting reality. Similarly, Winston's noble rhetoric about the spirit of man collapses when set against the incriminating tape-recorder and the accusing mirror. Winston's faith in man, however attractive, crumbles when tested. Neither Gulliver nor Winston can protect their consoling dreams against the hideous truth.

Yet Room 101 is the necessary final disclosure because, even after listening to the tape and looking at the mirror, Winston still clings to the possibility of self-transcendence through love. To love another person better than oneself is a provocation that the totalitarians of Oceania cannot abide. Winston still regards himself as such a lover, and with large justification, for the same tape that condemns him as a terrorist exalts him as a lover. He hates Big Brother so much that he is ready to commit any atrocity that may help to overthrow the tyrant, but, even for so blessed a consummation, he refuses to part with Julia – great as is his loathing for Big Brother, his love for Julia is greater still. In *The Devils* poor, foolish Stepan Verkhovensky achieves on his deathbed the key Dostoevskian insight: 'Love is higher than existence. Love is the crown of existence. And how is it possible that existence should not be subjected to it?'[31] It is not Winston's idiom but it is his sentiment. He makes the same commitment to Julia as Milton's Adam to Eve – 'Our state cannot be severed; we are one, / One flesh; to lose thee were to lose myself.'[32] The tape tells Big Brother what Winston regards as the best thing in the world, hence what must be destroyed so that O'Brien's vow to drain Winston of everything redemptively human may be fulfilled. The stage is set for the novel's final contest: the best thing in the world versus the worst thing in the world, love versus Room 101.

That is why Winston's final self-discovery is so appalling. He savours the full shame of his selfhood, acknowledging the humiliating truth – that his stinking, rotting carcase is the most precious thing in the universe, that he will grovel to any abomination, sacrifice any love, if only the panel between his face and the rats stays closed. 'If you want to keep a secret you must also hide it from yourself.'[33] Room 101 is the confessional where every secret is laid open and the self admits the truth. That is why O'Brien refuses to tell Winston what he must do to save himself. No other agent must intervene and such help is, in any case, redundant, for the self always, infallibly, knows what to do. O'Brien, pedantically discoursing on the antiquity of the torture, is deaf to Winston's frantic appeals, supplies only the simple assurance: 'You will do what is required of you.' Without tuition. The words carry the same chill inevitability as those of Aschenbach's menacing boatman: 'The signore will pay.'[34] In each case the prophecy is shockingly fulfilled.

This moment of shameful self-recognition is almost a trademark of modern literature, though its pioneer is the Swift of Gulliver's last voyage. All of those travels culminate in the resolution of an identity crisis when Gulliver at last discovers who he truly is, and in this Swift fathers a tribe of parallel revelations in our own time from Conrad and Mann to Camus and Golding. What Kurtz learns in the jungle, Aschenbach on the lido, Jean-Baptiste Clamence on a Seine bridge, is the same harsh lesson enforced on Winston in Room 101. Our forbears, in their ancient terminology, would have called it a conviction of sin, the sudden, shattering awareness bequeathed by Adam to all his sons of a shamefully indefensible nakedness. The spirit is willing but the flesh is weak: in some such terms they would have explained the sense of failure. In Orwell even this unequal contest has become a fiction, for there is, finally, no spirit to challenge matter, only a flesh reliably feeble and a self dependably insufficient: 'you *will* do what is required of you'.[35]

How does a man respond to this revelation of disgrace? There are a number of competing strategies and the choice defines the man. Othello opts for heroic, Flory for squalid, suicide, Kurtz for horrified despair, Gide's immoralist for defiant self-assertion, Clamence for cynical malevolence, Parolles for equable acceptance: 'Simply the thing I am / Shall make me live.' Winston is at once more anguished and depressing, for he cannot die nor justify himself nor live in amnesic insouciance. The worst thing in the world is that there is no death in Room 101, neither heroic nor expiatory; Winston is condemned to life, a life drained of value or virtue. He survives (that is what is so appalling) to suffer an unbearable antinomy: he has behaved shamefully and he could not help it. An inexpiable guilt, a sense of personal vileness that locks the door to any remedial action – this (it is Clamence's discovery too) is the worst torment of all.

In their final books Orwell and Camus address the same ethical dilemma: how can man recover innocence? Confessing one's guilt brings, in itself, no absolution. 'It is not enough to accuse yourself in order to clear yourself';[36] so insists Camus's remorseless *juge-pénitent*, and Orwell's faithless lovers agree. Each admits the fact of betrayal, but in such a way as to intensify self-disgust rather than bring relief or pardon. Comedians like Parolles may pardon themselves, but where can a failed Prometheus or a perjured Romeo find absolution? The only confessional belongs to the enemy and one goes there to be degraded, not redeemed. Swift, Camus and Orwell all explore the humiliation of man: Gulliver looks in the pool and knows himself, Clamence hears the cry from the river and hurries on, Winston learns in Room 101 whom he truly loves.

'Do it to Julia'; Winston screams out Big Brother's triumph and his own abasement – much more worrying, our abasement too. Having sided with him in his rebellion, it is difficult to extricate ourselves from his defeat. At what point did he go wrong? At which test would we have done better? The trap is as cunningly malicious as any set by Swift, for we have been manoeuvred into a distressing complicity which we cannot easily repudiate without appearing to adopt the self-righteousness of the Pharisee. It is a representative defeat, with all men falling in Winston as they did in Adam. Even in the *Travels* Gulliver exempts his sextumvirate of moral supermen from the general indictment, but Orwell is much more ruthless in denying that anyone, however heroic, can overcome Room 101. Winston knows in his dream that his mother and sister must die so that he may live, for this is 'part of the unavoidable order of things'.[37] Egoism is the law of life. When, no longer dreaming, he remembers his mother beseeching him not to be selfish, he remembers too the futility of her appeal: 'it was no use'.[38] How can decency resist an empty belly? He snatches all the food and condemns his sister to death. The shame afterwards is just another pointless crucifixion, for it is the shame of being human – we are all bags of filth and there is no more to be said: 'all you care about is yourself'.[39] Hemingway makes of the self a cornerstone for stoic fortitude: 'you have only yourself', but if you are Santiago what more do you need?[40] Winston is no Santiago; the peculiar anguish of *Nineteen Eighty-Four* is that there is only the self versus Big Brother, and the self is, cruelly, not enough.

It strikes Winston that 'in moments of crisis one is never fighting against an external enemy, but always against one's own body',[41] and it is the pain-shunning body, swelling to fill the universe, that betrays the would-be idealist. In battle the great, noble issues give way to brute preservation; only those ensconced in cosy armchairs dream of self-transcendence, just as only those companioned by fear and want know the untameable strength of the animal desire to survive. Well-fed people have no problem in conquering the pangs of hunger. Once again there is an almost despicably easy escape for any reader determined to evade the accusation in Orwell's text, namely, to insist that the insufficient self in *Nineteen Eighty-Four* is simply Winston's and that his failings are no index of our fortitude; his collapse is a purely personal one – when *we* reach Room 101 we shall show him what he should have done.

Yet the text will not allow us to arraign Winston as the sole culprit or isolate him as a sad exception. On the contrary, he is, all too distressingly, the universal representative. In the Ministry of Love a skull-faced man, clearly dying of starvation, is given some bread by a fellow-prisoner who is at once brutally beaten by a guard for his act of charity. The skull-faced man, ordered to Room 101, begs obscenely for reprieve, and, searching frantically for a substitute victim, fixes naturally upon his benefactor, hysterically accusing him of having whispered treason as he gave the bread. Orwell's modern rendition of the parable focuses less upon the charity of the Good Samaritan than upon the degrading ingratitude of the recipient. If the ultimate proof of love is to die for another, the nadir of self-love is to use the benefactor's body as a shield.

Nor is the skull-faced man to be regarded as a monster of depravity, for, within the text, he is a normal man acting as all men do when put to the test, as the Good Samaritan will act too when *he* is summoned to Room 101; we may feel ashamed only on condition of recognising the guilt as universal. Room 101 is where humanity is found lacking, not where cowards are separated from heroes. In *Nineteen Eighty-Four* there are no Sydney Cartons or Thomas Mores, no heroes or martyrs, for these are simply the mistakes of an inefficient penology, of blundering executioners who take them at their word that they prefer death when they are really fake suicides, inadvertently killing themselves in an obstinate attempt to make it look real. It is essentially a matter of chronology, of being on hand at the inevitable moment when the hero has seen through his own sham and the martyr is screaming to be saved from himself. Nothing is finally more important than one's own skin. 'All you care about is yourself', says Julia, explaining her treachery as a single instance of a universal law, and Winston, the betrayed betrayer, taught by his own experience, agrees.[42] Orwell's characters do as they must and despise themselves for it. They are in the desperate condition described by St Paul, quoting from the *Psalms*, in his *Epistle to the Romans*: 'There is not one just man . . . . All have gone astray together; they have become worthless. There is none who does good, no, not even one.' Paul, however, has a remedy where *Nineteen Eighty-Four* offers none. Oceania's God is no redeemer but the guarantor of man's degradation. O'Brien predicts Winston's future: 'We shall crush you down to the point from which there is no coming back . . . . Everything will be dead inside you. Never again will you be capable of love, or friendship, or joy of living, or laughter, or curiosity, or courage, or integrity. You will be hollow. We shall squeeze you empty, and then we shall fill you with ourselves.'[43] It is a promise devastatingly kept. At the end of Orwell's dark prophecy the self has not only ceased to be sufficient – it has ceased to exist.

6

The Fall: Living in the Little-Ease

To come from *Nineteen Eighty-Four* to *The Fall* is as short a literary journey as one could make in the twentieth century. Only eight years separate these texts, but the propinquity goes far deeper than a matter of mere chronology, for both exhibit all the marks of a parallel disillusionment and dread in the face of the same disaster. There are, indeed, a number of persuasive parallels between Orwell and Camus. Both won fame as heroes of truth, sworn to an uncompromising honesty which scorned to found the Just City upon a lie, however pious or well-intentioned; both were extolled as atheistic saints whose purity of thought was redemptive in a world dominated by one-eyed ideologues and party *apparatchiks*. Yet at the same time some found only confusion, even doublethink, in these alleged truth-tellers and sceptically rejected the celebrated integrity as a mask for reactionary views; others, less censorious, nevertheless maintained that both men, in their refusal to make an unreserved commitment to the revolutionary cause, were, however inadvertently, supporting an unjust status quo. Both in their admirers and in their detractors, in the reasons advanced for praise and censure alike, the parallelism persists.

One obvious link is that each was primarily a moralist who unremittingly subjected the world of politics to a keen ethical scrutiny, unprepared to make exemption in favour of extremism or terrorism. Camus's fall from intellectual favour in the sixties recalls the opposition to Orwell a decade earlier and it is indisputable that a decisive factor in fuelling these antipathies was the emphatically unselective moral stance of both writers. When Orwell proclaimed a willingness to attack Stalin as the litmus test of moral courage for those on the left, when Camus in his Nobel Prize speech declared that he had always condemned the use of terror, each was affirming the primacy of ethics over ideology.[1] When, at the close of *The Road to Wigan Pier*, Orwell rebuked doctrinaire leftists for disparaging certain bourgeois values, thereby foolishly allowing the Fascists to pose as their champions, when Camus announced that he would defend his mother before justice, each was defiantly flouting the prime commandment of the new religion: thou shalt not have strange gods before me. These anachronistic allegiances, Orwell's to his class, Camus's to his mother, were both denounced as disservices to history. Their enemies had small sympathy for moralists, least of all moralists who looked suspiciously upon collective action, detested violence, and scrutinised with increasing disfavour the innocence that the revolutionary ideology encourages in militant minds. Writers who upheld the cultural heritage of the past against rancorous egalitarians or who invoked filial piety against total commitment to Algerian liberation were unlikely to find favour with those who required literature to endorse their hatred of any institution that tied them to abhorred tradition.

Camus's 'defection' was the more offensive because he had seemed so securely on the revolutionary side. His career and reputation were linked to a defiance of right-wing tyranny. Andrei Sinyavsky once said that he owed his vocation to the KGB. Camus might equally have thanked the Nazis, for, in imposing upon Europe a reign of terror, they gave *The Myth of Sisyphus* and *The Plague* a far greater vogue than they might otherwise have enjoyed. At the end of the war, Camus's revolutionary fervour seemed as fierce as ever. He vehemently opposed Mauriac's plea for leniency, a national amnesty, in the uncompromising accents of a modern Saint-Just: 'Who would dare speak here of pardon?' He sided with his future foe, Sartre, in demanding death for collaborators; what else should the guilty expect, now that the long-tormented virtuous ones had finally triumphed? By 1946, however, sickened by the 'virtuous' terror of post-liberation France, he had crossed over to Mauriac and was pleading that there should be *'ni Victimes ni Bourreaux'*, neither victims nor executioners. In the less passionate atmosphere of post-war Britain Orwell attacked those on the left who wanted to take revenge upon their defeated enemies – even the Fascist Mosley should not be kicked when down.[2]

The parallels multiply the more we read. The claims of honesty are pressed to the point of discomfort and even pain. When Clamence, speaking for his creator, permits us to have slaves if we must, but only on condition that we stop calling them free men, it echoes Orwell's denunciation of doublethink: no attacking the British Empire while sharing in its dividends or advocating paci-

fism behind the shield of the Royal Navy or espousing egalitarian-
ism while sending one's children to public schools.[3] Reform
yourself before you reform the world – it is the demand most
calculated to enrage the dedicated revolutionary. Yet another point
of resemblance is their common detestation of Stalin and what his
cult implied. Orwell identified power-worship as the salient
iniquity of our times and linked it, astonishingly in view of his own
undeviating atheism, to the fact of religious decline – the atheist
intellectual, prostrating himself before Stalin, is indulging an up-
market form of the same emotions as the slum boy idolising Al
Capone.[4] Clamence utters the same provocative accusation when
he remarks that every intelligent man dreams of being a gangster
and makes the same scandalous tie-up between atheism and
modern servitude: 'one must choose a master, God being out of
fashion'.[5] Behind these criticisms is the indignation of inflexible
moralists sickened at the ease with which so many modern intellectuals put their gifts at the service of tyrants. Orwell and Camus
would have no part in this *trahison des clercs*.

Most pertinent of all to the present argument is the intriguing
affinity between their last books, extending to the sense of anger
and betrayal that they provoked in so many of their readers. The
outrage is certainly intelligible at what so many could only interpret
as a sell-out, for, undeniably, these texts were gleefully seized upon
and lauded for their insight by people whom the authors had spent
their lives opposing. In *Nineteen Eighty-Four* the crystal spirit is as
irreprievably shattered as Winston's paperweight, the last man in
Europe is crushed and the only prospect for humanity is a boot in
the face for ever. It is a strangely dispiriting message to come from a
man whose whole life had been a crusade for the underdog, for the
book condemns man to be an underdog for all time. But the shock of
betrayal was even greater for the readers of *The Fall*. Orwell had
always been something of a desponder; a melancholy, even a lugu-
briousness, is detectible from *Burmese Days* on, and he was, after
all, a dying man when he wrote his pessimistic masterpiece – those
scandalised could always placate themselves by attributing the
despair to a terminal illness; the book reflected the sad condition of
its author's lungs rather than the world either as it is or might
conceivably be.

No such refuge offered itself with Camus. That *The Fall* is a
surprising book is proved by the fact that everyone was suprised by
it, and with full justification. The very title was an affront, offensive

from anyone, outrageous from the man who, even in a century of death, had achieved fame as the singer of happiness. Meursault is happy even in the death-cell; the closing sentence of *The Myth of Sisyphus* commands us how to feel as we watch the absurd hero grapple yet again with his unmasterable, unleavable rock: 'one must imagine Sisyphus happy'.[6] Camus once told an interviewer that 'when I come to look for what is fundamental in myself, I find a taste for happiness', and in his early book of essays, *Noces*, he declared that 'happiness itself is a duty'.[7] The fact is that up to the writing of *The Fall*, happiness is, for Camus, inseparable from innocence and innocence is the datum from which his analysis of the human condition begins. He had always regarded innocence as the supreme good, had established his reputation as the apologist of man – like prelapsarian Clamence, Camus, too, is a defence lawyer. Man, he insists, is not guilty, whatever reactionaries say. Even in the earlier works, the phase of the stranger, dealing with the conflict between the *isolato* and his absurd surroundings, there is no condemnation of the criminal. Despite killing the Arab, Meursault is presented as an innocent man whose conviction indicts his society, not himself. Whether the stranger was viewed in contemporary, historical or mythological garb, as Meursault, Caligula or Sisyphus, whether he shot an Arab, terrorised a state or offended Zeus, Camus insisted on seeing him as victim, insulted by the absurdity of existence and determined to deny the agreed mendacities within which his fellows sheltered from the inane sky.

The next phase, the phase of heroic brotherhood, enhanced even more Camus's claim to be humanity's champion. In *The Plague* he moves from solipsism to solidarity as men band together to defy evil in all its manifestations: disease and occupation, guilt and superstition, rats and judges, Nazis and Jesuits. How account for the somersault from this celebration of heroism to a book like *The Fall*? 'What we learn in a time of pestilence: that there are more things to admire in men than to despise' – so asserts Dr Rieux in *The Plague*.[8] Clamence tells us the opposite: there is nothing but malice and nastiness in the human soul and the only basis for a perverse solidarity is the fellowship of the fallen and the community of the corrupt. Having discovered his own debasement, Clamence now slakes his Everest complex, his need to look down on other men, by gloatingly convicting others of the guilt that festers in his own soul. For the truth is that everyone is guilty, and guilty beyond all hope of recovery. This is the message of the new Baptist crying in the Dutch wilderness, but promising, instead of salvation, attaint and humiliation. Most monstrous of all, Camus seems to collude with the misanthrope in his hellish project to ensnare other men; the text will not permit us simply to dismiss him as a madman – Clamence is horribly right because things are horribly wrong, and if it is easy to dislike him, it is painfully difficult to deny the truth of what he says, a loathsome truth but no easier to evade on that account. 'We felt, alas, that by telling his story, Michel had made his action more legitimate. Our not having known at what point to condemn it in the course of his long explanation seemed almost to make us his accomplices. We felt, as it were, involved.'[9] The reluctant complicity experienced by the friends of Gide's Immoralist is intensified to agony point by a reading of *The Fall*. Michel defies us to condemn him, but Clamence condemns himself as a means of incriminating us; the Immoralist's story simply secures an acquittal where Clamence's touches a nerve.

Of course, as with Gulliver and Winston Smith, discrimination is essential, for we must not carry identification too far, joining Gulliver in the stable or Winston in gin-soaked despair or Clamence in venomous spite; but neither are we to detach ourselves too cheaply from their compromising company, thanking complacently whatever God we believe in that we are not like other men. The problem common to all of these texts is precisely this: at what baffling point in the narration can we break the relationship without incurring the charge of Pharisaism? If the problem is difficult to the point of being insoluble, this is surely because the writers have cunningly contrived it so: we are trapped and it will take all our intelligence and integrity to break free. Simply asserting one's superiority is too glib, denying the relevance of these lives to our own is mere evasion – that is the way, not to freedom, but to deeper entanglement.

The 'hero' of *The Fall* is an especially awkward adversary, for he is the supreme exponent of a dishonest honesty in his consummate strategy of the *juge-pénitent* – self-accusation as a device for incriminating others, ultimate trick in the repertoire of the malign polemicist. 'I meant no harm by it, believe me', he apologises, but the phoney politeness only makes him an even more dangerous predator.[10] It is much more difficult to resist someone who invites you to confess your sins, having just handsomely confessed his own, than to send packing a self-righteous bully like Alceste who claims a purity that everyone else lacks. Clamence is a much trickier opponent, for he leaves you with two equally unattractive options: to confess your guilt, accepting, with Winston Smith, that you *are* a bag of filth, or to join the Duchess of Buckingham in affronted proclamation of your Pharisaical blamelessness.[11]

Beneath the surface candour is the malicious entrapment of Baudelaire (*o hypocrite lecteur, mon semblable, mon frère!*), the treacherous courtesy of Gulliver's appeal to the 'gentle reader'. 'The portrait I hold out to my contemporaries becomes a mirror';[12] as David with Nathan, we have been lulled into believing that the shameful deeds are another's when they are really our own; thou art the man. It is our own tale we have unwittingly listened to and Clamence has been patiently preparing throughout for that climactic moment when he can launch his devastating demand: 'Then tell me, please, what happened to you one night on the quays of the Seine and how you managed never to risk your life.'[13]

We can, if we wish, dismiss Clamence, as some have dismissed Gulliver and Winston Smith, as a mistaken or perverted man whose aberrations are his own regrettable concern. Sympathy for a poor, afflicted soul aside, why should it trouble us if he has got himself hopelessly entangled in pointless, neurotic guilt? Why should it touch us if Gulliver has lost his wits among the horses or if Winston has behaved shamefully in Room 101 or if Clamence has had bad luck on bridges? And yet there is that accusatory epigraph adopted from Lermontov for the sole purpose of making us confess kinship: 'Some were dreadfully insulted, and quite seriously, to have held up as a model such an immoral character as *A Hero of Our Time . . . A Hero of Our Time*, gentlemen, is in fact a portrait but not of an individual; it is the aggregate of the vices of our whole generation in their fullest expression.' Could anything be plainer? We may continue to feel insulted but not to assume that we do so with Camus's approval. Like it or not, it is unarguable that Camus accosts us in the same mood as Hamlet does his mother:

> Come, come, and sit you down; you shall not budge.
> You go not till I set you up a glass
> Where you may see the inmost part of you.

To take refuge in indignation or to pronounce the speaker mad because we resent the message is scarcely what Camus or Shakespeare desires.

Yet, however undeniable, this leaves us with the problem still to solve. Why should Camus of all men have written a book about guilt and condemnation, providing us with one of the most searing presentations of the dark epiphany in our times? 'At the heart of my work there is an invincible sun',[14] he had once declared, but his sun is now totally shrouded in the murky mists of a Dutch city. So startling is the paradox that some readers are tempted to treat the whole work as pure satire, a joke at its misanthropic narrator's expense with Camus inviting us to join him in deriding the purveyors of gloom and guilt. It *must* be a joke, since the views it expresses cannot be reconciled with its author's previous opinions – Clamence's pessimistic appraisal of man is precisely what Camus does *not* want his readers to adopt. But apart from the fact that this marks the surrender of criticism to biography, it undermines the seriousness of the book's intent. We are challenged to show where Clamence is wrong, not to assume he is – it is discrimination that is demanded, not this easy evasion of judgement. Camus's best novel must be engaged in an altogether different way. 'The idea that comes most naturally to man, as if from his very nature, is the idea of his innocence.'[15] Niebuhr is puzzled as to how men can continue to cherish this idea while acting as they do, but, whatever we believe, in the century of Hiroshima, Auschwitz and the Gulag, it is no laughing matter and we can be sure that *The Fall* was not written to make us laugh. Its target is not guilt but bogus innocence; it denounces the self-righteous, the Pharisees, those who insist that innocence exists and that they have the monopoly. It is the delusion of innocence that must be destroyed; no one is to go on cossetting the myth of his own blamelessness, for the sinner is man, not capitalist man nor colonialist man nor western man nor any other conceivable subset, and the Pharisee lives in every band of the political spectrum. No wonder *The Fall* infuriated so many of those who read it.

To say that the book derides nineteenth-century doctrines of innocence based upon Rousseau will not explain the outrage it provoked. Certainly, Rousseau is implicitly rejected. As in Hugo's *Les Miserables* everything hinges on one dramatic moment: Clamence is as irrevocably lost in that fatal lapse on the bridge as Valjean is redeemed in that instant when the saintly bishop treats him like a brother. In *The Fall* the descendant of Hugo's saint receives a very different return for his charity; the disembowelled pacifist at once casts an ironic light upon the bishop's facile success in redeeming the brutalised convict and exposes the nineteenth-century dream of salvation for the sentimental nonsense it is.[16] But exposing Rousseauistic sentimentalism hardly accounts for the scandal of Camus's last book.

Complexity comes from the difficulty of identifying the target, for the target is chameleon, altering disconcertingly as we aim. There is general agreement that it is an acute analysis of Pharisaism, but dispute as to who the Pharisee is. Clamence has been identified as Camus himself, the novel interpreted as a personal *mea culpa*, an exercise in self-chastisement. Despite his assertion in another context that 'a character is never the writer who created him',[17] there is ample internal evidence that Clamence is to a considerable degree modelled upon his creator. The epigraph from Lermontov indicates as much: 'others shrewdly noticed that the author had portrayed himself'. Camus was presumably reacting against his own cult in embarrassed rejection of the excessive adulation paid to him as the godless saint, the one just man. No one could have lived up to such overblown tribute, but to his enemies Camus appeared to be both pretentious and self-righteous, and Sartre rapidly became the leader of those who told him so. Clamence is above all a debunker and derider (*diabolos*), a modern Thersites railing against all virtue as a racket, and it is hard not to detect in all this an element of self-ridicule. Camus joins his detractors in baring his feet of clay. If Clamence is not wholly Camus, neither is he just a separate creation; he is a fusion of autobiography and art, evidence of Camus's unease at his beatification by over-enthusiastic admirers.

Hence the book's confessional form, its pervasive Christian imagery, its obsession with guilt and insistence that the admission of one's own sins is the first step in any progress towards truth – Camus acts as devil's advocate towards the cause of his own virtue. But, as deviously as his own 'hero', Camus turns his confession into an attack upon his attackers; the novel moves in contradictory directions at the same time, is simultaneously self-criticism and self-defence. In *A Modest Proposal* Swift denounces the satirist, i.e. himself, in order the more effectively to denounce his enemies: landlords, English government, Irish people. Camus, similarly, admits his faults but only so that he can retaliate the more devastatingly upon his critics – 'but just think of your life, *mon cher compatriote!*'[18] The latter is undoubtedly Sartre – Sartre, who recognised only the sins of other men, especially Americans, while denying his own failings and those of his Russian allies. Sartre was not loath to proclaim his own innocence; Camus invites us to consider who the real Pharisee is. Pilloried for posing as the right-eous man, told to climb down from his moral pedestal, Camus does so in the guise of Clamence, but immediately converts the portrait into a mirror to incriminate his critics.

But if the book were no more than a personal vendetta, it would not be the masterpiece it is. Clamence transcends Sartre to become representative of the elitist intellectual in the tradition of Dos-toevsky's Grand Inquisitor, justifying slavery in the name of realism. The new theme announced in Camus's work by *The Rebel* and *The Fall* is the increasing violation of the rights of the indi-vidual by society and a fear that political realism could so easily be used to justify tyranny. Camus refused Sartre's assurance that the only threat came from the right: 'Over the dead body of innocence the judges swarm . . . those of Christ and those of the Anti-Christ, who are the same anyway, reconciled in the little-ease.'[19] One of the most dismaying moments in modern literature occurs at the end of *Animal Farm* when the victimised animals, looking through the window, can no longer tell the difference between pigs and men, and the greatest political shock of our times is the revelation that there is nothing to choose between the atrocities of left and right, that it matters not at all whether Jones or Napoleon sends you to the knacker. Camus attacks totalitarians of every hue. Orwell speaks of intellectuals itching to get their hands on the whip;[20] Camus, ex-plaining how the intellectual becomes a PR man for Stalin, traces it to the fascination which power exercises on the mind of the seden-tary thinker and detects behind this a frustrated desire to rule society by force. Since this dream is impossible for the individual, 'one generally relies on politics and rushes to join the cruellest party'.[21]

The chorus of disapproval that greeted *The Fall* will not surprise us, once we recognise that, not Rousseau's, but another doctrine of innocence provoked Camus's attack: the twentieth-century inno-cence of the revolutionary ideology, dividing the world into elect and reprobate, and indemnifying the former for every act whereby they sought to cleanse the world of their enemies. Camus finally wrote against innocence because he feared what the belief in inno-cence was being used to legitimise in our own time. The terrible paradox is that innocence had become an instrument of murder. If it is God who is under attack in *The Plague*, it is man in *The Fall*. No wonder Sartre felt threatened, for it was his doctrine of innocence that was being arraigned. The sense of injury experienced by Boling-

broke confronting *Gulliver's Travels* has its parallel in the resentment of the revolutionary ideologues as they looked into Camus's
mirror to find the face of guilt staring back. The Communist
Malraux declared revolutionary action to be Manichaean, a strict
segregation of the world into sheep and goats, the children of light
and the sons of Belial. Sartre, speaking in 1975 and still answering
The Fall, exemplifies the attitude perfectly: 'I have never felt guilty,
and I am not.'[22] The woman taken in adultery should be grateful
that Sartre was not present when Christ issued his challenge.

'After prolonged research on myself, I brought out the basic
duplicity of the human being':[23] it is, as Clamence says, his key
discovery. Sartre deplored such morbid introspection as a blind
alley, a styptic to revolutionary action, and offered instead an
infallible creed as the cure for this stultifying psychology. From
Saint-Just to Lenin the revolutionary encouraged a flight from the
dubieties of self into the certainties of inquisition and the search for
a salvation beyond individuality. In *The Rebel* Camus summarises
the apocalyptic-terrorist process as killing God to build a church.[24]
Kolakowski argues that politics in our time is a pursuit of the old
religious questions in new guise, and Camus is so urgent an inter-
preter of contemporary history because of his intuition that twentieth-century politics has increasingly become the pursuit of
religion by other means.[25] Thus the individual who devotes himself
to overthrowing a wicked society, a kingdom of darkness, is
absolved from all guilt in the means he employs to achieve that
blessed consummation. History is a grateful deity to her servants;
those willing, better still, eager, to dirty their hands in this service
are not merely exonerated but beatified as the saints of the revolutionary hagiography. For all their differences, the ideologues from
1792 to 1917 dreamed the same dream of a new dispensation that
would license the faithful to commit virtuous murder; history, as
beneficiary of the violence, could be trusted to pardon the perpetrators. That Camus took a very different view is plain if we contrast
his play *Les Justes* with Sartre's play *Les Mains sales*. Kaliayev and
Dora believe that there are limits imposed by basic humanity upon
revolutionary action; it is the chill Stepan who says that there are no
limits, since the revolution justifies everything.[26] Hoederer,
Sartre's hero, likewise insists that everything is permitted and is
prepared to do anything that will advance the cause, for the end
justifies the means. *Les Justes* is Camus's answer to Sartre, and in
The Rebel and *The Fall* he attacked the whole moral infrastructure

upon which the doctrine of revolutionary innocence was based.

But the quarrel with Sartre and the recoil from a murderous innocence carried Camus beyond the confines of an historical period, however crucial, to a reflection upon the essential meaning of the human being; *The Fall* is as timeless as *Gulliver's Travels*, for each transcends the purely historical conditions that produced them. The more we learn about Whigs, Tories and freethinkers, about Cold War and Parisian literary politics, the better for us, but this kind of knowledge, valuable though it be, is finally irrelevant to the enduring significance of these texts. It is a matter of permanent truth rather than of transient political excitement. To set *The Fall* in this wider perspective, to understand fully the cultural catastrophe which is its subject and to open it to larger debate, we do better to leave Sartre and turn to Freud.

In an essay published in 1915 entitled 'Thoughts for the Times on War and Death', Freud adumbrates in general terms the problem particularised by Camus in the person of Clamence.[27] Freud's fall is that of a whole civilisation, the descent of cultured Europe into the maelstrom of world war. For war to have occurred at all among the leading civilised nations was in itself a scandal. Throughout the nineteenth century the notion of a new and wider fatherland, a common culture transcending national boundaries, had taken root among educated Europeans and the idea of this comity tearing itself apart in war seemed to many inconceivable; but, even if the worst happened and war came, it would surely be a restrained and gentlemanly affair in which the suffering would be held to an unavoidable minimum. When, in shocking rebuttal, the war proved to be as cruel and implacable as any previous conflict, its devastation far worse in consequence of improved technology, the dismay among cultured Europeans was all the greater. The European states, so exacting in the moral demands levied internally upon their citizens, were thoroughly immoral in their external dealings with each other, commanding their peoples to do for the various fatherlands deeds which would have been draconically punished if performed by a private individual for himself. Worse still, these peoples, so long and ostensibly so securely civilised, were only too ready to obey the appalling orders. It was no surprise that dismay and disillusion descended upon those still immune from the war hysteria.

Yet it is these and not the perpetrators of atrocity that Freud paradoxically criticises. The shock caused by the reversion to savagery is, for him, unjustified, since belief in man's civilised self is mere illusion. The fallacy springs from imagining that the process of civilisation entails the eradication of evil, when 'in reality, there is no such thing as "eradicating" evil'.[28] Even at his civilised best, man remains the same instinctual creature suffused with the same primal needs and desires; these have simply been transformed through the influence of two factors, one internal, the other external, working in the same direction. The first is the tempering of the egotistic instincts by erotism, which Freud defines as 'the human need for love, taken in its widest sense'.[29] Man wants his own way in all things, but he also wants the good opinion and affection of his fellows: 'we learn to value being loved as an advantage for which we are willing to sacrifice other advantages'.[30] The second factor is the pressure of the cultural environment as it moulds and compels the individual to behave in certain socially-approved ways. Society unites with erotism to produce civilised man; throughout the individual's life there is a reciprocal, reinforcing process – the renunciation of instinctual satisfaction and the constant replacement of external by internal compulsion.

It is, however, according to Freud, the external factor which is paramount in this transmutation of egoism into altruism: the coercive force of society, not man's innate disposition to win his fellows' love, is the decisive agent. Our 'susceptibility to culture', i.e. our readiness to enter into the contract of civilisation, owes more in a majority of people to external conditioning than to any process of internal conversion. But since this distinction is not visible to an outward scan, all the observer sees is a civilised people all behaving more or less in obedience to the requirements of culture; consequently, he tends to assume, quite erroneously, that they are all civilised in exactly the same way. His confusion is compounded by society's slovenliness in declining to track to its discreditable, perhaps even shameful, source the reprehensible motive of many an ostensibly 'noble' action. Society doesn't care why a man acts as he does provided the act itself is beneficial; we must not make windows into men's souls just so long as their outward behaviour is decorous – it is the lesson that Mandeville had long since delivered in *The Fable of the Bees*. But the business of the psychoanalyst (and in this he is heir to the Calvinist theologians of the sixteenth and seventeenth centuries) is precisely to make windows into men's souls, exposing the dark roots, not merely of our vices, but, far more unnervingly, of what we deludedly presume to regard as our virtues: for there is not one that does good in the sight of the Lord. Gulliver holds, at the end, this cardinal Calvinist tenet: let man continue an irremediably filthy Yahoo on condition he abandon pride and see himself for what he truly is. Pride and the myth of a false innocence are our gravest affronts – not the evil we do but the Pharisaism with which we do it is the unforgivable, exasperating offence. In La Rochefoucauld's words, 'almost all our failings are more pardonable than the means we employ to hide them'.[31]

By this route Freud reaches his bleak conclusions. We have no right to be shocked by atrocities, for men are simply acting in accord with their real natures, and they do so the more gratefully because the force normally restraining them is actually ordering the gratification of long-suppressed instinct – what a relief, what liberation it is to unleash at last the tabooed desires. We have, as the war has proved, grossly exaggerated the number of human beings who are internal converts to civilisation, 'transformed in a cultural sense'; in the vast majority the savage instincts have simply been playing possum, waiting the opportunity to erupt, the opportunity so avidly grasped when society gives these instincts the nod. For orders are not necessary, permission alone is enough.

Freud characteristically harvests some consolation from his grim discovery. We were wrong about civilisation and the war has at least opened our eyes; our flattering perception of our fellows was mere illusion and it is always an advantage to be rid of illusion. Disaster itself may be educative. 'In reality our fellow-citizens have not sunk so low as we feared, because they have never risen so high as we believed.'[32] There has been no fall, for there was never an ascent; man is pretty much where he has always been, despite the optical illusions of civilisation. Above all, so-called civilised man has 'a special capacity for involution – for regression . . . the primitive stages can always be re-established; the primitive mind is, in the fullest meaning of the word, imperishable'.[33]

What is perhaps surprising is Freud's equanimity in the face of his dark discoveries, his stoic imperturbability as he charts the catastrophe. Even if he is right in insisting that disillusionment is the child of exorbitant expectations, isn't he too impassive, too scientifically neutral, towards the demoralising truths he unearths? Orwell remarks, *a propos* of power-worship, that it is impossible to be impartial about a disease one is dying from, but Freud seems queerly untroubled as he shatters the myth of civilisation and rejects its ability to control the destructive drives forever fermenting beneath its showy surface. Nietzsche derides civilised man as a mere cartoon, a fragile overlay that the authentic Dionysian self so easily tears to shreds. Freud comes close to saying the same thing as when he asserts that civilised man is, consciously or not, a hypocrite, forever living beyond his psychological means, continually acting in opposition to his instincts and commensurately elated when war or some equivalent social breakdown gives him the chance to do his own uninhibited thing. Civilisation is simply the individual writ large – one vast system of organised hypocrisy which would crack apart 'if people were to undertake to live in accordance with psychological truth'.[34] But where Nietzsche is fiercely apocalyptic, Freud is composedly scientific, noting coolly that civilisation is based upon hypocrisy or observing that 'there are very many more cultural hypocrites than truly civilized men'.[35] Reading his essay, one might fairly conclude that civilisation is a fraud and civilised man a sham, that the whole civilised enterprise is the supreme manifestation of bad faith. What more dire communication could one receive?

Yet all this is conveyed in the calm idiom of the detached scholar, for, as Gulliver concludes his catalogue of human depravities, 'this is all according to the due course of things'.[36] In Freud's terminology, 'the transformation of instinct, on which our susceptibility to culture is based, may also be permanently or temporarily undone by the impacts of life',[37] and war is assuredly one such impact. Freud would have denied that he was under any obligation to console and there is certainly small consolation in the assurance that, once the war is over, the mass of those now behaving with such unrestrained ferocity will quietly resume civilised ways, their instincts re-ennobled with the restoration of peace. Quite apart from the innocent victims and the unpunished atrocities, all this tells us is that we are safe till the next time, but in the age of the bomb next time may be the last time that men will be permitted to gratify their destructive urges. Freud's concept of civilisation offers no guard against annihilation and his assurance that the fanaticism of war will wane when peace returns seems almost smug. Just as in sleep, so too in war (but with far more perilous results) we strip ourselves of our hard-won morality to emerge as the naked, unembellished creatures we are, not Lear's poor, vulnerable victim but Hobbes's unrestrained animal: so Freud tells us and it is meagre comfort to hear that all this will be expunged in smooth reversion to the status quo, a status quo, moreover, already exposed as one vast hypocrisy.

But if Freud's sense of outrage seems inadequate to his own disclosures, the same cannot be said of the artists of the dark epiphany. There is no easy return to civilisation for Marlow after *his* penetration of the heart of darkness, while Winston Smith is devastated by the self he encounters in Room 101, so much so that hostile critics use terms like hysteria, neurosis and mysticism of cruelty to condemn his reaction to the revelation. It is, however, in *The Fall* that we find the perfect dramatisation of Freud's thesis. The misanthrope's story demonstrates how an excessively high valuation of human nature must end in disillusion, how pride goes before a fall. The major divergence is that there is not, as in Freud, calm acceptance of the depressing truth. Men are not as good as they think they are: Freud's insight is a simple scientific statement with no hint of reproach, no summons to penance or self-contempt; the sensible scientist has no quarrel with truth. Clamence, however, is, like his creator Camus, a moralist and when he discovers that he is not as good as he thought, the shock is traumatic. How can he live with this shameful self? Freud's war criminals have the blessed ability to forget and return; Clamence, psychologically speaking, can never go home again.

'Ah, this dear old planet! All is clear now. We know ourselves; we now know of what we are capable.'[38] This emphasis upon a specific historical moment is revealing, indicating as it does the mental landscape of Europe after the end of the Second World War and the full revelation of its abominations. But, as with Freud, a particular historical catastrophe becomes a lens for seeing the abiding truths of human nature, for understanding man as he was, is and always will be. The bitterness is inseparable from a sense of betrayal: man is a fraud, virtue an illusion, exorbitant expectations jar with reality and turn into despair. The Grand Inquisitor rebukes Christ for thinking too highly of men and Freud levels the same charge against his contemporaries in 1915. Clamence likewise discovers that his cherished goodness is a bogus thing, easily produced when the cost is small and the gratification great, but evaporating when the test is real and the price painful. Anyone can be a hero when there is no danger, as Sartre's Garcin in *Huis Clos* so tormentedly realises.

'I am malicious because I am miserable.'[39] Frankenstein's Creature can teach us why Clamence turns so vindictively upon virtue, innocence and happiness – it is because the shock of his own corruption reveals that there are illicit ways of being happy, bogus ways of being good and spurious ways of being innocent. We scan in vain the pages of Camus's earlier novels for such perceptions. The book opens with Clamence as polite predator, poised in the seedy Amsterdam bar to pounce upon the first unwary prey that comes along. It is, we soon learn, a familiar routine and even from the start, courtesy notwithstanding, flashes of malevolence appear. But the story he tells is chronological and it begins when he was a happy, self-satisfied man, working in Paris as an admired and much sought-after defence lawyer whose life is one long, delightful indulgence in virtuous deeds and altruistic enterprises. He enjoys being good: he defends the poor without payment, consoles widows, befriends orphans, goes about eagle-eyed to help beggars and blind men. The account that he gives of his life before the catastrophe entitles us to link him with pre-Houyhnhnmland Gulliver, two happy, genial men complacently at ease in their social roles. True, Gulliver is a respectable family man, a husband and father, while Clamence has a string of complaisant mistresses, but, given the change in sexual mores, this, far from being cause for reprehension, merely enhances his sense of accomplishment and provokes envy in his admiring contemporaries – the brilliant lawyer and zealous philanthropist are complemented by the polished lover; we could not have a better instance of man as all-rounder. Gulliver and Clamence are men perfectly adapted to their environments, untroubled men with no shadow of a cloud on their social horizons. Gulliver lives contentedly in England but Clamence, ostensibly in Paris, is really resident in Eden: 'I took pleasure in my own life and in my own excellence.'[40] Adam before the fall undoubtedly felt the same.

With a bit of luck Gulliver and Clamence might have gone to their graves blissfully undisturbed, loving their fellow-men so easily because they love themselves so much. But Gulliver goes on his fourth voyage and Clamence walks home over the bridge and catastrophe occurs. Can we seriously regret this or lament that they did not stay the obtuse, complacent men they were? Would it have been better for Gulliver to continue jingoistically blind to the faults and follies of his dear native land or for Clamence to have gone on hugging the myth of his own goodness? Isn't their very honesty, their initial wholeness of self, a limitation which they do well to abandon, and if each becomes *une âme déchirée* (as Rousseau described himself) isn't this very disintegration the paradoxical proof of their ascent to a higher level of self-awareness? Surely we must agree that it is good that they stopped being the men they were, even if we still have grave doubts about the men they become. Such doubts will result not from the discoveries they make but from what they make of the discoveries. After the incident on the bridge, Clamence can no longer maintain, at least in their old form, the twin beliefs that have made him happy: that he is good and that he is superior. Yet neither can he complain that no warning of the test to come was given, that he was taken unawares by the challenge for which he was so unfairly ill-prepared. Already, some years before the cry from the river, he had been shaken by a mysterious, untraceable laugh on another Seine bridge, and deep within he senses uneasily that the laugh is on him.

But why should anyone presume to laugh at so triumphant a man, half Cerdan, half de Gaulle? The encounter with the motor-cyclist, from which he emerges feeling so foolish and humiliated, might have supplied the clue had not self-love worked to prevent the lesson being learned.[41] But after the second bridge incident (no wonder he shuns bridges in Amsterdam) the truth is inescapable and he is forced to review his whole life in the light of this epiphany: 'my dream had not stood up to facts'.[42] He is a fake, a mere play-actor; all of his 'good' deeds were performances, for the sake of the public's applause and his own self-esteem. He recalls how he used to tip his hat to the blind men he escorted across busy streets — who else was that intended for but the admiring audience? Beneath this sham is the true self, vicious and nasty. Every memory, once treasured as proof of his worth, now torments him as proof of his worthlessness; the significance of the perplexing laugh now dawns on him — it is the universe deriding the gross counterfeit. Like Gulliver schooled by the Houyhnhnms to despise what he had once prized, so Clamence retrospectively appraises his life and finds that what used to be lustrous is now leprous. La Rochefoucauld is right: there may be 'virtuous' actions but never 'virtuous' motives. The very word 'justice' infuriates Clamence; he dreams of tripping up blind men, wrecking invalid cars, slapping children, he orders the restaurant manager to drive away the beggar who is making him feel uncomfortable as he eats his meal. It is a transformation as total as Gulliver's. The latter learns that he is a Yahoo, Clamence that he is a Pharisee. What does a Pharisee do when he see through the fraud of his own virtue? He lies in wait for his brethren to trap them into confessing their own sins.

To ask why Clamence doesn't repent and try to become a better man is to miss the point of this pessimistic book. Why doesn't Rastignac, having gazed into the corruption of Paris, retire to a cave in the country? Because he hasn't changed, he still wants Paris and what it stands for, he means to conquer the city, not forsake it. The self as a bondage, as Pascal says – *le moi est haïssable* – and in Clamence we see egoism so ineradicable that it survives unabashed the worst disgrace and the deepest infamy. 'I, I, I is the refrain of my whole life':[43] the very form of the narrative, the monopolistic monologue that denies the auditor's right to respond, supports stylistically this psychological fact. As much as Winston Smith, Clamence is impotent before the claims of self-transcendence. Bernanos, counselling against self-hatred, tells us that grace means forgetting oneself, but it's easier said than done.[44] Even in the safety of the Chestnut Tree Café, the smell of rats, recalling the moment of his shameful survival, mingles with the smell of Winston's gin.[45] Clamence claims that there is nothing extraordinary in his story: every man is a shabby Narcissus. Both men are stuck with their sordid selves forever, though Clamence still characteristically strives, in the greatest of literary *tu quoques*, to make even this discovery a source of superiority, while Winston, by contrast, is as drained as O'Brien promised to make him.

Only externally for Clamence do things change; essentially he remains the same. True, the erstwhile 'good' man has now become actively malicious, almost as if Winston had joined the Thought Police, but this is simply a new strategy to achieve the same old end. The need to dominate is strong as ever; when he discovers his own ignominy, this drive simply takes a more devious, underground route for its gratification. Herostratus sought fame through infamy: better to be known for burning the temple of Diana than accept nonentity – to be the centre of attention is all, the reason for it is secondary. There is a hint of Herostratus in Clamence: if he can no longer be the Thespian of virtue, he will be the impresario of vice. Given that 'society is entirely made up of assumed personalities',[46] that all the world's a stage, the only thing that matters is to grab a leading role. Even in such intimate transactions as death and love, grief and orgasm, man puts on a show. Everything stems from vanity and affectation. La Rochefoucauld observes that 'perfect valour consists in doing without witnesses what one would be capable of doing before the world at large',[47] though nowhere in the

Maxims does he suggest that such valour really exists. *The Fall* is even more pessimistic in insisting that the imposture needs no other audience than the self; his own applause persuades Clamence that he is a good man; he is his own deluded, deluding spectator. Unfortunately, this is not enough to guarantee the performance. On a bridge crammed with spectators, he *might* have dived into the water; with nobody to impress, he thinks of the risk and hurries away from the scene because it isn't one. The failure is decisive; henceforth impersonation is impossible.

   The Fall marks a partial return to the moral outlook of the religion which Camus had long since repudiated. At its Augustinian extreme, Christianity pronounced virtue impossible; man was a sink of iniquity whose only hope was to be granted a grace he could never merit. In its more moderate form, it still regarded virtue as extremely difficult, for within man Satan's fifth columnist was firmly entrenched – every victory for good was sorely won in an unceasing psychomachia which split the self into two warring factions. On such a view there is something distinctly worrying about the easy way the prelapsarian Clamence zestfully notches up his triumphs for goodness. The sharp contrast between himself and his 'very Christian friend' towards the beggar is instructive.[48] The friend has to subjugate the old Adam in forcing himself to be charitable towards the beggar; Clamence exults when he sees a beggar approaching and he scans the ground for blind men as avidly as a trickster for fools. This passion for liberality is akin to a miser's for gold or a lecher's for women, and La Rochefoucauld teaches us how to assess such benevolence: 'What is called generosity is the more often just the vanity of giving, which we like more than what we give.'[49] Such virtue is really self-indulgence, for the hurt which is the proof of true goodness is ominously absent. The way to heaven is hard; it is the primrose path that leads to the everlasting bonfire.

   In the eighteenth century Shaftesbury, anxious to refute the black legend of Augustinian-Hobbesian man, proposed instead as his ideal good man one who finds pleasure in the happiness of others and who strives to promote and extend that happiness. Fielding's Mr Allworthy is the clearest fictional representation of this ideal, but Gide's criticism of Fielding shows how the Shaftesburian model conflicts with other views of the moral life.[50] Gide faults Fielding for his inability to conceive a saint, i.e. someone who has to battle with himself to be good, overcoming the enemy within who is far more difficult to circumvent than all the external hindrances added together. Allworthy has no enemy within; at worst, he makes mistakes, errors of judgement, going wrong as a man does when he fails to solve a quadratic equation – he *wants* the right answer but fails to see it. But this is not the manner in which Macbeth goes astray. *Video meliora proboque, deteriora sequor*: here is the key to Macbeth's anguish – the corrupt will and not the defective intelligence. Macbeth is a divided man, Allworthy (as his name implies) is a unity.

So too is the unfallen Clamence: 'I enjoyed my own nature to the fullest and we all know that therein lies happiness . . . few creatures were more natural than I. I was altogether in harmony with life.'[51] To live in harmony with oneself and nature is to be resident in Eden; to have no sense of self-division is the privilege of pre-lapsarian man, to live without consciousness of defect is to inhabit a mental landscape far removed from that of Ovid or St Paul: the good that I would do I do not, and the evil that I would not do I do. The fall occurs when a sense of unity gives way to a realisation that the self is double, that Janus is the presiding deity of man's nature. At the moment of crisis Clamence discovers that he is not one but two: 'I told myself that I had to be quick and I felt an irresistible weakness steal over me.'[52] It is the first intimation of this 'essential discovery', the revelation of 'the basic duplicity of the human being' which finally dawns on him 'after prolonged research on myself'.[53] Henceforth, oxymoron is, for Clamence, the figure under which man reveals himself: Christian landowner, adulterous humanist, *juge-pénitent*. Contemplating the various trade-signs of the old merchants in the streets of Amsterdam, Clamence proposes the sign for the house of man himself – a charming Janus, a double face – and supplies the appropriate motto: 'Don't rely on it.'[54] The disciple of Shaftesbury has deserted to Augustine.

With this realisation of division and duplicity comes the loss of harmony and the exit from Eden. 'Indeed, wasn't that Eden . . . no intermediary between life and me?'[55] Unfallen man needs no intermediary, for not until accusation does one need to brief defence counsel. The peculiar torment of the story Clamence tells is that he starts out needing no redeemer and ends up unable to find one: 'there is no lamb and no innocence any longer'.[56] Salvation is a fiction but the need is more clamant than ever. Clamence has fallen out of Eden into duplicity; the joy of stretching freely, the delicious liberty of the unconfined limbs, is lost and Clamence is condemned forever to living in the little-ease. His one recourse is to ensure that nobody else continues to enjoy his old innocence of movement: 'I have accepted duplicity instead of being upset by it. On the contrary, I have settled into it and found there the comfort I was looking for throughout life.'[57] Since we are in hell, let's make the best of it.

Man is trapped inescapably in the little-ease, the finely appropriate home for one who begins his story, in hubristic abandon, by declaring that he 'felt like a king's son, or a burning bush'.[58] Clamence's dream is an even more blasphemous aspiration than Gatsby's and it is fitting that he should be undone in a manner that would have been approved by ancient and Christian moralist alike. He has just enjoyed an excellent day: a blind man helped, a reduced sentence secured, a grateful client's homage, a brilliant improvisation among friends on the sins of other men, a hard-hearted governing class, hypocritical leaders. Walking alone afterwards on the bridge, he feels in harmony with himself and the world: 'I dominated the island. I felt rising within me a vast feeling of power and – I don't know how to express it – of completion, which cheered my heart.'[59] The ancient Greeks would have identified this as hubris; it is thus that Oedipus strides onto the stage, resolved to detect the sinner, who is, of course, some other man, for how could it be himself? With such an attitude nemesis is a certainty; so conceited a man cannot avoid being exposed as polluted. Nor can the alert Christian fail to recall Christ's fulminations against the Pharisees, those smug servants of God, all show without, whited sepulchres within. It is this moment of arrogance that is punctured by the unaccountable laugh which is the beginning of a radical unsettlement.

Yet *The Fall* cannot be called Christian, since the essential element of salvation is absent. It is yet another point of resemblance to *Nineteen Eighty-Four*, for both texts deal with the ubiquity of guilt and the unavailability of pardon. Winston and Clamence can neither shrive themselves nor find absolution. Guilt becomes exasperated before the vacancy of heaven, man is left facing the unavailing stare of his fellows. The psychoanalyst's craft is futile, for to become innocent it is not enough to accuse oneself;[60] advertising one's infamies does not in itself bring relief and may well intensify the sense of self-contempt. Winston and Julia admit betrayal but in the dull despair that they would do it all over again. Clamence is left 'strangely aching' by his failure to dive but does not know where to find the healing balm.[61] La Rochefoucauld puts the problem in a form pleasing to the humanist exasperated by fairy-tales of divine deliverance: 'When you cannot find your peace in yourself it is useless to look for it elsewhere.'[62] How mistaken, as Feuerbach explains, to look to the sky for the help that is really within. Hence the scandal of *The Fall*, exhibiting the problem of the anguished atheist, finding absolution nowhere and solace only in multi-plying, like a malevolent leper, the number of fellow-sufferers.

In spiteful mockery Clamence tells of the man who slept on the floor in sympathy with his imprisoned friend, but knows no one who could emulate such self-sacrifice: 'Who, *cher* Monsieur, will sleep on the floor for us? Look, I'd like to be and I shall be. Yes, we shall all be capable of it one day and that will be salvation.'[63] It echoes Swift and Orwell – the Swift who despised *rationis capax* as yet another shift of devious man, a promise to be good in the future made all the more worthless by the resolve to go on being shame-lessly Yahoo in the present. We detect in Clamence's words the same cracked and jeering note, the yellow note that the broken Winston hears in the mocking music at the café: heroic self-sacrifice is an illusion; we look after ourselves, whatever the cost. Clam-ence's vow of future heroism is as idle as the promises of O'Neill's derelicts in *The Iceman Cometh*, and he knows it – hence the aggres-sive derision of his tone.

Guilt is forever: there is no do-it-yourself absolution kit, no amnesiac return to the old life with the shameful deeds forgotten. On his recuperative sea-trip Clamence is shocked to see a body far out on the waves. It turns out to be a piece of flotsam, but he now knows that his sin will haunt him forever. He is at the same time too honest to take comfort in the lie that a second chance is all he needs; if by some miracle the bridge should come again, the result would be exactly the same. The coward who redeems himself is a Holly-wood cliché; the penitent thief, whether in the gospel or Victor Hugo, is a sop to sentimentalism. Clamence knows that the future is simply a repetition of the past and he knows how he has acted in the past: 'I drank the water of a dying comrade'[64] – and did so, moreover, fortified by the good old utilitarian argument that only by saving himself could he be of any service to those depending on him. Clearly, some people are more important than others and so have a greater right to survive; join this conviction of superiority to a raging thirst and it easily becomes nonsensical to waste the precious water upon an inferior man who is, in any case, dying. It was in a very different spirit that Sir Philip Sidney gave *his* water to the wounded soldier or that Captain Oates walked into the storm. But these instances of self-transcendence belong to an older concept of man which in the age of the dark epiphany seems either inconceivable or so unrepresentative as to be no norm for everyday life or ordinary men.

Winston Smith is still seared with sterile guilt over the chocolate snatched from his dying baby sister many years before – dying comrades and sisters have no chance against thirst and hunger, and in Winston's case the boy is father to the man; the childhood act of self-preservation is a rehearsal for the betrayal in Room 101. The book implies that it is our shame, too, that we will all cave in when put to the test, interposing our own Julias between us and the horror. Clamence similarly ends his story by making it ours, inviting us vindictively to tell him, in turn, how *we* managed never to risk our lives. In each case the trap for the reader is cunningly sprung: we refuse Winston and Clamence absolution, but who are we to refuse it? Like Claudius, we, too, are 'guilty creatures, sitting at a play', and entrapment is as much the aim of Camus and Orwell as it is of Hamlet.

What distinguishes the works of the dark epiphany from Freud is the very different reactions which their discoveries evoke. Freud seems altogether too casually permissive in describing the easy return from atrocity to civilisation. To reply that this is, in fact, what really happens is not much help, for this tranquil resumption of the old, interrupted life is more outrageous than the outrages themselves: after such knowledge, what forgiveness? Gulliver, Marlow, Aschenbach, Smith and Clamence are much more serious in their awareness that everything is altered, that their journeys to the interior have taken them forever from the old lives, and here, at least, they surely have their creators' support: why write books which leave us where we started out?

Clamence begins his story with the quiet assertion that 'we are at the heart of things here'.[65] 'Here' is Amsterdam, a Dutch hell, dismal and rainswept, where the doves alight on no heads, for the Paraclete is forever absent, and where the predator lurks – 'that's where I wait for them' – to lead his victim ever deeper into the damned circles until escape is impossible: 'Now I shall wait for you to write to me or to come back. For you will come back, I am sure!'[66] This journey is in the opposite direction from that described by Dante; no one emerges from this inferno to look once more upon the stars. Nevertheless, the text forbids us to repudiate even this place in favour of the bland mendacities of Paris. Paris, with its false innocence and deluded happiness, is behind us forever; too many truths, however hideous, stand between us and renewed residence in the city of lies.

It is an appropriately Swiftian conclusion to a Swiftian book. 'Admit, however, that today you feel less pleased with yourself than you felt five days ago?'[67] Or, as in the *Travels*, four voyages ago. To vex the world was precisely Swift's vocation; his satire, like *The Fall*, is a critique of happiness and virtue, an attempt to revoke unearned content and to instil guilt where a conviction of innocence had been. When, near the end, Clamence brutally tots things up and tells us that we are all incorrigible evil-doers, 'just like that. Just as flatly',[68] we recall Gulliver's similar list of depravities and similarly insulting conclusion: 'this is all according to the due course of things'.[69] Both men will permit no appeal against the undeniable evidence of our daily lives: 'That's the way man is, *cher* Monsieur.'[70] When Clamence extols the perverted genius that invented the little-ease and the spitting-cell, he echoes Gulliver praising the invention of gunpowder or deliberately omitting all mention of the refined debaucheries unknown to the Yahoos of Houyhnhnmland but cultivated by their European brethren.

We approach the final paradox of these two writers. The little-ease is undoubtedly a diabolic invention, yet Swift and Camus alike scheme to catch their readers in its literary equivalent, for their texts are traps which we serenely enter only to find our comfort cancelled and our exit barred. *The Fall* leads us to the little-ease and leaves us there. Clamence declares it to be our abiding home and recommends us to reconcile ourselves to it. The text implicitly challenges us to prove him wrong, but this means breaking the prison, not pretending that it isn't there. Hugo's escape route is too facile, Sartre's too frightful. The greatness of *The Fall* is that it shows just how immensely difficult escape will be.

7

Lord of the Flies: Beelzebub's Boys

There are a number of reasons why this study of the dark epiphany should end appropriately with *Lord of the Flies*, for it recapitulates in a fable immediately resonant to a twentieth-century sensibility the themes that we have traced from Swift onwards: the dread that civilisation is simply a veneer over bestiality; that the self is no more than the fragile product of a particular conditioning which, when the matrix alters, is unnervingly at the mercy of the new situation; that orgiastic surrender to a dark irrationalism is always a temptation and sometimes a fate; that we are shockingly obliged to give psychological house-room to strangers who claim kinship, to the Yahoo, the Pharisee and the sadist, all of whom disconcertingly seem to have equal residential rights with our more decorous, benevolent selves. In its final scene the book supplies us with one of the most explicit renditions of the dark epiphany in modern literature when the newly-rescued Ralph, to the embarrassed incomprehension of his superficial saviour, breaks down and, in thoroughly un-English style, weeps for the end of innocence and the darkness of man's heart.

Golding, as much as his book, seems the apposite terminus for our investigation. If, in fulfilment of Adrian Leverkühn's promise, the twentieth century has pursued a policy of revocation towards the work of its predecessor, it is Golding who has proved himself the most overt and deliberate of revokers. Almost all of his early work is a taking back, a rescinding of certain long established views and *idées reçues*. His second novel, *The Inheritors*, sets out to invalidate the optimistic view of human development held by H. G. Wells; its epigraph is provided by *The Outline of History* in which Wells celebrates the coming of *homo sapiens* and his victory over Neanderthal Man. Wells presents the latter as a half-witted, bloodthirsty creature, prototype of the cannibalistic ogre of folk-tale, while his supplanter is shown as thoughtful and resourceful, fit

138

ancestor of our superior selves. Even more pertinent to the plot of Golding's book is Wells's short story *The Grisly Folk*, in which the Neanderthal monsters steal a human child and are then, with Wells's total approval, hunted down and destroyed by the new men in an act at once retributive and progressive. *The Inheritors* stands Wells on his head by depicting the Neanderthals as gentle and innocent, the newcomers as vicious and aggressive – man still imagines today that progress and the extermination of his enemies are the same thing. It is man who ruins the garden by introducing evil into it – the serpent is redundant in Golding's revision of Genesis.

His third novel, *Pincher Martin*, does to *Robinson Crusoe* as a myth of human fortitude and tenacity what *The Inheritors* does to *The Grisly Folk*, and is equally outrageous in the reversal it proposes. From Prometheus onward we have come, through culture and inclination alike, to cherish the hero who, rejecting capitulation or despair, pits his isolated, unconquerable self against the overwhelming tyranny of external circumstance. How can we withhold admiration from these champions of the self who cry no surrender even to inexorable reality? Pincher, clinging to his ocean rock after being torpedoed, seems for much of the book yet another irresistible candidate for heroic apotheosis, a worthy son of Prometheus ; only gradually do we become aware that another, very different view of the situation is being pressed upon us. A series of flashbacks reveals a nasty, competitive person, bent on self-gratification even if it means destroying others. The snarling man, defying sea and sky, involved in his fierce and cunning struggle to survive, is simply exhibiting the same thraldom to appetite, the same wicked infatuation with his precious self, that caused so much agony to others before his shipwreck. He is not a hero but a damned soul; we learn that he has, in fact, been dead from the first page and that the speciously heroic stand against the self's extinction is, properly understood, a timid and childish refusal to face the truth. What we have deludedly prized as our noblest quality is revealed as a sordid bondage, making us such a woe to ourselves and such a menace to others.

But it is his first and best-known novel, *Lord of the Flies*, that reveals Golding as the supreme revoker, the most obvious abrogator in modern literature, employing the dark discoveries of our century to disclaim the vapid innocence of its predecessor. The target is R. M. Ballantyne's *The Coral Island* and Golding points up the ironic contrast by lifting even the names of his boys from the earlier work. Ballantyne's book could be used as a document in the history of ideas, reflecting as it does a Victorian euphoria, a conviction that the world is a rational place where problems arise so that sensible, decent men can solve them. God has his place in this world but his adversary is pleasingly absent and, with him, the sin which is his hold on humanity. The Home Counties come to the jungle and win easily. Difficulties are confidently overcome, fire is acquired easily and safely, pigs are hunted and killed with neither guilt nor bloodshed. The only troublesome things (cannibals and pirates) come from outside and are bested by British grit and commonsense. What cannibal is so foolish as to eat human flesh in preference to roast pork? All he needs is the proper culinary advice and Ballantyne knows the boys to give it. They, in turn, know nothing of Beelzebub: they are cleanly, godly, sensible, decent and efficient, and their island adventure is gratifying proof that they are just about ready to assume the blessed work of extending the British Empire throughout the savage world.

Lord of the Flies was conceived in a very different moral landscape and Golding himself tells us that the horrors of the Second World War were crucial in producing this alteration. When Sammy Mountjoy in *Free Fall* remarks that 'the supply of nineteenth century optimism and goodness had run out before it reached me' and goes on to describe the world as 'a savage place in which man was trapped without hope',[1] one senses an authorial reinforcement behind the words. *Lord of the Flies* springs from the cultural catastrophe of our times and not, as has been foolishly alleged, from the petty rancour of an arts graduate peeved because the scientists today have all the jobs and all the prestige. To attribute the book to a sullen distaste for the contemporary world, to see Golding as another Jack, who, when he can't have his own way, won't play any more and goes off in a huff, all because the scientist has displaced the literary intellectual as leader of society, is dignified by describing it as a *niaiserie*. But it does, at least, help us to focus our attention on Golding's attitude to science. He had started to read science at university on the twin assumptions that 'science was busy clearing up the universe' and that 'there was no place in this exquisitely logical universe for the terrors of darkness'.[2] But the darkness stubbornly refused to scatter and Golding came to suspect (as Bertrand Russell likewise did[3]) that science by itself could not be our saviour and might well, in the wrong hands, become our enslaver. The war confirmed that 'the darkness was all around, inexplicable, unexorcised, haunted, a gulf across which the ladder (science) lay without reaching to the light'.[4] It is, allowing for the heightened mode of expression, much the same perception as Freud's towards the previous war, and no one, surely, is going to accuse Freud of being a disgruntled arts graduate envious of the scientists' acclaim.

Golding's explanation of how his book came to be written seems infinitely more convincing: 'I set out to discover whether there is that in man which makes him do what he does, that's all . . . the Marxists are the only people left who think humanity is perfectible. But I went through the War and that changed me. The war taught me different and a lot of others like me.'[5] Among the lessons learned was that Ballantyne was retailing illusions: namely, that man is basically noble and decent, that reason must extend its empire over darkness, that science is the prerogative of the civilised man. *Lord of the Flies*, by contrast, 'is an attempt to trace the defects of society back to the defects of human nature. Before the war, most Europeans believed that man could be perfected by perfecting his society. We saw a hell of a lot in the war that can't be accounted for except on the basis of original evil.'[6] Orwell's nightmare is a boot in the face forever, a world dedicated to cruelty for its own sake; Camus invites us to contemplate the little-ease and the spitting-cell, the one an ingenious medieval invention, the other the equally masterly device of the most civilised nation in modern Europe.[7] Golding's is the same dilemma as he seeks to discover 'that in man which makes him do what he does'; to dismiss these men as a literary cave of Adullam, a gang of petulant and disaffected *littérateurs* miffed at a scientific takeover, is as foolish as it is impertinent.

Golding has perhaps encouraged his own devaluation by describing himself as a parodist and parody as depending on the mean advantage of being wise after someone else's event.[8] There is a similarly ungenerous self-depreciation in his allusion to a pint-sized Jeremiah, almost as though he were colluding with those who dismiss him as a peddler of doom, content to describe the ruins around us.[9] But *Lord of the Flies* is more than just an inversion of *The Coral Island*, a retelling in realistic terms of a nineteenth-century fantasy, and it is when Golding is most creative that he is also most interesting. *Joseph Andrews* becomes the comic masterpiece it is when Fielding stops burlesquing Richardson and liberates his own imagination. The real triumph of *Lord of the Flies* is not its parodic demolition of Ballantyne but the innovative skill that is most evident in the creation of Piggy, Simon and Roger; it is this that makes it an original work of art, the authentic expression of its age, and not simply a spoof deriving its second-hand force from the work of another era. How sin enters the garden; it is, after all, the oldest story in western culture and Golding's contemporary rendition is a worthy continuation of the tradition.

Piggy is a much more complex character than the simplistic interpretations so regularly adduced will allow; the very fact that his unhesitant commonsense would have chimed in so well with Ballantyne's ethos might make us pause before acclaiming him as the book's hero. This commonsense is evident from the start as when he organises the meeting and tries to make a list of everyone present. It is, significantly, the first question put by the rescuing officer; he wants to know how many boys there are and is disappointed and a little shocked to hear that English boys in particular have not made even this elementary calculation. Yet Piggy is a doubtful hero who, no sooner met, has to rush away from us in a bout of diarrhoea; in addition, he wears spectacles, suffers from asthma, is fat through eating too many sweets in his auntie's shop, can't swim, and, most important of all, his abysmal English reveals him as unmistakably working-class. What, one wonders, was he doing on the plane with boys so clearly his social superiors? Neither Ralph nor Jack would ever have met Piggy back in England except as their employee, for while they are so obviously, in their respective ways, officer material, Piggy is just as obviously born to be an underling all his days.

Yet it is he who has a monopoly of commonsense and practical intelligence. Jack, instinctively recognising him as an inferior and a target of abuse, orders him to be quiet, yet no one else talks such consistent good sense. Ironically, in the increasingly hysterical atmosphere, that turns out to be as much a handicap as his bad eyesight. Yet nowhere is Orwell's description of England as a family with the wrong members in control more visibly demonstrated than in the way the leadership contest becomes a straight two-way fight between Ralph and Jack, with Piggy not even considered, far less chosen.[10] Yet who better to elect, given that clear thinking, with a view to maximising the chances of rescue, is the main priority? Jack knows that he should be leader and tells the others why he can sing high C. The utter irrelevance of this is not meant to expose Jack's folly but his menace: the *Führer's* lust for power needs no other justification than his own irrational conviction of merit. Yet the choice of Ralph, as Golding makes plain, is just as irrational.[11] Ralph becomes leader because he looks like one – he gets the job on appearance and not ability. His very stillness is charismatic; he only has to sit and look the part.

Piggy lacks the looks but has the know-how. The trouble is that he knows but cannot do, and is relegated, in accordance with Shaw's dictum, to being at best a teacher. He cannot blow the conch himself – the asthma again – but he sees its possibilities and shows Ralph how to do it. He never advances his own claims to leadership nor even thinks of doing so, but is happy to be Ralph's adviser, the thinker and framer of policy. *Lord of the Flies* does not, like *The Admirable Crichton*, depict the rise of a meritocracy, when, following the social upheaval of shipwreck, the supremely efficient butler takes over as leader from the feckless aristocrats and only relapses into subordination when the party is rescued and taken back to the Home Counties from the jungle. Ralph and Jack are the leaders in the jungle as they would be in England. Barrie's aristocrats, recognising the demands of reality, resign themselves to accepting a social inferior as their natural leader; Golding's boys would laugh at the idea of taking orders from Piggy.

What is interesting is the skilful way in which Golding employs the prejudices of the English class system to support his allegorical intention. The allegory requires that the boys should undervalue, ignore and even despise commonsense. How shrewd, in that case, to embody commonsense in a fat, bespectacled, unathletic, working-class boy who is the natural target of upper-class contempt. The language barrier is the crucial thing. Crichton, after all, did at least speak immaculate English, but what gentleman could ever bring himself to take orders from someone who talks like Piggy? Piggy can aspire, at most, to advise and he is to begin with the best adviser that Ralph could get. We must not, of course, push the allegory to the absurd extreme of saying that the working-class have all the commonsense, but we are entitled, even obliged, to point out that the task set commonsense in the book becomes infinitely more difficult by making its representative a working-class boy among upper-class companions.

The allegorical insistence throughout the book that men prefer passion to practicality and glamour to commonsense (*plutôt la barbarie que l'ennui*) is reinforced by the realism of social antipathy.

Piggy, trained to know his place, does not protest, far less rebel against this. From the moment Jack turns up, commonsense takes a back seat, and the reason is unarguably connected with the English class system. Piggy at once stops taking names for his list: 'He was intimidated by this uniformed superiority and the offhand authority in Merridew's voice. He shrank to the other side of Ralph and busied himself with his glasses.'[12] Piggy knows he is inferior just as Ralph and Jack take their superiority for granted. It is this sense of inferiority that makes him deliver himself into the hands of his class enemies right from the start when he foolishly tells Ralph his derisory nickname and even more foolishly asks him to keep it a secret. It is perhaps unfair to say that Ralph betrays him, since betrayal implies a confidence solicited and a promise broken, and Ralph does neither, but at almost the first opportunity Ralph blurts out Piggy's secret to the whole world. Even Ralph, so straight and decent, is not above meanness, and his tears at the close for Piggy are an act of contrition for all the insults and injuries, climaxing in murder, which the boys have inflicted right from the start upon their inferior companion. In Ralph, at least, class contempt is gradually and thoroughly overcome; he weeps for the true, wise friend who came to him originally in such an unprepossessing guise.

That Piggy does to some extent bring his troubles upon himself leaves unchallenged his claim to be *the* sensible person on the island. He himself never makes this claim because he only partially realises it. One of his limitations is a tendency to credit others with his own good sense. He keeps attributing to Ralph his own practical insights when it is plain to the reader that Ralph is still fumbling around in the dark. He rebukes the other boys for distracting Ralph from what he was about to say and then puts the words into his bemused leader's mouth. There is nothing devious or disingenuous in this. He shares Ballantyne's confidence that commonsense can master any problem and he believes that most people, given the chance, are as logical as himself.[13] When, after Ralph's first speech – Piggy admires it as a model of succinct good sense – the other boys, led by Jack, run off in disorganised excitement to light the signal-fire, Ralph and Piggy are left alone with the conch; then Ralph, too, scrambles after 'the errant assembly', leaving disgusted common-sense on its own. All Piggy can do is toil breathlessly after them while venting his exasperation in the worst reproof he can imagine: 'Acting like a crowd of kids!'[14] But that's what they are. The book shows that you only get an old head on young shoulders when the shoulders are those of a podgy, unhealthy boy. The adult the boys so desperately need is among them but disguised so impenetrably that there is no hope of his being recognised, let alone heeded. Piggy's continual annoyance and even less justified continual surprise at the foolish behaviour of his companions should surely have led him to suspect that his own commonsense was not so widely distributed as he had imagined, yet right up to his destruction he goes on believing in the power of reason to tame the beast. His most fervent exhortation to the others is that they should stop being kids and instead try to think and act as adults do, for he believes that therein lies salvation. One of the book's major ironies is that the boys finally take his advice: they act like adults and kill him.

Yet in this ambivalent book in which everything is double – fire is both good and bad, faces lit from above are very different from faces lit from below, nature is both beautiful and menacing, the human being is at once heroic and sick[15] – it is fitting that Piggy's handicaps, most notably the asthma, all those things which qualify him as the target for ridicule, should be, in another sense, compensations. Sickness brings its own insights – Simon is, of course, an even more dramatic exemplification of this psychological truth. Long before anyone else Piggy senses the menace of Jack and the element of self-interest in this intuition makes it no less valid. Allegorically, it represents the fact that reason and commonsense are the prey of fanaticism. Piggy is stricken when Ralph talks despairingly of surrendering to Jack: ' "If you give up", said Piggy in an appalled whisper, "what'ud happen to me? . . . . He hates me. I dunno why." '[16] On the naturalistic level this is perfectly credible; a little boy, with every cause to be frightened of a bully, expresses his own personal fears, but allegorically we note the impotence of commonsense to check the progress of demented totalitarianism – when Jack is frustrated his eyes are described as bolting, blazing or mad.

Orwell, in what was almost a kind of parricide, attacked H. G. Wells for complacently dismissing Hitler as a jumped-up nonentity doomed to defeat because he was the enemy of reason.[17] Winston Smith has all the commonsense truths of arithmetic and history on his side but they do him no good against O'Brien's fanaticism. Golding shifts the conflict to a school playground, emptied of all teachers, to enforce the same lesson. Piggy perceptively associates his fear of Jack with the sickness from which he suffers: 'You kid yourself he's all right really, an' then when you see him again; it's like asthma an' you can't breathe.'[18] When Ralph tries to pooh-pooh this as exaggeration, Piggy confides the source of his superior insight: 'I been in bed so much I done some thinking. I know about people. I know about me. And him.'[19] If the grammar is faulty, the psychology is sound: Piggy does know about Jack, long before anyone else does, and his knowledge springs from the kind of boy he is. The same thing that has stopped him from being an athlete has encouraged him to be a thinker, though, as we shall see, a thinker of a limited kind.

There is certainly much to admire in Piggy. His liberal-democratic outlook and sense of fair play lead him to the honourable idea that everyone, however lowly, has a right to speak – even a littlun who wants the conch must be given it.[20] Again Jack is the adversary: 'We don't need the conch any more. We know who ought to say things.'[21] This leads straight to a kind of Asiatic court where only the tyrant's voice is heard because all dissenters have been put to death; Piggy supports a polyphonic society, Jack a society of mutes, since men require only ears to hear the master's command.

Piggy, too, is the first to recognise that life entails making certain choices and establishing certain priorities. Ralph, by contrast, tells the boys what mankind has always wished to hear: that there is no troublesome competition among our desires but that all can be simultaneously gratified, that the world will complaisantly minister to all our wishes, that, psychologically speaking, we are like pampered guests in a Hilton hotel where the whole *raison d'être* of the establishment is to provide whatever we want. 'We want to be rescued; and of course we shall be rescued.'[22] Such brash optimism is presumptuous enough, for even though the assembly is 'lifted towards safety by his words', we know that words alone are futile and that the comfort they provide is delusive. But Ralph compounds his offence by presuming still more: 'We want to have fun. And we want to be rescued.'[23] (Fun is a word worth watching in *Lord of the Flies* for on the three important occasions when it is used – here by Ralph, by Beelzebub in his warning to Simon, and finally by the unseeing officer – it sets alarm bells ringing.) The conjunction used by Ralph implies a confidence that we can have both things – fun *and* rescue – together. The boys have had a happy accident: they will have a delightful, unexpected, adult-free holiday, with rescue just around the corner the moment boredom begins.

It is the practical Piggy who jarringly introduces the reality prin-ciple into this dream of pleasure: 'How can you expect to be rescued if you don't put first things first and act proper?'[24] The grammatical solecism should not conceal the psychological wisdom. Life is not the Hilton but a succession of harsh choices and necessary sacri-fices; at the very best, if you are lucky, you will get what you deserve, but windfalls are a pipe-dream. It is the Judaeo-Christian premise upon which western civilisation once rested. You can eat the apple or stay in Eden; not both. You will reach the Promised Land but only after the discipline of an arduous journey through the wilderness. Do you want fun *or* rescue? Piggy introduces the unpleasant idea of an incompatibility between desires; if rescue is our first priority, then fun must come a poor second. If we are serious about rescue, that means work, and work is what we would prefer someone else to do for us: lighting and maintaining fires, building shelters, and all the other tedious chores that the little folk in fairy tales perform for a bowl of milk. Civilisation, says Freud, is based upon the renunciation of instinctual gratification and Piggy is the only Freudian on the island. *Lord of the Flies* depicts, initially, the disintegration of a society whose members play rather than work.

Self-denial is the infallible litmus-test. When Jack goes hunting, he is clearly doing something that is both demanding and dan-gerous – instinctual gratification is not necessarily immersion in sybaritic hedonism. The point is that Jack is doing what he wants, not what he ought; he relishes the danger of the chase and the excitement of the kill. Piggy does not criticise Jack for doing what is easy, but for putting his own pleasure above the priority of rescue. Stalking pigs is thrilling, tending a fire is dull, so Jack opts for Yahoo excitement in preference to Houyhnhnm tedium – that's what makes him the foe of civilisation and Piggy alike. The trouble is that Jack is more representative than Piggy and his outlook prevails, even though not all of the defaulters are pursuing pigs with the indefatigable hunter – many have plumped for Tahiti, for fruit, swimming and sunbathing. At assemblies they all vote duti-fully for the laudable resolutions because people love to talk, but they do not love to work: 'We decide things. But they don't get done . . . people don't help much.'[25] And so the huts, vital to civilised survival, are either unbuilt or ramshackle. It is hard to be civilised, deleteriously easy to be savage. Work is irksome, and, in terms of this Kantian definition, Jack is a layabout, even if he chased pigs from dawn to dusk.

We must, accordingly, be careful not to be too harsh on Piggy for being such a bore; even Ralph, despite their growing friendship, sees this failing: 'his fat, his ass-mar and his matter-of-fact ideas were dull'.[26] Piggy *is* depressingly literalist, totally lacking in a sense of humour, taking everything so seriously. But the book exists to demonstrate the superiority of dull decency to the heady intoxication of evil – the Yahoos pay a swingeing price for all that life they are supposed to possess. The two worlds are strikingly contrasted when Jack, the bloodied knife in his hand, fresh from his first, elated kill, confronts Ralph, fuming because the chance of rescue has been lost: 'the brilliant world of hunting, tactics, fierce exhilaration, skill' versus the antithetical world of 'longing and baffled common-sense'.[27] We *must* choose between pigs and huts, hunters and builders, fun and rescue. If Piggy is dull, he is also right.

Only to a certain degree, however, because Piggy's intelligence is seriously limited. The sole, damaging occasion when he agrees with Jack is to deny the beast's existence. Jack initially insists, with fine positivist arrogance, that there is no beast – he has hunted all over the island and 'if there were a beast I'd have seen it'.[28] Piggy ominously joins his enemy in scouting the idea of a beast – 'of course there isn't nothing to be afraid of in the forest' – though he approaches Simon's intuition in stating that 'there isn't no fear . . . unless we get frightened of people'.[29] But Piggy is handicapped by an unfounded trust in a rational universe administered by rational man: 'Life is scientific, that's what it is . . . . We know what goes on and if there's something wrong, there's someone to put it right.'[30] Everything comes right in the end: it is the root fallacy of the liberal mind that Orwell identified and pilloried in *Nineteen Eighty-Four*. Piggy has joined up with the complacent optimists he formerly rebuked.

It is Simon, a character not to be found, however faintly, in Ballantyne's story, whom Golding uses to highlight Piggy's short-comings. The distance separating Piggy from Simon (who clearly embodies Golding's highest values) is indicated in Piggy's shocked incomprehension when Simon hesitantly suggests that perhaps there *is* a beast and that 'maybe it's only us'.[31] Piggy indignantly rejects this as 'Nuts!' Simon's mystical speculations are beyond

Piggy's limitedly sensible mind; he cannot and, more to the point, will not assist Simon in the latter's inarticulate effort to express man's essential illness. For Piggy, man is *not* ill – he just has a foolish but corrigible habit of following Jack when he should be taking Piggy's sensible advice. Piggy is still handing out this sensible advice when the stone crushes him to death. Simon's stumbling attempt to explain the beast provokes general derision in which Piggy participates, but, as the book shows, it is Simon who is right and the mockers who are wrong.

Ralph reveals a similar incapacity for Simon's insight and reproaches him for voicing such a distressing thought: 'Why couldn't you say there wasn't a beast?'[32] Tell us what we want to hear or say nothing at all. But Piggy characteristically supplies the rationale for dismissing Simon as demented. There is no beast for the same reason that there are no ghosts. "Cos things wouldn't make sense. Houses an' streets, an' – TV – they wouldn't work'.[33] Piggy will pay for this empty faith with his life, but, even as he speaks, the argument is sorrily unconvincing. Golding ironically emphasises this by having the other boys, led by Jack, chant and dance like savages while Piggy is making his pitiful profession of faith.

Ralph and Piggy both fail to see that, in silencing Simon, they are in effect delivering themselves into Jack's hands. The book traces three routes for mankind: Piggy's commonsense, Jack's irrationalism, and Simon's mysticism. But commonsense is intimidated by irrationalism – Piggy is terrified in Jack's presence. The paradox is that the mystic way, which strikes Piggy as outrageous mumbo-jumbo, is the only sensible, practical solution. That the mystic is, astonishingly, the practical man is made evident when the boys huddle in crazed despair after the appalling discovery of the beast on the mountain. Ralph has just gloomily announced that there is nothing to be done when Simon reaches for the conch. Ralph's irritation is plain: 'Simon? What is it this time?'[34] Bad enough to be leader in such a predicament without having to listen to a crackpot, but what Simon says takes the all-time gold medal for sheer looniness: 'I think we ought to climb the mountain.'[35] Piggy receives this with open-mouthed incomprehension and no one even bothers to answer the idiot when he asks, 'What else is there to do?' Piggy's solution, applauded by the boys as a stroke of intellectual audacity, is to concede the mountain to the beast and shift the signal-fire to a safer place. Yet Simon's is the truly intrepid invitation in every sense of the word, intellectually, morally and psychologically, for it *is* the only thing to do: we must outstare Medusa, face and outface whatever we fear or be afraid forever. Either the beast rules us or we rule it – surrendering the mountain to the beast is admitting that the contest is over. One might as well go the whole way and join Jack in devil-worship, in full propitiation of the demon.

Simon knows how to deal with the beast because he knows who the beast is: 'However Simon thought of the beast, there rose before his inward sight the picture of a human at once heroic and sick.'[36] Piggy is incapable of such an intuition. In his secret place among the leaves Simon's recognition of the beast enables him to solve the problem that leaves the others in baffled anguish. It is while Simon is unlocking the secret that Ralph is asking why things have gone so terribly wrong and making one more vain appeal to commonsense. Surely if a doctor told the boys to take medicine or die, they would do the sensible thing? Why, then, can't they see the equal importance of the signal-fire? Why do you have to beg people to save themselves? The mystery tortures him without respite: 'Just an ordinary fire. You'd think we could do that, wouldn't you? Just a smoke signal so we can be rescued. Are we savages or what?'[37] It echoes Swift pondering in angry perplexity the insensate behaviour of the self-destructive Irish. Ralph appeals piteously to Piggy: 'What's wrong? . . . what makes things break up like they do?', but Piggy's answer shows how sadly limited his own understanding is, for all he knows is to blame Jack.[38] This is true only in the allegorical sense, but Piggy, of course, not knowing that he's a character in an allegory, blames Jack as an individual and this is totally inadequate. Jack is to blame only in the sense that he lives in all of us, that we are all guilty because mankind is sick.

Simon is the one exception to this general condemnation. The epileptic is the one spiritually sound person on the island, and, further paradox, it is his sickness that helps to make him a saint. Simon is not interested in leadership or any other form of competitive self-assertion – the nature of reality, not the promotion of the self, is his preoccupation. He is one of the meek, of the poor in spirit, who are promised the kingdom of heaven, not the congratulations and rewards of earthly assemblies. He is a surprising and anachronistic addition to the one-time commonplace tradition which affirmed the peculiar sanctity of the sick, the weak and the dying. His very debility is to be seen as a mark of the divine at work in him. While Ralph and Piggy wrestle in vain with the *mysterium iniquitatis*, Simon is shut up in audience with the Lord of the Flies.

Piggy is only partially right: there is nothing to fear in the forest because the beast is within man; the only forest to fear is the heart of darkness. 'Fancy thinking the Beast was something you could hunt and kill! . . . I'm part of you? Close, close, close! I'm the reason why it's no go? Why things are what they are?'[39] From the first men in *The Inheritors* to the atomic killers of our own day persists the same root delusion: evil is external and other; we, innocent and threatened, will pursue and destroy it. Beelzebub warns the boy who has broken the secret not to interfere with the 'fun' about to take place or else 'we shall do you', and it is significant that the 'we' includes Piggy and Ralph as well as Jack and Roger; Simon is the sole immaculate conception in Golding's fable. When he ignores the threat and tries to bring the good news to the other boys, Beelzebub's promise is hideously fulfilled.

'What else is there to do?' Despite Beelzebub's warning and the indignation of his companions, Simon climbs the mountain to face the beast and finds instead the rotting parachutist, 'harmless and horrible'. He at once sets out to bring to the others as quickly as possible the news of salvation, and, stumbling into the predicted 'fun', is murdered by his frenzied friends, Piggy and Ralph included. The representatives of commonsense and decency are just as eager as anyone else to take a place in the ritual of 'this demented but partly secure society'. Simon is killed while 'crying out something about a dead man on a hill',[40] and, however different from Christ the parachutist is, the words cannot fail to evoke an image of the corpse on Calvary, with Simon's own death just as clearly intended as a recapitulation of that ancient sacrifice. Nothing changes in the way men treat their redeemers.

Despite the fact that *Gulliver's Travels* was written by the Dean of St Patrick's, and despite *The Fall*, with its significant title and its pervasive Christian themes and images, it is, of all the texts we have considered, *Lord of the Flies* that is closest in spirit to Christianity. There is no hint of redemption in *The Fall* and it is pointless to speculate as to what Camus might have gone on to write had he not been so tragically killed. His last book is unrelievedly pessimistic and we have no right to assume that in producing so dark a text Camus was either propelling us towards the church door or preparing to enter it himself. It may be a propaedeutic for Christianity but it may also be nothing of the kind. *Lord of the Flies* is different and the difference is Simon, for either he is imbecile or he has a 'supernatural' insight into reality denied to the other boys. The novel forbids the first alternative. Simon clearly *has* some mystical, prophetic power, as when he tells Ralph that he *knows*, in some incommunicable way, that Ralph will get home again – Ralph, be it noted, not himself. Simon is awkward in that he confounds all simplistic interpretations of the novel, for example, that it is an Augustinian or 'tory' book, arguing for law and order against anarchic misrule and licentious freedom.[41] All of the boys, so it is argued, removed from the pinfold of civilisation, inevitably regress to savagery. But Simon doesn't regress to savagery; it is in the jungle that he become prophet and redeemer, and it would be foolish in the extreme to argue that he inherits these roles as a result of a sound education in the Home Counties. Simon is not one up for civilisation in its quarrel with nature – if anything, the beautiful resumption of his body by the ocean might lend support, here, if nowhere else, to nature's advocates.

But it is misleading to use him as a counter in the culture versus nature debate, for he transcends both to become, in the religious sense, a new creation. Why did Golding create him and why is the hideous death followed by so beautiful a *requiescat*, in almost brutal contrast to the curtly realistic disposal of the dead Piggy? Only the determinedly deaf will miss the religious reverberations echoing through the passage describing the transfiguration of the dead Simon – the gentle escort of his body towards the infinite ocean is as close to a resurrection as any novel dare come, is far more truly 'religious' than Sydney Carton's self-sacrifice, despite the explicitly Christian context in which Dickens invests the latter. Simon's transformation – the silvering of the cheek and the sculptured marble of the shoulders[42] – is, to begin with, beautiful in the way that the transformation described in Ariel's song in *The Tempest* is beautiful. But more than simply a sea-change is depicted in Simon; this beauty is clearly the servant of some greater purpose – it points to an alternative world opposed to the nightmare world of blood and taboo, a world, in Hopkins's words, charged with the glory of God. The passage provides a sacramental guarantee that creation is not just some haphazard collision of atoms but the product of an organising power, a power which promises not simply rest but resurrection to those who sacrifice themselves for its sake. The rhythm and imagery make it impossible to believe that Simon's death is merely another bloody atrocity, pointless and inane, clinching proof in this dark book that life is a tale told by an idiot. The sense of peace informing the passage is not simply that which Macbeth envies in

Duncan. Simon *is* out of the madness, *is* at rest – after the fever of the island he sleeps well – but not just in the negative sense of Macbeth's longing; the peace that concludes Simon's sacrifice is much more akin to the promise of the Sermon on the Mount: blessed are the pure in heart for they shall see God. Simon is now at one with whatever strong, beautiful power it is that sustains creation, the power that will continue to maintain 'the steadfast constellations' when all the hagridden acolytes of Jack have followed Macbeth to vacuous death.[43] It is an arresting *peripeteia*: the dark epiphany is pierced by a shaft of light from that other epiphany promising salvation and for once Dame Julian's assurance that all shall be well is echoed in the century of revocation.

But only momentarily. We are taken from the glory of resurrection back to fallen humanity, to the 'befouled bodies' of Simon's friends, Ralph and Piggy.[44] It is now that Piggy's moral limitations are most fully exposed: the failure to climb the mountain is a metaphor for the failure to face truth. He will not even talk about Simon: 'We got to forget this. We can't do no good thinking about it, see?'[45] Truth must be placatory or it is unwelcome. He searches desperately for any defence against the accusation, for the essential thing is to maintain one's innocence. The darkness, the dancing, the storm all combined to thrust the boys into an act they never intended. One recalls Swift's icy disdain for the shifts of alibi-seeking men, incriminating Satan for their own misdeeds. Ralph, more honest than Piggy, denies that he was afraid and seeks in vain to name the emotion that drove him to attack Simon – the reader has no difficulty in identifying it as bloodlust. 'Didn't you see what we – what they did?' The change of pronoun deceives no one, himself included, for even as he speaks 'there was loathing, and at the same time a kind of feverish excitement in his voice'.[46] Piggy denies complicitly: he wasn't in the circle and his poor eyesight prevented him from seeing what happened. By now he is hopelessly entangled in evasions, contradictions and lies: perhaps Simon isn't dead, perhaps he was only pretending, the boys' fear absolves them from all responsibility, it was an accident, Simon deserved what he got for crawling out of the dark. Any one of these excuses on its own would be flimsy – jumbled together in one self-exculpating torrent they are pitiful, indicating merely his frantic attempt to blot out the memory of what happened.

Ralph is frightened 'of us', but Piggy still insists that he is victim and not culprit, and he finally persuades Ralph to tell the lie that preserves innocence: 'I was on the outside too.'[47] We did and saw nothing; Jack and the others committed the crime – it is always the others who are guilty. Yet the Lord of the Flies included Ralph and Piggy among those who would 'do' Simon, and this is one occasion when the father of lies speaks true. And the boys know it: when Piggy touches Ralph's bare shoulder, Ralph shudders at the human contact.[48] Simon in death is proved correct; there is no salvation for those who will not climb the mountain. Jack is just as evasive; they didn't kill Simon, for it was really the beast in disguise and the beast is unkillable. But Piggy's self-deception is much more hurtful, for, while Jack's irrationalism thrives on lies, Piggy's practical intelligence must respect truth or it is good for nothing.

Piggy starts off short-sighted, becomes one-eyed and, finally, his glasses stolen, is completely blind; it is, in terms of the allegory, a depressing view of the value of commonsense. His reverence for the conch is at once exemplary and absurd, touching and ludicrous. As with his commonsense, he tends to attribute his own values to everyone else. Thus, despite Jack's unconcealed contempt for the conch from the start, Piggy foolishly believes that the purpose of Jack's raid was to seize the conch and not the glasses. To the end Piggy clings to the delusion of legitimacy. The blind boy demands, with heroic obtuseness, to be led by his friends to the fortress of the savage chief where he will confront the tyrant with 'the one thing he hasn't got', i.e. the precious conch.[49] He will use decency to shame power; right will confront might and right will prevail. Piggy's passionate willingness to carry his talisman against all the odds is at once a tribute to his liberal commitment and the guarantee of his eventual destruction. No wonder the savages giggle derisively when Ralph tells their chief that he isn't 'playing the game', that in stealing Piggy's spectacles Jack has broken some schoolboy code.[50] Has Ralph forgotten that he's speaking to Simon's murderer? The twins' protest at being taken prisoner is equally absurd: 'Oh, I say!' It would be farcical if it were not tragic, for what have these gentlemanly reproaches got to do with the demented doings of the island? Appealing to Jack's sense of decency is like asking for fair play in Dachau. Piggy's commonsense is still trying to prevail in bedlam: 'Which is better – to be a pack of painted niggers like you are, or to be sensible like Ralph is? . . . '[51] The logic is irrefutable but the questions are addressed to the wrong company, as misplaced as they are reasonable. Piggy insists on treating the savages like a crowd of scatter-brained kids, implying that if only they behaved like adults all would be well. When Roger, looking down on the bag of fat that is his view of Piggy, releases, 'with a sense of delirious abandonment',[52] the great rock that kills the advocate of adult commonsense, he is not acting like a kid but like the corrupt adults who have plunged the world into atomic war in the first place. Commonsense and the conch perish together and there is nothing healing or transfiguring about this death.

Yet, even after all this, the frenzied slaughter of Simon and the calculated killing of Piggy, Ralph still tries to persuade himself that the savages will leave him alone. His first thought, remembering his dead friends, is to assume that 'these painted savages would go further and further', but it is a thought too hideous to entertain and he instinctively rejects it: 'No. They're not as bad as that. It was an accident.'[53] It is easy to believe what we want to believe. His wish to think well of his fellows, despite all the contrary evidence, springs from fear for himself, for if they *are* as bad as their actions, he is as good as dead. The incentive to repeat Piggy's mistake of denying truth for the sake of comfort is massive – there can be a vast emotional investment in delusion when the truth is too terrible to accept. Only when he hears the chilling news that Roger has a stick sharpened at both ends does he brace himself for the appalling truth that his erstwhile friends intend to treat him as they did the pig: skewer, roast and eat him while leaving his head as an offering to the Lord of the Flies. Both Golding and Orwell know that the worst thing in the world can and will happen unless man unearths some undisclosed resource, some as yet untapped or neglected potency, to deflect the disaster.

This deliverance is shown by the text to be far more difficult than some of its more simplistic interpreters will allow. It is facile to present the book as a straight opposition between civilisation and savagery, city and jungle, with Golding unholding the former and all its salutary disciplines against the chaotic free-for-all of the latter. Certainly, this opposition is present but the solution is not nearly so easy as the mere election of one over the other. The first page presents the two states, jungle and Home Counties, which are apparently so remote from each other. The boys are ecstatic at their miraculous relocation. To be on an adult-free, coral island means 'the delight of a realized ambition', conveyed in the 'bright, excited eyes' and 'glowing' faces, the elated boyish exclamations, the sense of glamour and adventure at escaping civilisation.[54] We hear that 'the cause of their pleasure was not obvious', for Ralph, Jack and

Simon are at this point hot, dirty and exhausted, but that only makes it more plain that internally they feel exhilaratingly emancipated. It is a good island and it is theirs, empty of adult restriction. 'Until the grown-ups come to fetch us we'll have fun.'[55] The island is not to be a permanent home but a storybook holiday.

Almost immediately reality breaches the idyll. The marvellous sun burns, the convenient fruit causes diarrhoea, irrational fears come with darkness. The bigger boys deride the littluns' terrors – 'But I tell you there isn't a beast!'[56] – but privately they share them. Soon taboos have infiltrated paradise: 'snakes were not mentioned now, were not mentionable';[57] 'the glamour of the first day' wears increasingly thin. The jungle is now threat rather than playground; even Jack, besotted with hunting, senses that in the forest he shockingly exchanges the role of hunter for hunted, 'as if something's behind you all the time in the jungle'.[58] Ralph is scandalised, but Jack's personal courage is never in question and no one knows better than he the jungle atmosphere. The holiday camp becomes a hellhole as the idyll plummets towards nightmare. 'The best thing we can do is get ourselves rescued.'[59] Life in a real jungle educates the boys to appreciate civilisation: the rescue once so casually postponed is now ardently desired, the missing adult supervision is no longer cause for celebration but grief.

'With a convulsion of the mind', Ralph discovers dirt and decay.[60] Everything breaks down: the shelters collapse, the simplest repairs are too taxing, the basic rules of hygiene are ignored, the habit of disciplined work is lost as lazy, feckless man succumbs to nature. The boys understandably blame this collapse on the absence of adults, but the text denies the reader so simple an explanation. Ralph, Piggy and Simon, left alone as the others slide into savagery, can be forgiven for craving 'the majesty of adult life', for believing that with adults in control none of the insanities would have occurred.[61] Adults, they assure themselves, would not quarrel or set fire to the island; what the boys fail to see is that children are but men of a smaller growth, that the child is father to the man, for they would not be on the island at all but for the fact that adults have quarrelled in an atomic war which may set the whole world ablaze. It is the discovery analogous to that announced by Freud relating to the First World War. The state, which insists on internal peace, is externally the greatest criminal of all; the adults who would make the children behave, handle their own enemies with a sophisticated ferocity that makes Jack look like a mere dabbler in destruction. When the boys pray for a sign from the adult world – 'if only they could get a message to us'[62] – their prayer turns into an ambush. 'A sign came down from the world of grown-ups'[63]; the dead parachutist descends upon the island and is cata-lystic in toppling the already disintegrating society into gibbering demon-worship.

Everything has come full circle. Ralph pines now for the once unheeded benefits of civilisation like a bath or toothbrush, while Simon the prophet can bring Ralph no more joyous tidings than to assure him that 'you'll get back to where you came from'.[64] The island is now a prison, Eden become Gehenna. Ralph's dreams reflect his altered view of reality and the reversal of priorities which the island experience has produced in him. He turns away from wild Dartmoor and its wild ponies – 'the attraction of wildness had gone'; far better 'a tamed town where savagery could not set foot'.[65] *Lord of the Flies* was clearly not written to encourage a flight to the jungle, and the nature it exhibits is certainly very different from that mediated by Wordsworth or Rousseau. Yet it would be unwise to conclude that it must be a plea for civilisation, at least in its existing form, for, just as clearly, it exposes the delusion that 'civil-isation' is civilised and that Jack can only be found in the jungle.

Jack is not a proponent of savage disorder but of stern totalitarian discipline. Far from disliking rules, he loves them too much and for the wrong reasons: ' "We'll have rules!" he cried excitedly. "Lots of rules! Then when anyone breaks 'em – " '[66] Those critics who find the book upholding Augustine against Pelagius should reflect that Jack is a confirmed Augustinian with a zest for retribution. From the outset his authoritarianism is glaringly evident. That is why it is such a disastrous concession when Ralph, to appease his defeated rival, tells him that 'the choir belongs to you, of course'.[67] Jack, as leader of the hunters, becomes invincible as the lord of the food supply. The need to hunt and kill leads to the formation of an army and the democratic process is undermined by this alternative power-structure. Ralph's bitterness when he lashes the hunters for throwing away a chance of rescue should include himself as target, for he is not blameless. Nor does he emerge with credit from his showdown with Jack, for he finds the lure of meat as irresistible as anyone else. His resolve to refuse the costly meat crumbles and he is soon gnawing as voraciously as the others. It is a crucial victory for Jack, as his triumphant cry announces; 'I got you meat!'[68]

This is not, as is sometimes mistakenly said, a slide from society into savagery, but the replacement of one kind of society by another. Jack's exultant claim is the announcement of a new totalitarian contract in which freedom is the price of meat. The Grand Inquisitor (who was certainly not advocating a return to nature) declared that men will fall down and worship anyone who guarantees to feed them and his chief complaint against Christ is that he will not use food to secure obedience. Jack would have won the Grand Inquisitor's approval. The provision of meat becomes a key element in the establishment of his new society. The democrats can stay and get diarrhoea with Ralph or defect to Jack and a full table, at the trifling cost of their freedom. The meat-giver wins hands down; a hungry democracy cannot compete with a well-fed tyranny. The meat which in Ballantyne is the means of redeeming cannibals becomes in Golding the infallible resource for transforming citizens into slaves – slaves rather than savages. Even Ralph and Piggy, all their fine principles notwithstanding, are driven by hunger towards Jack's camp where he sits among piles of meat 'like an idol'.[69] The dictator, as lord of the feast, contemptuously permits the shamefaced pair to eat. When, later, the quarrel rekindles and Ralph attacks them for running after food, Jack needs only to point to the accusatory bone still in Ralph's hand. It is analogous to that devastating moment in *Nineteen Eighty-Four* when O'Brien, exploding Winston's claim to moral superiority, plays back the incriminating tape on which the 'good' man has promised to commit the very atrocities which he denounces Big Brother for committing. In each case, the hero, in compromising himself, has forfeited the right to condemn his opponent.

Those who cite the book as proof of how people, removed from the ramparts and reinforcements of civilisation, so easily regress into savagery, have failed to see that, for Golding, our much vaunted civilisation is little more than a sham in the first place. 'We're English; and the English are best at everything.'[70] Such hubris is asking to be chastised and the book duly obliges. Our alleged civilisation is, at best, a mere habit, a lethargy, a conditioned reflex. Jack, longing to kill the piglet yet unable to do so, is simply unlearning a tedious half-taught lesson; three chapters later he has overcome the rote indoctrination as he sniffs the ground while he tracks his prey, obsessed with a lust to kill, more avid for blood than for meat. The island, like a truth-serum, makes us tell the truth about ourselves, the truth that hitherto lay hidden within – it is, in the etymological sense, an education, and its prime lesson is to confirm Renan's belief that we are living on the perfume of an empty vase. Roger is simply the most frightening instance of the emptiness of civilisation; to say that he retreats from it misleadingly implies that he was ever there at all. But the island does not change people so much as liberate them to be their real selves. Jack would be just as arrogant in England, though his aspiration to command would necessarily take a different route. Roger would have the same sadistic drives at home but the island allows them to be indulged with impunity, as he finds himself in the serendipitous position of a psychopath promoted to chief of police. It is, however, not only in the jungle that psychopaths become chiefs of police.

To begin with, Roger, throwing stones to miss, is still conditioned by a distant civilisation now in ruins. The old taboo is still just barely effective. Lurking darkly behind a tree, 'breathing quickly, his eyelids fluttering', longingly contemplating the vulnerable littlun, so temptingly defenceless, Roger is a masterly depiction of barely controlled perversion.[71] Even Ralph, in the roughhouse of the mock ritual, is not immune from the 'sudden, thick excitement' of inflicting pain on a helpless creature.[72] But what is a shocking, fleeting visitation for Ralph is Roger's permanent condition. It is appropriate that, during the killing of the sow with its explicit sexual overtones, he should be the one to find a lodgement for his point and to force it remorselessly 'right up her ass!' Who else but the pervert should lead those pursuing the sow, 'wedded to her in lust', and, at her death, collapsing 'heavy and fulfilled upon her'?[73] Orgasmic release for Roger is always a matter of hurting someone else.

He is a much more frightening figure than Jack, for whereas the latter's cruelty springs from fear – the unfortunate Wilfred is going to be beaten because the chief is angry and afraid – Roger's sadism is the pure, unadulterated thing, with pleasure as its motive. When he hears the delectable news of Wilfred's beating, it breaks upon him like an illumination and he sits savouring the luscious possibilities of irresponsible authority; it is a sadist's elysium – absolute power and a stock of defenceless victims. The rescuing officer arrives just in time to prevent a supplantation, for, as the connoisseur in pain, Roger is already beginning to shoulder the chief aside to practise his hellish craft. Significantly, the sharpened stick meant to take Ralph's life is carried by Roger and not Jack. But we do the island an injustice if we blame it for producing Roger, for he exhibits, rather, the two ostensibly contradictory truths which the book advances: how far the boys have moved away from civilisation and what a tiny journey it is. By the book's close little Percy Wemys Madison has completely forgotten the talismanic address chanted throughout to console him in his ordeal;[74] it is a sign at once of how perilously fragile the civilised life is and of how thoroughly abandoned it can become.

Whatever flimsy excuse can be offered for missing the implicit indictment of civilisation recurring throughout the text is irreprievably cancelled by the unmistakable irony of the climax. Yet some readers uncomprehendingly dismiss this as a gimmick, Golding sacrificing the text's seriousness to a piece of sensationalism.[75] The truth is that the final startling change of perspective is integral to the book's meaning. Ralph, fleeing in terror, falls, rolls over and staggers to his feet, 'tensed for more terrors and looked up at a huge peaked cap'. The long desiderated adult has finally arrived and the bloodthirsty savages seeking Ralph's life dwindle to a semicircle of little boys indulging in fun and games; Jack, from being a manic dictator, is reduced to a dirty little urchin carrying some broken spectacles at his waist. This has been astonishingly misinterpreted as an unprincipled evasion of the problems posed by the fable: the horror of the boys' experience on the island is finally only a childish, if viciously nasty, game; adult sanity has returned and the little devils will have to behave themselves again. Human nature cannot be so irremediably bad if the arrival of one adult can immediately put everything to rights – the problem is, apparently, a mere matter of classroom control.

But such obtuseness in face of the text's irony is inexcusable. Ralph is saved but that does not exempt us from scrutinising his saviour or assessing the fate that awaits the rescued boy. The officer seems a doubtful redeemer; his cruiser and sub-machine gun are the sophisticated equivalent of the primitive ordnance used by Jack and his followers. Killers are killers, whatever their implements, sharpened stick or atomic missile, and it is no more a proof of progress to kill technologically than it is for a cannibal to use a knife and fork – the unkempt savages are the counterparts of the trim sailors, not their opposites. We must be gullible indeed to be taken in by evil simply because it comes to us well groomed and freshly laundered. The officer stands embarrassed as Ralph weeps – English boys should surely behave better than this – but this merely betrays his imperception, which is replicated in that of certain critics. Ralph, weeping for the end of innocence and the darkness of man's heart, is weeping for all men, the officer and his crew included. Because the officer cannot see this does not entitle the reader to be equally blind. The idea that when the cruiser arrives the beast slinks back abashed into the jungle to wait for the next set of castaways is so preposterous that it scarcely deserves refuting.

There is no happy ending nor anything optimistic about the final scene. Whatever we may wish, it is not legitimate to infer from the text that society, the *polis*, is man's salvation. The book is not an implicit tribute to the humanising power of social institutions nor does it offer us the city as a refuge from the jungle. Perhaps the city *is* essential, but it very much depends what kind of city it is – Cain's city will not help us. If man regresses in nature, that does not mean that social man is necessarily good; Swift detests the Yahoo but abhors the 'civilised' Yahoos of London and Dublin even more. Of course, man needs a structured community in which to develop his humanity; of course, the city should be the safe and decent haven. But 'should' is not 'is'; in *King Lear* the castle is where man should be safe, the wild heath where he should be endangered, but Lear and Gloucester do not find it so. Golding likewise knows that all too tragically in our century the city itself has become, paradoxically, a jungle, the wild place in which man finds himself born. In any case, Golding's concern is with the defects of man and not those of society, because man is more important than society. Simon is again the decisive figure, for, while not anti-social, he cannot ultimately be defined in social terms – when he goes apart from his fellows to meditate alone, Golding is affirming the superiority of man to men. This is an auspicious point upon which to end this study. Salvation is not in the city but exists, if anywhere, within man himself, the individual human being transcending social roles, however important those may be. From Swift to Camus we have contemplated the darkness of man's heart. *Lord of the Flies*, continuing this tradition, supplies yet another striking instance of the dark epiphany, but shows, too, the possibility of a brightness within. It would be presumptuous to demand more. Dame Julian may seem altogether too serene for a troubled century like ours; but, if we cannot be certain of salvation, perhaps it is enough to sustain us if we know that the darkness need not prevail.

Notes

NOTES TO CHAPTER ONE: INTRODUCTION

1. G. M. Hopkins, *Poems and Prose of Gerard Manley Hopkins*, selected with an Introduction and notes by W. H. Gardner (Harmondsworth, Middx: Penguin, 1958) p.62.
2. Fyodor Dostoevsky, *The Brothers Karamazov*, trans. Constance Garnett (London: Heinemann and Zsolnay, 1948) p.263.
3. Graham Greene, *Collected Essays* (Harmondsworth, Middx: Penguin, 1970) p.21.
4. *W. H. Auden: A Selection*, ed. by Richard Hoggart (London: Hutchinson, 1963) p.112.
5. Mary Shelley, *Frankenstein*, ed. by Maurice Hindle (Harmondsworth, Middx: Penguin, 1985) p.141.
6. George Eliot, *Middlemarch*, ed. by W. J. Harvey (Harmondsworth, Middx: Penguin, 1965) p.789.
7. Ibid., p.808.
8. Ibid., p.465
9. Charles Dickens, *A Tale of Two Cities*, ed. George Woodcock (Harmondsworth, Middx: Penguin, 1970) p.403.
10. Charles Dickens, *Hard Times*, ed. David Craig (Harmondsworth, Middx: Penguin, 1969) p.314.
11. Charles Dickens, *David Copperfield*, ed. Trevor Blount (Harmondsworth, Middx: Penguin, 1966) p.950.
12. Charles Dickens, *Our Mutual Friend*, ed. Stephen Gill (Harmondsworth, Middx: Penguin, 1971) p.892.
13. Charles Dickens, *Little Dorrit*, ed. John Holloway (Harmondsworth, Middx: Penguin, 1967) p.895.
14. Charles Dickens, *Dombey and Son*, ed. Peter Fairclough (Harmondsworth, Middx: Penguin, 1970) p.940.
15. *Revelations of Divine Love Recorded by Julian of Norwich*, ed. Grace Warrack (London: Methuen, 1901) p.57.
16. Thomas Mann, *Notizbuch*, quoted by Lieselotte Voss, *Die Entstehung von Thomas Manns Roman 'Doktor Faustus'* (Tubingen: Max Niemeyer Verlag, 1975) p.15. (My translation.)
17. Angus Wilson, 'Evil in the English Novel', in *Diversity and Depth in Fiction: Selected Critical Writings of Angus Wilson*, ed. Kerry McSweeney (London: Secker and Warburg, 1983) pp.3–24.
18. Johann Wolfgang Goethe, *Faust*, trans. Philip Wayne (Harmondsworth, Middx: Penguin, 1973) Part Two, p.277.

19. Thomas Mann, *Doctor Faustus*, trans. H. T. Lowe-Porter (Harmondsworth, Middx: Penguin, 1971) pp.458–9.

20. Ibid., p.470.

21. Karl Jaspers quoted by Erich Heller, *The Disinherited Mind* (Harmondsworth, Middx: Penguin, 1961) p.35.

22. Ibid., pp.33–55.

23. Mann, *Doctor Foustus*, p.470.

24. Ibid., p.465.

25. Jean-Paul Sartre, *What Is Literature?* (London: Methuen, 1950) pp.160–2. See also Anthony Burgess, *Urgent Copy* (Harmondsworth, Middx: Penguin, 1973) pp.204–12.

26. Albert Camus, *The Fall*, trans. Justin O'Brien (Harmondsworth, Middx: Penguin, 1957) p.11.

27. Graham Greene, *The Quiet American* (Harmondsworth, Middx: Penguin, 1962) p.84.

28. George Orwell, *The Collected Essays, Journalism and Letters*, ed. Sonia Orwell and Ian Angus (Harmondsworth, Middx: Penguin, 1970) vol. IV, pp.340–1. (Hereafter *CEJL*.)

29. William Golding, quoted by Francis E. Kearns, 'Golding Revisited', in *William Golding's 'Lord of the Flies': A Source Book*, ed. William Nelson (New York: Odyssey Press, 1963) p.166. (Hereafter *Nelson*.) (Kearns is rejecting an optimistic exegesis of the ending of the novel advanced by Luke M. Grande, 'The Appeal of Golding', in *Nelson*, pp.156–9, 163.)

30. *The Correspondence of Jonathan Swift*, ed. by Harold Williams (Oxford: Oxford University Press, 1963) vol. III, p. 183. (Hereafter *Corr.*)

NOTES TO CHAPTER TWO: *GULLIVER'S TRAVELS*

1. T. S. Eliot, ' "Ulysses", Order and Myth', *Dial*, vol. LXXV (1923) p.481; Patrick Reilly, *Jonathan Swift: The Brave Desponder* (Manchester: Manchester University Press, 1982) pp.1–19.

2. *The Prose Works of Jonathan Swift*, ed. Herbert Davis (Oxford: Basil Blackwell, 1939–68) vol. XII, p.117.

3. John Milton, 'Areopagitica', in *Selected Prose*, ed. C. A. Patrides (Harmondsworth, Middx: Penguin, 1974) p.219.

4. *Corr.* vol. III, p.118.

5. Peter Gay, *The Party of Humanity: Essays in the French Enlightenment* (New York: Alfred A. Knopf, 1964) pp. 111–13, 114–16.

6. Quoted by R. S. Crane, 'Suggestions Towards a Genealogy of the "Man of Feeling" ', *Journal of English Literary History*, vol.1 (1934) pp.222–3.

7. Quoted by T. O. Wedel, 'On the Philosophical Background of *Gul-*

liver's Travels', *Studies in Philology*, vol. 23 (1926) p. 436.

8. Quoted in Roland Stromberg, *Religious Liberalism in Eighteenth-Century England* (Oxford: Oxford University Pres, 1954), p.144 (footnote).

9. See Wedel, 'On the Philosophical Background of *Gulliver's Travels'*, p.439; Ernst Cassirer, *The Philosophy of the Enlightenment*, trans. Fritz C. A. Koelln and James P. Pettegrove (Boston, Mass: Beacon Press, 1960) pp.137–60.

10. *The Poems of Jonathan Swift*, ed. Harold Williams (Oxford: Oxford University Press, 1963–5) vol.II, p.497.

11. Reinhold Niebuhr, *The Nature and Destiny of Man* (London: Nisbet, 1946) vol.I, pp.100–1.

12. *Corr*, vol.V. p.4.

13. Quoted by Wedel, 'On the Philosophical Background of *Gulliver's Travels'*, p.438.

14. Ibid., p.435.

15. 'Lectures on the English Poets', in *The Collected Works of William Hazlitt*, ed. A. R. Waller and Arnold Glover (London: J. M. Dent, 1902) vol.V, pp.110–1.

16. *The Works of Jonathan Swift*, ed. Sir Walter Scott (London: Bickers and Sons, 1883), vol.I, p.315.

17. W. E. H. Lecky, Introduction to the *Prose Works of Jonathan Swift*, ed. T. Scott (London: G.Bell and Sons, 1897) vol.I, p.lxxxviii.

18. *The Works of William Makepeace Thackeray* (London: Smith, Elder, 1869) vol.XIX, pp.162–3.

19. Edmund Gosse, *A History of Eighteenth-Century Literature* (London: Macmillan, 1889) pp.161–2.

20. Jonathan Swift, *Gulliver's Travels*, ed. Peter Dixon and John Chalker with an Introduction by Michael Foot (Harmondsworth, Middx: Penguin, 1967) p.40.

21. *Prose Works of Jonathan Swift*, vol.IX, p.263.

22. *Corr.*, vol.II, p.430.

23. *The Poems of John Dryden*, ed. James Kinsley (Oxford: Oxford University Press, 1958) vol.1, p.33.

24. Daniel Defoe, *Robinson Crusoe*, ed. Angus Ross (Harmondsworth, Middx: Penguin, 1965) pp.143, 153; Swift, *Gulliver's Travels*, p.325.

25. Swift, *Gulliver's Travels*, p.267.

26. Blaise Pascal, *Pensées*, trans. with an Introduction by Martin Turnell (London: Harvill Press, 1962) p.175.

27. Swift, *Gulliver's Travels*, p.267.

28. R. C. Elliot, 'Gulliver as Literary Artist', *English Literary History*, vol. XIX (1952) pp.49–63.

29. Swift, *Gulliver's Travels*, p.271.

30. Ibid., p.271.

31. Jonathan Swift, *A Tale of a Tub and Other Works*, ed. Angus Ross and David Woolley (Oxford: Oxford University Press, 1986) pp.133–4.

32. *The Poems of Jonathan Swift*, vol.II, p.497.

33. Ibid., vol.I, p.297.

34. Swift, *A Tale of a Tub*, pp.78-80.

35. Swift, *Gulliver's Travels*, p.270.
36. Quoted by R. W. Frantz, 'Swift's Yahoos and the Voyagers', *Modern Philology*, vol. XXIX (1932) p.55.
37. Swift, *Gulliver's Travels*, pp.276, 277.
38. Ibid., p.285.
39. Ibid., pp.306, 283–4.
40. Ibid., p.282.
41. Ibid., p.282.
42. Ibid., p.285.
43. Ibid., p.277.
44. Ibid., p.339.
45. *Prose Works of Jonathan Swift*, vol. IV, p.251.
46. Swift, *A Tale of a Tub*, p.84.
47. Swift, *Gulliver's Travels*, p.303.
48. Ibid., p.304.
49. Ibid., p.305.
50. Swift, *A Tale of a Tub*, p.104.
51. Ricardo Quintana, *The Mind and Art of Jonathan Swift* (London: Methuen, 1953) p.65.
52. Swift, *Gulliver's Travels*, p.327.
53. Ibid., p.345.
54. Ibid., pp.314–15.
55. Ibid., p.315.
56. Ibid., p.335.
57. Ibid., p.338.
58. Ibid., p.342.

NOTES TO CHAPTER THREE: *HEART OF DARKNESS*

1. Joseph Conrad, *Heart of Darkness*, ed. with an Introduction by Paul O'Prey (Harmondsworth, Middx: Penguin, 1984) p.86.
2. Ibid., p.55.
3. Ibid., p.46.
4. Ibid., p.85.
5. Ibid., p.85.
6. Ibid., p.85.
7. *Prose Works of Jonathan Swift*, vol. IX, p.244.
8. Swift, *Gulliver's Travels*, p.241.
9. *Prose Works of Jonathan Swift*, vol. IX, p.152.
10. *Joseph Conrad on Fiction*, ed. Walter F. Wright (Lincoln, Nebr.: University of Nebraska Press, 1964) pp.208–9.
11. *Heart of Darkness*, ed. Robert Kimbrough (New York: W. W. Norton, 1971) pp.141, 140. (Hereafter *Kimbrough*.)
12. Conrad, *Heart of Darkness*, p.87.
13. Ibid., p.52.
14. Joseph Conrad, *Under Western Eyes* (Harmondsworth, Middx: Penguin, 1957) p.52.

15. Conrad, *Heart of Darkness*, p.64.
16. Ibid., p.71.
17. Ibid., p.69.
18. Ibid., p.70.
19. Ibid., p.69.
20. George Steiner, *In Bluebeard's Castle: Some Notes Towards the Redefinition of Culture* (London: Faber and Faber, 1974) p.31.
21. Sigmund Freud, 'The Future of an Illusion', in *Civilization, Society and Religion* (Harmondsworth, Middx: Pelican Freud Library, 1985) vol.12, p.221.
22. Conrad, *Heart of Darkness*, p.69.
23. Quoted in *Kimbrough*, p.189.
24. Conrad, *Heart of Darkness*, p.84.
25. Quoted in *Kimbrough*, p.122.
26. Bertrand Russell, *Portraits from Memory and Other Essays* (London: George Allen and Unwin, 1956) p.82.
27. Conrad, *Heart of Darkness*, p.48.
28. Ibid., pp.84, 89.
29. Ibid., p.120.
30. Ibid., p.32.
31. See *Kimbrough*, p.122.
32. Conrad, *Heart of Darkness*, p.64.
33. Joseph Conrad, *Nostromo: A Tale of the Seaboard* (Harmondsworth, Middx: Penguin, 1963) p.310.
34. Conrad, *Heart of Darkness*, p.76.
35. Ibid., p.97.
36. Ibid., p.95.
37. Lilian Feder, 'Marlow's Descent into Hell', in *Kimbrough*, p.183, Stewart C. Wilcox, 'Conrad's "Complicated Presentations" of Symbolic Imagery', in *Kimbrough*, p.189: Robert O. Evans, 'Conrad's Underworld', in *Kimbrough*, p.218, Robert F. Haugh, 'Heart of Darkness: Problem for Critics', in *Kimbrough*, p.163; Albert J. Guerard, 'From Life to Art', in *Kimbrough*, p.122; Jerome Thale, 'Marlow's Quest', in *Kimbrough*, p.176; Kenneth A. Bruffee, 'The Lesser Nightmare', in *Kimbrough*, p.234.
38. Conrad, *Heart of Darkness*, p.49.
39. Quoted by Matthew Arnold in *Essays in Criticism* (London: Dent, Everyman's Library, 1969) p.7.
40. Conrad, *Heart of Darkness*, p.102.
41. Ibid., p.98.
42. Ibid., p.107.
43. Ibid., p.107.
44. Ibid., p.111.
45. Ibid., p.112
46. Ibid., p.112.
47. Quoted in *Kimbrough*, p.152.
48. Conrad, *Heart of Darkness*, p.113.
49. T. S. Eliot, 'Baudelaire', in *Selected Prose*, ed. by John Hayward (Harmondsworth, Middx: Penguin, 1955) p.194.

50. Graham Greene, *Brighton Rock* (Harmondsworth, Middx: Penguin, 1957) pp.128–9.
51. Conrad, *Heart of Darkness*, p.113.
52. Ibid., p.113.
53. Conrad, *Under Western Eyes*, p.210.
54. Swift, *Gulliver's Travels*, p.146.
55. Conrad, *Heart of Darkness*, p.113.
56. Swift, *Gulliver's Travels*, p.173.
57. Conrad, *Heart of Darkness*, p.86.
58. Ibid., p.86.
59. Ibid., p.113.
60. Ibid., p.92.
61. *Prose Works of Jonathan Swift*, vol. x, p.4.
62. Conrad, *Heart of Darkness*, p.114.
63. Ibid., p.116.
64. Quoted in *Kimbrough*, p.155.
65. Ibid., p.129.

NOTES TO CHAPTER FOUR: *DEATH IN VENICE*

1. Thomas Mann, *Tonio Kröger*, in *Death in Venice*, trans. H. T. Lowe-Porter (Harmondsworth, Middx: Penguin, 1957) p.156.
2. Quoted by Steiner, *In Bluebeard's Castle*, p.18.
3. Thomas Mann, *The Magic Mountain*, trans. H. T. Lowe-Porter (Harmondsworth, Middx: Penguin, 1969) pp.491–4.
4. Friedrich Nietzsche, *The Birth of Tragedy and the Genealogy of Morals*, trans. Francis Golffing (New York: Doubleday, 1956) p.26.
5. Ibid., p.34.
6. Mann, *Death in Venice*, p.53.
7. Ibid., p.57.
8. Mann, *Tonio Kröger*, pp.185, 188–9.
9. Mann, *The Magic Mountain*, pp.72, 207; see also pp.129–30.
10. Ibid., pp.265–6.
11. Mann, *Death in Venice*, p.13.
12. Ibid., p.25.
13. Ibid., p.48.
14. Ibid., p.48. See Homer, *The Odyssey*, trans. E. V. Rieu (Harmondsworth, Middx: Penguin, 1954) p.79.
15. Mann, *Death in Venice*, p.8.
16. Ibid., p.8.
17. Ibid., p.9.
18. Ibid., p.67.
19. Ibid., p.9.
20. Ibid., p.9.
21. Ibid., pp.9–10; Conrad, *Heart of Darkness*, p.69.
22. Mann, *Death in Venice*, p.56.
23. Ibid., p.78.

24. Ibid., p.19.
25. Ibid., p.53.
26. Ibid., p.54.
27. Ibid., p.80.
28. Ibid., p.80.
29. Ibid., p.81.
30. Ibid., p.30.
31. Ibid., p.34.
32. Ibid., pp.34–5.
33. Ibid., p.35.
34. Ibid., p.63.
35. Ibid., pp.33, 40.
36. Ibid., p.41.
37. Ibid., p.44.
38. Ibid., p.44.
39. Ibid., p.45.
40. Ibid., p.54.
41. Ibid., p.54.
42. Nietzsche, *The Birth of Tragedy*, p.45.
43. Ibid., p.124.
44. Mann, *The Magic Mountain*, p.465
45. Mann, *Death in Venice*, p.73.
46. Ibid., p.73.
47. Ibid., p.74.
48. Ibid., p.74.
49. Ibid., p.74.
50. Ibid., p.80.
51. Ibid., p.55.
52. Ibid., p.47.
53. Ibid., p.56.
54. Nietzsche, *The Genealogy of Morals*, p.120.
55. André Gide, *The Immoralist*, trans. Dorothy Bussy (Harmondsworth, Middx: Penguin, 1960) p.137.
56. Ibid., p.19.
57. Ibid., p.51.
58. Ibid., p.51.
59. Ibid., p.51.
60. Mann, *Death in Venice*, p.83.

NOTES TO CHAPTER FIVE: *NINETEEN EIGHTY-FOUR*

1. *CEJL*, vol. IV, pp.257, 261.
2. *CEJL*, vol. I, p.56; vol. III, pp.246–60; vol. IV, pp.201–2, 203, 205–6, 214–15.
3. George Orwell, *Down and Out in Paris and London* (Harmondsworth, Middx: Penguin, 1963) p.20.
4. *Marx and Engels: Basic Writings on Politics and Philosophy*, ed. Lewis S. Feuer (London: Fontana, 1969) p.288; see also p.84.

5. Quoted in Peter Singer, *Marx* (Oxford: Oxford University Press, 1980) p.38.
6. 'The Eighteenth Brumaire of Louis Napoleon', in *Karl Marx and Friedrich Engels: Selected Works in Two Volumes* (Moscow: Foreign Languages Publishing House, 1950) vol.1, p.249.
7. *Marx and Engels*, ed. L. S. Feuer, p.284.
8. *CEJL*, vol. II, p.33; vol. III, p.121.
9. *CEJL*, vol. II, pp.304–5.
10. George Orwell, *A Clergyman's Daughter* (Harmondsworth, Middx: Penguin, 1964) p.258.
11. Ibid., p.240.
12. *Complete Shorter Poems of John Milton*, ed. John Carey (London: Longman, 1981) p.209.
13. Orwell, *Down and Out*, p.147.
14. Ibid., p.148.
15. Ibid., pp.22, 27, 48, 120; *CEJL*, vol. I, p.66.
16. *CEJL*, vol. II, p.306
17. *CEJL*, vol. I, p.301.
18. George Orwell, *Coming Up for Air* (Harmondsworth, Middx: Penguin, 1962) p.224.
19. Orwell, *Down and Out*, p.22.
20. *CEJL*, vol. IV, p.465.
21. *CEJL*, vol. II, p.297.
22. *CEJL*, vol, II p.170
23. *CEJL*, vol. I, p.419.
24. *CEJL*, vol. I, p.414.
25. *CEJL*, vol. I, p.395.
26. *CEJL*, vol. I, pp.413–14; vol. II, p.297; vol. III, p.177.
27. George Orwell, *Nineteen Eighty-Four* (Harmondsworth, Middx: Penguin, 1958) p.136.
28. Ibid., pp.27–8.
29. *CEJL*, vol. II, p.161; vol. III, p.160.
30. *CEJL*, vol. I, p.64.
31. Fyodor Dostoevsky, *The Devils*, trans. David Magarshack (Harmondsworth, Middx: Penguin, 1967) p.655.
32. John Milton, *Paradise Lost*, ed. Alistair Fowler (London: Longman, 1976) p.494.
33. Orwell, *Nineteen Eighty-Four*, p.225.
34. Mann, *Death in Venice*, p.27.
35. Orwell, *Nineteen Eighty-Four*, p.229.
36. Camus, *The Fall*, p.70.
37. Orwell, *Nineteen Eighty-Four*, p.27.
38. Ibid., p.132.
39. Ibid., p.235.
40. Ernest Hemingway, *The Old Man and the Sea* (St Albans, Herts: Triad-Panther Books, 1976) p.43.
41. Orwell, *Nineteen Eighty-Four*, p.85.
42. Ibid., p.235.
43. Ibid., p.206.

NOTES TO CHAPTER SIX: *THE FALL*

1. *CEJL*, vol. III, p.237; quoted by Conor Cruise O'Brien, *Camus* (London: Fontana – Collins, 1977) p.75.
2. *CEJL*, vol. IV, p.456.
3. Camus, *The Fall*, p.36; *CEJL*, vol. I, p.589; vol. II, pp.197, 200; vol. II, pp.113, 271; vol. III, pp.158–9; George Orwell, *The Road to Wigan Pier* (Harmondsworth, Middx: Penguin, 1962) pp.139–40.
4. *CEJL*, vol. IV, pp.201–2, 203, 205–6.
5. Camus, *The Fall*, p.98.
6. Albert Camus, *The Myth of Sisyphus*, trans. Justin O'Brien (Harmondsworth, Middx: Penguin, 1975) p.111.
7. Maurice Cranston, 'Camus', *Encounter*, Feb.1967, pp.43, 45.
8. Albert Camus, *The Plague*, trans. Stuart Gilbert (Harmondsworth, Middx: Penguin, 1960) p.251.
9. Gide, *The Immoralist*, p.157.
10. Camus, *The Fall*, p.15.
11. See Stromberg, *Religious Liberalism in Eighteenth-Century England*, p.144.
12. Camus, *The Fall*, p.102.
13. Ibid., p.107.
14. Cranston, *Encounter*, p.43.
15. Camus, *The Fall*, p.60.
16. Ibid., p.11.
17. Albert Camus, *The Rebel*, trans. Anthony Bower (Harmondsworth, Middx: Penguin, 1962) p.33.
18. Camus, *The Fall*, p.49.
19. Ibid., p.85.
20. *CEJL*, vol. IV, p.212.
21. Camus, *The Fall*, p.42.
22. Quoted by Frederick Brown in review of Patrick McCarthy, *Camus*, in *The New York Review of Books*, vol. XXIX (18 Nov. 1982) p.14.
23. Camus, *The Fall*, p.62.
24. Camus, *The Rebel*, pp.74–5.
25. Leszek Kolakowski, 'The Priest and the Jester: Reflections on the Theological Heritage of Contemporary Thinking', in *Marxism and Beyond* (St Albans, Herts: Paladin, 1971) pp.31–40.
26. Albert Camus, *The Just*, trans. Justin O'Brien (Harmondsworth, Middx: Penguin, 1970) pp.30–1.
27. Freud, *Civilization, Society and Religion*, pp.61–89.
28. Ibid., p.68.
29. Ibid., p.69.
30. Ibid., p.69.
31. François, Duc de La Rochefoucauld, *Maxims*, trans. L. W. Tancock (Harmondsworth, Middx: Penguin, 1959) p.85.
32. Freud, *Civilization, Society and Religion*, p.72.
33. Ibid., p.73.
34. Ibid., p.72.
35. Ibid., p.72.

36. Swift, *Gulliver's Travels*, p.345.
37. Freud, *Civilization, Society and Religion*, p.74.
38. Camus, *The Fall*, p.35.
39. Shelley, *Frankenstein*, p.186.
40. Camus, *The Fall*, p.20.
41. Ibid., pp.39–41.
42. Ibid., p.41.
43. Ibid., p.37.
44. George Bernanos, *The Diary of a Country Priest*, trans. Pamela Morris (London: Fontana, 1977) p.251.
45. Orwell, *Nineteen Eighty-Four*, pp.231–2.
46. La Rochefoucauld, *Maxims*, p.67.
47. Ibid., p.62.
48. Camus, *The Fall*, p.18.
49. La Rochefoucauld, *Maxims*, p.68.
50. André Gide, 'Notes for a Preface to Fielding's *Tom Jones*', in *Twentieth Century Views: Fielding: A Collection of Critical Essays*, ed. by Ronald Paulson (Englewood Cliffs, N.J.: Prentice-Hall 1962) pp.81–3.
51. Camus, *The Fall*, pp.17, 22.
52. Ibid., p.52.
53. Ibid., p.62.
54. Ibid., p.36.
55. Ibid., p.22.
56. Ibid., p.95.
57. Ibid., p.103.
58. Ibid., p.23.
59. Ibid., p.30.
60. Ibid., p.70.
61. Ibid., p.13; 'The absurd is sin without God': Camus, *The Myth of Sisyphus*, p.42.
62. La Rochefouchauld, *Maxims*, p.110.
63. Camus, *The Fall*, p.25.
64. Ibid., p.93.
65. Ibid., p.13.
66. Ibid., p.103.
67. Ibid., p.103.
68. Ibid., p.97.
69. Swift, *Gulliver's Travels*, p.345.
70. Camus, *The Fall*, p.26.

NOTES TO CHAPTER SEVEN: *LORD OF THE FLIES*

1. William Golding, *Free Fall* (Harmondsworth, Middx: Penguin, 1963) p.171.
2. William Golding, *The Hot Gates* (London: Faber and Faber, 1965) p.172.
3. Bertrand Russell, *Fact and Fiction* (London: George Unwin, 1961) p.32.

4. Golding, *The Hot Gates*, p.174.
5. D. M. Davis, 'A Conversation with William Golding', *New Republic*, 4th May 1963, p.28.
6. Quoted in *Nelson*, p.142.
7. Camus, *The Fall*, pp.80–2.
8. William Golding, 'It's a Long Way to Oxyrhynchus', *Spectator*, 7 July 1961, p.9.
9. William Golding, 'Androids All', *Spectator*, 24 Feb. 1961; see also Martin Green, 'Distaste for the Contemporary', in *Nelson*, pp.75–82; John M. Egan, 'Golding's View of Man', in *Nelson*, pp.145–7.
10. William Golding, *Lord of the Flies* (Harmondsworth, Middx: Penguin, 1960) p.22.
11. Ibid., p.22. Ralph recognises his inferiority: 'I can't think. Not like Piggy' (p.74).
12. Ibid., p.20.
13. See Frank Kermode, 'Coral Islands', in *Nelson*, p.40; see also Kermode, 'The Novels of William Golding', in *Nelson*, pp.107–20.
14. Golding, *Lord of the Flies*, p.37.
15. Ibid., pp.74, 99.
16. Ibid., p.89.
17. *CEJL*, vol. II, pp.167–70.
18. Golding, *Lord of the Flies*, p.89.
19. Ibid., p.89.
20. Ibid., p.34.
21. Ibid., p.97.
22. Ibid., p.36.
23. Ibid., p.36.
24. Ibid., p.44.
25. Ibid., pp.76, 52.
26. Ibid., p.62.
27. Ibid., p.68.
28. Ibid., p.79.
29. Ibid., p.80.
30. Ibid., p.80; see also Carl Niemeyer, '*The Coral Island* Revisited', in *Nelson*, pp.90, 91–2.
31. Golding, *Lord of the Flies*, p.85.
32. Ibid., p.89.
33. Ibid., p.88.
34. Ibid., p.122.
35. Ibid., p.123.
36. Ibid., p.99.
37. Ibid., p.161.
38. Ibid., p.133.
39. Ibid., p.137.
40. Ibid., p.145; see also Wayland Young, '*Letter from London*', in *Nelson*, p.18.
41. See G. C. Herndl, 'Golding and Salinger: a Clear Choice', *Wiseman Review*, Winter 1964–5; F. E. Kearns, 'Salinger and Golding: Conflict on the Campus', in *Nelson*, pp.148–55. Kearns, 'Golding Revisited', in *Nelson*, pp.165-9.

42. Golding, *Lord of the Flies*, p.146.

43. Ibid., p.147. Golding claims that Simon is at once a saint and a proof of God's existence; only sophisticated literary people will, in Golding's view, fail to see this. See Kermode, in *Nelson*, pp.110, 112. See also Peter Green, 'The World of William Golding', in *Nelson*, p.176; C.B. Cox, 'Lord of the Flies', in *Nelson*, p.84; Sam Hynes, 'Novels of a Religious Man', in *Nelson*, p.72.

44. Golding, *Lord of the Flies*, p.148.

45. Ibid., p.149.

46. Ibid., p.149.

47. Ibid., p.149.

48. Ibid., p.149.

49. Ibid., p.162.

50. Ibid., p.169.

51. Ibid., p.171.

52. Ibid., p.172.

53. Ibid., p.175.

54. Ibid., pp.8, 10. 29, 38.

55. Ibid., p.34.

56. Ibid., p.36.

57. Ibid., p.50.

58. Ibid., p.51.

59. Ibid., p.51.

60. Ibid., p.73.

61. Ibid., p.90.

62. Ibid., p.90.

63. Ibid., p.91.

64. Ibid., p.106.

65. Ibid., p.156.

66. Ibid., p.32.

67. Ibid., p.22.

68. Ibid., p.71.

69. Ibid., p.141.

70. Ibid., p.42; see also Peter Green, in *Nelson*, p.175.

71. Golding, *Lord of the Flies*, p.60.

72. Ibid., p.109.

73. Ibid., p.129.

74. Ibid., p.191.

75. James Gindin, ' "Gimmick" and Metaphor in the Novels of William Golding', in *Nelson*, pp.134, 132-40; reprinted in *Post-War British Fiction: New Accents and Attitudes* (London: Cambridge University Press, 1962). But see also C. B. Cox, *Lord of the Flies*; in *Nelson*, p.88; and Margaret Walters, 'Two Fabulists: Golding and Camus', in *Nelson*, pp.98–9.

Index